Getting It
Right
the First
Time

Getting It
Right
the First
Time

Creating
a Healthy
Marriage

**BARRY McCARTHY, Ph.D.
and EMILY J. McCARTHY**

BRUNNER-ROUTLEDGE
NEW YORK AND HOVE

Published in 2004 by
Brunner-Routledge
29 West 35th Street
New York, NY 10001
www.brunner-routledge.com

Published in Great Britain by
Brunner-Routledge
27 Church Road
Hove, East Sussex
BN3 2FA
www.brunner-routledge.co.uk

Brunner-Routledge is an imprint of the Taylor & Francis Group.
Printed in the United States of America on acid-free paper.
Typesetting: Jack Donner, BookType

10 9 8 7 6 5 4 3 2 1

Library of Congress Cataloging-in-Publication Data

   Getting it right the first time : creating a healthy marriage /
Barry McCarthy and Emily McCarthy
          p.   cm.
Includes bibliographical references and index.
   ISBN 0–415–94829–0 (Paperback)
   1. Marriage. 2. Interpersonal relations. 3. Intimacy (Psychology) 4. Family.
5. Stress management. I. McCarthy, Emily J. II. Title.
   HQ734.M44234 2004
   646.7′8—dc 22

                                                        2003022169

CONTENTS

CHAPTER 1

What to Do after You Say "I Do"

We have more scientific information about marital processes and outcomes than at any time in history. So why is it so difficult to create a healthy, stable marriage? Human behavior is multi-causal and multidimensional; there are no simple answers. There are no hard-and-fast rules that guarantee a happy, secure marriage. If that is what you are hoping for, you have the wrong book (any book that promises guaranteed marital success is aimed at selling copies, not at being honest or empowering you to create a healthy marriage).

This book provides information, guidelines (not rules), and strategies based on scientific and clinical studies of successful marriages. Unfortunately, there is clearer understanding of what does not work than of what does. One of the frustrations in psychological research is that it is easier to pinpoint problem behavior and predict what will fail than what will succeed. There is *not* "one right way" to be married.

Marriage is the most popular voluntary institution in our culture. Although the United States has one of the highest divorce rates in the world, it also has one of the highest marriage and remarriage rates. A healthy marriage meets needs for intimacy and security better than any other human relationship.

For such a highly valued institution, little attention is paid to developing and maintaining a satisfying, stable marital bond. Love songs, peer discussions, and self-help books emphasize finding the right person to marry. The naive assumption is that once a couple are married, love will overcome all problems. Love is *not* enough. The marital bond of respect, trust, and intimacy must be developed, nurtured, and reinforced. Marriage cannot rest on its laurels. Marriage is an ongoing process: You cannot be complacent after 5, 15, 25, or even 55 years.

Couples come into their marriage from quite different backgrounds and living experiences. Some have known each other for less than a year, others have been a couple for over 5 years; many are cohabitating, others would not think of having intercourse until marriage; most do not have a child, but many have a child from a previous relationship or marriage; for most this is a first marriage for both, but for many one partner had previously been married. Although you need to consider these guidelines from the unique experience of your lives and relationship, newly married couples face very similar challenges.

A wise partner choice is only the first step in creating a satisfying, stable marriage. Those who believe marrying the right person is all there is to marriage are in for a rude awakening. People think divorce occurs after many years of marriage, the major causes being falling out of love or having an affair. Empirically, that is wrong. More couples divorce in the first 2 years of marriage than at any other time. The median year for marriage to end in divorce is the 7th. After 20 years of marriage the divorce rate is relatively low. Folklore pushes the myth that having a child stabilizes a troubled marriage. In fact, the opposite occurs—the most common time a couple separate is 3 months before or 3 months after the birth of a first child.

The first 2 years are crucial in building a solid marital foundation. The guideline of waiting at least 2 years before the birth of a child provides time to develop a strong, vital marital bond. The most important relationship in a family is the husband-wife bond, which needs at least 2 years to mature.

"Romantic love," idealization of the partner and relationship, is transformed into mature intimacy and a respectful bond. Idealization changes to realistic acceptance of the spouse for the person he is, with strengths and stellar characteristics, as well as weaknesses and vulnerabilities. At its core, marriage is a respectful, trusting friendship. Emotional and sexual intimacy energize your marital bond and reinforce special feelings. Realistic acceptance means acknowledging weaknesses and problems, but not allowing these to subvert your marriage. There are no perfect people and no perfect marriages. Optimism and commitment are based on mature acceptance and willingness to address problems, not on pretending or idealizing.

What Do You Know about Marriage?

How much do you really know about marriage? Many people believe it is common sense and they know it all. Are you willing to take a test? Do not worry about performance anxiety—you will not be graded.

TRUE-FALSE TEST

1. The honeymoon is a great way to start a marriage, especially sexually.
2. The "honeymoon phase" lasts at least 6 months.
3. The first year of marriage is the happiest.
4. Having a baby during the first year results in greater marital stability.
5. If you communicate and love each other, everything will be fine.
6. Couples who establish a good premarital sexual relationship find marital sex requires little additional effort.
7. The biggest problem couples face is dealing with in-laws.
8. Sex is most satisfying during the first year of marriage.
9. Couples find it easy to develop a money management and budgeting system.
10. Avoiding conflicts and patching over disagreements is the best way to maintain marital harmony.
11. Traditional roles for men and women (for example, he mows the lawn and she does the cooking) are most satisfying.
12. When the wife earns more money, couples enjoy a better relationship.
13. Planning a child reduces sexual fun and spontaneity.
14. Same-sex friends give the most honest, best advice about marriage.

15. It is important to guard individuality and avoid interdependence.
16. It is crucial to merge as a couple and give up autonomy.
17. Having a child strengthens a shaky marriage.
18. The male should be the sexual initiator.
19. The couple need not discuss a 2- or 5-year plan, just let their lives evolve.
20. Maintaining individual friends and interests is a threat to the marriage.
21. Seeking couple therapy or attending a relationship workshop is an indication the marriage is in trouble.
22. People from different backgrounds have the most interesting and successful marriages.
23. The birth of a planned, wanted child heralds a time of greater couple intimacy.
24. Most affairs occur after 10 years of marriage.
25. Most divorces occur after 10 years of marriage.

Add the number of *true* answers you checked. This tells you the number of myths you believe about marriage. This was a marital myth test. All the items are false. Do not be embarrassed; the average number checked true is nine. Marital myths are rampant in our culture. "Pop psychology" books, talk shows, and discussions with same-sex friends add to the misinformation and confusion.

Although there has been a great deal of high-quality research and writing about marriage in the past 20 years, myths and confusion still abound. Naively optimistic myths have given way to cynical, jaded myths. Myths die hard. You can benefit from awareness and understanding of what a satisfying, stable marriage requires. Knowledge is power.

Core Couple Processes

Getting married is only the first step. The 2 major tasks during the first 2 years of marriage are to build a strong marital bond of respect, trust, and intimacy and to develop a comfortable, satisfying marital style. Establishing a mutually satisfying couple style, complementary, conflict-minimizing, best friend, or emotionally expressive, is a foundation for a healthy marriage.

There are four important things you need to do as a couple:

1. Develop a communication pattern in which you empathically listen, make clear requests, and give supportive feedback.
2. Identify conflicts and difficulties, discuss alternatives, problem-solve, and reach viable agreements.
3. Share emotional and sexual intimacy so your bond is nurtured and energized.
4. Enjoy each other, share activities and your lives.

Most couples, even those who have lived together for years or are in a second marriage, find it takes at least 6 months after marriage to develop a couple style. It might sound simple, but it is an individualistic, complex, multidimensional task that takes thought, communication, refinement, and feedback.

Developing a strong marital bond and a functional couple style are crucial tasks. If they are not successfully negotiated, you develop bad habits and destructive patterns of thinking, communicating, and dealing with problems that can subvert the most hopeful, loving marriage.

The cultural myth holds love is all you need. The scientific evidence is that loving feelings are necessary but are not sufficient. In fact, romantic love seldom lasts more than a year after marriage. Unless idealized romance is replaced by mature intimacy, the relationship degenerates into frustration and disappointment. A classic song, "You've Lost That Loving Feeling," reflects the myth that if love leaves, the relationship must be doomed. Idealized romantic love is better for songs, novels, and movies than for real-life marriages. A satisfying, viable marriage is based on developing and maintaining a bond of respect, trust, and intimacy. Romantic love marriages are exciting but unstable. Marriage cannot live up to romantic fantasies. Marriage is based on a respectful, trusting friendship made special and energized by emotional and sexual intimacy. A marriage based on romantic love is transient and unstable. Mature love is strengthened by respect, trust, intimacy, realistic expectations, and commitment.

Marital Poisons

Healthy marriage requires that you not only reinforce positive feelings and experiences but avoid traps that poison and destroy your relationship. Be aware of potential marital poisons. The factor most commonly mentioned is lack of communication. In fact, poor communication is not among the top five poisons. The main poisons are (a) losing respect for the spouse, (b) inability to deal with and resolve conflicts, (c) playing the "what if" or comparison game, (d) breaking the trust bond, (e) a sexual dysfunction or conflict. Rather than your hoping or praying your marriage will not experience problems, we urge prevention and early intervention.

Any marriage will be fine as long as everything goes well. The test of a viable marriage is the ability to successfully address differences and conflicts. Deal with differences and problems to ensure they do not turn into a marital poison. If you are disappointed or hurt by something your spouse has said or done, constructively address the issue rather than allowing destructive thoughts and angry feelings to fester. Accepting your spouse for her strengths *and* weaknesses is a sign of genuine respect. When you lose respect for the spouse, your marriage is in major trouble.

Fifty percent of marriages experience sexual problems— whether a dysfunction, extramarital affair, or fertility issue. Deal with this as an acute problem; work together to resolve it. If sex becomes a chronic problem, especially inhibited sexual desire, it turns into a poison that robs the marriage of intimacy and vitality. Couples fall into the guilt-blame trap that reinforces this self-defeating pattern. Address issues as a respectful, intimate team. Even if a conflict or problem cannot be successfully resolved, you can stop its poisonous effects.

Who We Are and Why We Wrote This Book

Barry and Emily have been married 37 years. We began writing together in 1980; this is our eighth coauthored book.

This has been an enjoyable book to write. In Barry's work as a clinical psychologist, marriage therapist, and sex therapist, he deals with people whose lives and marriages are experiencing major problems. Prevention truly is the best, cheapest, and most efficacious way to address marital issues. Our hope is that in your reading this book, discussing guidelines, engaging in exercises, being aware of traps, and learning from case studies, your marriage will be stronger and more satisfying.

When we married in 1966 we could have used a book like this. Although we would not have followed all the guidelines—we like to make our own decisions—we would have welcomed the chance to discuss issues and focus on what was relevant for us. This is what we hope you will do with our book.

Getting It Right the First Time is not meant to be read as a textbook. Each chapter is self-contained. The material can be read for information and ideas, but it is best used as an interactive learning medium. We encourage you to read together and discuss what is important for you. One technique is to take turns reading aloud, stopping at important points to discuss. Another method is for each person to underline or star the points he feels are relevant. Next the other person reads it, underlining or marking what is important to her. Then discuss issues. We encourage you to engage in exercises that are of interest and feel free to skip those which are not. Try relevant strategies, skills, and coping techniques.

This is a book of ideas, guidelines, and exercises, not a do-it-yourself therapy book. The more information and understanding you have, the better decisions you will make. Knowledge is power. We draw on case studies of clients Barry has treated (identities have been disguised) as well as personal experiences to provide concrete illustrations for concepts. Exercises help you assess and change attitudes, behaviors, and feelings. Exercises offer a specific, individualized approach to creating a satisfying, stable marriage.

A healthy marriage is a major contributor to psychological well-being. Being in a respectful, trusting, intimate marriage brings out the best in each person. Marriage meets needs for intimacy and security better than any other human relationship.

Marriage should not dominate your life or self-esteem. Ideally, a healthy marriage would contribute one-quarter to self-esteem. Self-esteem transcends marital status or even the quality of your marriage.

You deserve a marriage that promotes rather than subverts your psychological well-being. If this is not true for you, we strongly suggest seeking therapy (Appendix A offers suggestions for finding a competent, trusted marriage therapist). People think of marital therapy during a crisis or after they have been married many years. The most effective and cost-beneficial marital therapy is with new couples who have not developed bad habits or chronic problems. Early intervention is most effective when both people are motivated to deal with acute problems and strengthen their marital bond.

Throughout our marriage, we have continued to change as individuals and our relationship has grown. If we had known what we know now, there are a number of things we would have done differently, especially in the first 2 years of marriage. Neither of us grew up with marriages that were good models. We were committed to do better, especially not to engage in the physical violence or intimidating threats that characterized our families of origin. We take pride in having honored our agreement about violence. Avoiding "poisons" is crucial.

During the early years, we wish we had been better able to communicate feelings and requests, had better problem-solving skills, found more equitable ways to reach decisions, and emphasized nondemand pleasuring and intimate sexual experiences. We would have benefited from marital enhancement classes and groups, which are described in Appendix B. Our marriage survived because we were highly motivated to create a successful marital bond. Our bond did grow, although we stumbled on several occasions. Both of us worried (interestingly, about different issues), but neither threatened divorce nor tried to manipulate or intimidate the spouse. We adopted the "best friend" marital style during our second year, which fits us well.

Emily feels the major "glue" of our marriage is taking walks—sometimes we walk for companionship and exercise, often we walk and share thoughts, feelings, plans, and dreams. Sometimes we use walks to talk out differences and conflicts, other times walks are to emotionally connect. Walking and talking is our time to deal with personal and couple feelings. Barry feels a major resource has been our respect for individual styles and goals while continuing to put a high priority on coupleness. Our friends joke that we have the most individualistic marriage they know, while our adult children see us as having a traditional marriage. They complained we were too much of a parental team and did not portray our individuality. Both views are true—we are a close, intimate team and we value autonomy and individuality. Establishing a healthy balance between autonomy and coupleness is a chief task in creating a satisfying, stable marriage.

Your Marital Commitment

Choosing a spouse and saying "I do" is one of the easier parts of marriage. Marriage is not a movie where "The End" flashes on the screen. The ceremony is just the beginning. Creating a marriage that is satisfying and stable requires thought, time, communication, experimentation, feedback, and realistic expectations. The marital bond of respect, trust, and intimacy must remain vital.

Our favorite metaphor for marriage is a garden (Emily is an avid gardener and Barry contributes sweat equity). You choose a good spot, plant a variety of vegetables, herbs, and flowers, water regularly, diligently weed, pick and prune, enjoy the beauty of your garden, and at the end of the season rototill and prepare for next year. A garden requires thought, attention, and effort while providing food, seasonings, beauty, and the smell of flowers. It is important to choose a spouse whom you respect, trust, and can grow with. Marriage involves shared activities, interests, and values. Your relationship requires attention and nurturing, trust is reinforced, difficulties are addressed and problems solved, you share emotional and sexual intimacy, and individual and couple growth is welcomed. Your marital bond needs to be nurtured and valued if it is to remain vital, satisfying, and secure.

Closing Thoughts

The best time to work on a marriage is the first 2 years. The best strategy is prevention and the second-best is early intervention. If you build a solid base in the early years, you inoculate yourself against major problems in the future. It is not that transitions, differences, conflicts, and problems will not occur—they will. Dealing with problems, losses, and conflicts is part of marriage. Develop problem-solving skills, emotional resources, and positive, realistic expectations. Be open to and welcome change. This book with its information, guidelines, exercises, case studies, strategies, and skills will help you create a healthy, satisfying, stable marriage.

CHAPTER 2

Strengthening Your Bond: Respect, Trust, and Intimacy

The core of marriage is a respectful, trusting friendship. Emotional and sexual intimacy provides special feelings and energizes your marital bond. The central tasks in the first two years of marriage are to strengthen your marital bond and develop a comfortable, functional couple style. If the marital bond is weak or you do not develop a satisfying couple style, your marriage is vulnerable to dissatisfaction, dysfunction, and divorce.

In most marriage books, communication is given prime billing—especially communicating feelings. "Pop psychology" writers and media gurus promise that good communication guarantees a successful marriage. We believe in and advocate clear and honest communication, but empirical research demonstrates communication is *not* the prime element in a healthy marriage. The core element is developing and maintaining a marital bond of respect, trust, and intimacy. Communication is important but cannot substitute for a solid martial bond.

The core of your marital bond is respect for each other and respecting the marriage you have created. You trust the spouse has your best interest in mind, will honor agreements, and not do anything to intentionally subvert you or the marriage. You can enhance emotional openness and vulnerability while enjoying sexual intimacy. Within this context, the principles of open, clear, and direct communication are of great value. These same communication techniques in the context of a nonrespectful, nontrusting relationship with a gross power imbalance are destructive. For communication to be valuable, you need an equitable power balance, self-respect, respect for your spouse, and a trusting relationship. Otherwise, communication techniques can be used in a dishonest or manipulative manner.

Respect, Trust, and Intimacy

Respect, trust, and intimacy are the mantra for marriage. Each component is necessary with the whole being more than the parts. We discuss each separately and then examine how to integrate these core elements into your marriage. Although there are differences for each marital style, your bond has to be solid and secure.

Respect

Respect is the cornerstone of marriage. Respecting the spouse and accepting him with strengths and weaknesses is the basis for a healthy marriage. Knowing, understanding, and accepting your spouse for the person he is, with stellar as well as problematic characteristics, clashes with the cultural ideal of romantic love. Respect is based on a clear view of your spouse, different from the romantic love approach that idealizes the spouse and places him on a pedestal. Romantic love builds an idealistic, perfectionistic picture. Respect involves being aware of personal characteristics and behaviors that are problematic, rather than pretending they do not exist. Respect involves awareness of the person's positive and negative traits. Knowing your spouse, warts and all, and still being loving and respectful is a powerful personal validation that provides a solid marital foundation. This is very different from the romantic love myth of idealizing your partner and relationship. It is a powerful affirmation of self-worth and marital viability.

Respecting your spouse does not entail unconditional acceptance of her behavior—contrary to the romantic love admonition "Love means never having to say you're sorry." In a respectful, trusting marriage, you say you are sorry often; that is normal and healthy. Respect does not mean you agree with everything your spouse believes or does. It does mean listening in a respectful, caring manner. Validating your spouse's feelings does not mean you agree with the spouse on content issues. Each person has a right to her or his feelings. Marriages work best when you communicate empathy. You then negotiate changes and agreements based on a positive influence model. This contrasts with noncontingent acceptance on one extreme and intimidation or coercion on the other extreme.

It is crucial to not demean your spouse, especially in front of children, family, or friends. This includes not demeaning your spouse even in your own thoughts. You want to be a supporter, not a critic. When your spouse is experiencing a problem at work, a phobia, or depression—be empathic and supportive, not blaming or condescending. Be aware of and emphasize your spouse's strengths and coping abilities. Help him confront and deal with the problem; denying or pretending does not serve either the person or the marriage. People like us for our strengths and successes. Your spouse loves and respects you with strengths and weaknesses, successes and failures. For example, Barry's lack of skill with mechanical and perceptual motor tasks is a major deficit and source of embarrassment. Emily is a friendly, outgoing person who practically hyperventilates when faced with groups of 10 or more in a formal setting. We accept problem areas, realizing some are not changeable. We acknowledge weaknesses without decreasing love or respect. Difficult areas are monitored and addressed. Support your spouse through the change process. Marriage works best when based on a positive influence model that includes both acceptance and change.

Acknowledge problem areas without losing respect for your spouse. When there is a problem that needs to be dealt with, for example, Barry not monitoring his diabetes or Emily ignoring financial issues, these are confronted, discussed (hopefully, in a nonblaming manner), and problem-solved. Do not put down or punish your spouse. Avoid finger pointing or obsessing. Addressing problems helps maintain a sense of positive influence in your marriage. Maintaining an equitable power balance is crucial for personal respect, respect for your spouse, and respect for your marital bond.

A major task in the first 2 years of marriage is to create a viable couple style—whether complementary, conflict minimizing, best friend, or emotionally expressive. Respect your chosen marital style. Respect is a necessary, but certainly not sufficient, basis for a healthy marriage.

Trust

Trust is a crucial component. When people think of trust they focus on extramarital affairs and jealousy. These are important issues but are not the major element in a trusting marriage. The essence of trust is believing your spouse cares about you and has your best interest in mind. Trust involves both functional and emotional components. A trusting marriage includes the positive, reciprocal assumption that your spouse's intention is to promote your well-being and the well-being of the marriage. A trusting marriage means your spouse would not intentionally hurt you nor subvert the marital bond.

Trust is the emotional bedrock for a healthy marriage. Couples dealing with a crisis or chronic stress successfully cope as long as their sense of trust remains intact. Knowing you support and care about each other allows you to deal with crisis and loss. You trusting your spouse will help you deal with the pain and you will survive as a couple.

When the trust bond has been breached, it is difficult, although certainly not impossible, to rebuild. All couples experience negative feelings, hurt, disappointment, conflict, frustration, and anger because of different needs, perceptions, and preferences. That is a normal part of life and marriage. It is not negative feelings, stress, or conflict that disrupts trust. The spouse acting in a disrespectful or destructive manner is what breaks the trust bond. This includes emotional betrayal, personal put-downs, public humiliation, an extramarital affair, lying, or trying to coverup or deny a problem.

If trust is to be rebuilt, both the content issue and the trust process have to be addressed. It does neither of you nor the marriage any good to pretend the breach of trust did not occur. Rebuilding trust is crucial. Restate understandings and agreements and reinforce the importance of trust. Rebuilding your trust bond requires confronting the problem, taking responsibility for the trust breach, offering a genuine apology, and having a clear understanding about the meaning and value of trust in your lives and marriage.

Intimacy

Emotional and sexual intimacy generate special feelings that reinforce your respectful, trusting relationship. Emotional intimacy nurtures your relationship. Sexual intimacy energizes your marital bond. A chief ingredient of emotional intimacy is freely disclosing feelings, thoughts, perceptions, and desires. This includes both positive and negative feelings. Intimacy is highest in best friend couples and lowest in conflict-minimizing couples, but a sense of intimacy is vital for all marriages. Establishing a mutually comfortable level of intimacy is a major marital task.

Marriage manuals would have you believe the more intimacy the better. This is not true. Each couple establish their comfort zone—it is crucial to maintain personal boundaries and autonomy, and not feel overwhelmed by your spouse's feelings and needs. The balance between being an individual and being a couple, between autonomy and intimacy, is not the same for everyone. Couples find a comfortable place on the continuum, not falling into the extreme of isolation nor the extreme of enmeshment. Intimacy does not mean giving up your sense of self.

The traditional trap is when one spouse (usually the woman) pursues and demands intimacy, while the other withdraws and avoids to protect autonomy. You cannot demand intimacy; intimacy is voluntary and reciprocal.

Emotional intimacy involves a comfortable way to be with each other. Some couples relish sharing feelings, aspirations, concerns, hopes. Others do best when talking is combined with activities such as walking, playing board games, having dinner, working on a household chore, playing golf. Many couples enjoy talking about emotional topics and feelings. Others realize it is necessary but find it difficult. For some, integrating talking and affectionate touch is a crucial ingredient for intimacy.

Be there for each other through difficult and sad times, as well as sharing joyous and successful experiences. To paraphrase the poet-philosopher Kahlil Gibran: *There are many people you can laugh with, but treasure people you can cry with.* Intimacy includes celebrating successes and triumphs as well as supporting each other through painful or traumatic experiences. Being there through tough times makes your intimacy bond strong and resilient.

Sexual intimacy is special. Traditionally, the major function of marriage was procreation. Procreation is a potential function of sexuality, not its prime function. There is not one kind of sexual expression in marriage; there are a variety of ways to experience touching and sexuality that convey a range of meanings. Sexuality can be a shared pleasure, a way to deepen and reinforce intimacy, a tension reducer to cope with the stresses of life and marriage. A "quicky" can be as valuable as an extended, romantic experience. Sensual, gentle sex fits one circumstance; passionate, lustful sex another. The romantic ideal that all sex should be natural and spontaneous with equal desire, arousal, and orgasm is nonsense. It is a self-defeating performance criterion. Romantic love/passionate sex sells movies and novels, but is destructive for real-life couples.

A positive, realistic expectation is that sexuality enhances and energizes your marital bond. Sexual comfort and quality increase over time. Premarital experiences are fun and exciting, but marital sex is better quality, more intimate, and more satisfying. Marital sexuality is different from a premarital affair. Comfort, awareness, safety, intimacy, pleasuring, and eroticism can be integrated so that marital sex is satisfying and energizing.

Power in a Healthy Marriage

Traditionally, power issues were not discussed. The women's movement made us acutely aware of power issues. The traditional model where the man was in control of house, career, and financial matters because he was the sole income producer while the woman was a handmaiden in charge of cooking, cleaning, and children was never valid. Men believed that since they earned more money and money equaled power, they did not have to share in the mundane tasks of housecleaning, changing diapers, driving carpools. Our culture mistakenly equates money and power as a measure of worth, but that definitely should *not* be so in marriage.

A joke among marriage therapists is that the most difficult

couple to treat are two lawyers because each protects his/her bargaining position and will admit to no weakness or fault. They fall into a classic power struggle, so worried about losing and protecting themselves they forget about positive feelings and couple goals. Techniques that are appropriate in legal or business negotiations are harmful and self-defeating in marriage. Power plays, coercion, and intimidation have no place in a healthy marriage. They might get you what you want in a specific situation, but in the long run you weaken your marital bond. You win the battle but lose the foundation for a viable, satisfying marriage. Resentments build and lead to an attack-counterattack cycle. Manipulation and demands result in hollow victories at great expense to respect and trust.

You can develop an equitable way to share power that facilitates personal and marital satisfaction. Each person has domains in which he/she takes initiative and is dominant. The spouse's accepting the partner's initiative does not mean he is powerless. Equity does not mean all decisions are shared fifty-fifty. The equal power for all issues model is unworkable and sets unrealistic expectations. Each spouse has areas of interest, competence, and skill. Feeling comfortable with your sense of power and being aware of your spouse's areas of power facilitate marital equity. An equitable power balance enhances respect and trust.

Couples with a complementary marital style need to establish what is in each person's domain and appreciate your spouse's contributions. Conflict-minimizing couples have clear boundaries of who is responsible for what. Best friend and emotionally expressive couples spend time negotiating roles and responsibilities. Both people need to be satisfied with how roles, tasks, and power are shared.

5-to-1 Ratio of Positive-Negative Feelings and Experiences

A core concept for a satisfying, stable marriage is the 5-to-1 ratio of positive to negative couple feelings and experiences. Reinforcing positive attitudes, behaviors, and feelings toward your spouse is the crux of a healthy relationship. This needs to be a genuine process, not pretending or "faking good." You want to cherish the spouse for the person he/she is. Being in this marriage enhances your psychological well-being. This acknowledgment is shared with your spouse as well as couple friends and extended family. On a day-to-day basis, both verbally and nonverbally, each spouse reinforces the positive feelings and experiences that build marital respect and cohesion.

Marital Communication

Communication techniques facilitate marital functioning, but only when there is an equitable power balance existing in the context of a healthy marital bond. These same techniques can be used destructively or manipulatively if there is a power imbalance or a hidden agenda. The following are suggested communication techniques:

1. Empathic listening for feelings, attitudes, and content.
2. "Checking out," especially the spouse's intentions.
3. Empathic responding.
4. Using "I" communications, not "you" communications.
5. Making requests, not demands.
6. Using "going my way" skills of negotiation and problem solving.
7. Reaching "agreements" both can live with, not settling for unsatisfactory "compromises."

Healthy marital communication is a process that recognizes that each person's feelings and perceptions matter. You trust the spouse is negotiating in good faith rather than engaging in a power play or placating you. You reach understandings and agreements that can be successfully implemented, rather than make empty promises.

CAROLINE AND TOM

The wisest advice Caroline and Tom received was from their best couple friends who had been married 16 months—"the real work of marriage starts after the ceremony." Caroline and Tom had a lot going for them—they dated two years, talked about personal and couple plans, discussed issues of children, money, sex, careers, where to live; discussed strengths and weaknesses, liked each other's families and friends, confronted hard issues including Caroline's career dissatisfaction and tendency to procrastinate and Tom's brother who was physically and emotionally handicapped; Tom's desire to pursue his hobby of glider flying that meant he would be less available on weekends. Caroline's parents divorced when she was 9, mother was in a successful second marriage, but father's second marriage was marginal. Tom's parents remained married until his father died 3 years ago, but they were not a good marital model. Both Tom and Caroline were committed to developing a healthy, secure marriage. They were surprised how much time and energy were needed to develop a couple style and strong marital bond.

When they were dating, Caroline and Tom felt they were best friends; love and intimacy meant everything to them. If they had clung to this, they would have been a disappointed and frustrated couple at their first-year anniversary. Tom valued Caroline and their marriage, but also valued autonomy, especially enjoying gliding and friendships with others who shared this hobby. Although Caroline had flown with Tom on occasion, she did not find it interesting and had no desire to take lessons. Nor was she interested in hanging around the airfield.

Caroline focused time and energy on a career change. She trained as a computer systems analyst because that is where job opportunities existed. However, she did not find it interesting nor did she feel competent. Caroline enrolled in a career planning program through a women's center. After thought, research, and information-seeking interviews, Caroline discovered she could be successful at and enjoy being a technical consultant in computer marketing. This entailed taking in-service courses and switching companies. Tom was supportive emotionally and practically (it would be at least 2 years before her salary returned to the base, although in the long run this would be a lucrative and satisfying career).

Tom and Caroline divided roles and responsibilities, including household chores and family activities. They valued couple time and sex was an integral part of their marriage. Caroline and Tom no longer emphasized being best friends above everything else. Tom respected Caroline's courage in deciding to change careers and perseverance in taking courses while maintaining a full-time job. Tom would have a hard time if roles were reversed. Tom had a complicated, time intensive system of computer software to manage their finances. Caroline understood and could utilize the system, but decided that since Tom had more interest they would follow traditional gender roles and finances would be his domain. She respected Tom's competence and appreciated his doing this task.

Tom and Caroline were in work and hobby situations that provided opportunity for extramarital affairs. They had seen this happen with friends and were not so naive as to pretend it could never happen to them. They had an up-front agreement not to do anything that would be harmful to the spouse or marital bond, which included an extramarital affair. They agreed to discuss any high-risk person or situation. This is a powerful technique, along with awareness of personal vulnerability to certain types of people and situations, to reduce the probability of "falling into an affair."

Emotional intimacy cannot be taken for granted, nor can the marriage rest on its laurels. Caroline realized Tom loved her and was loyal, but she worried he would fall into the traditional male trap of settling for a marginal marriage. Tom admitted he had low marital expectations. Discussing expectations about the marriage is not a one-shot exercise but an ongoing process, especially crucial during the first 2 years. Caroline and Tom found a comfortable balance between autonomy and coupleness. Tom was afraid Caroline would be dependent and challenged her to value her time and worth. He did not respect people who cannot function autonomously. Being a fully functioning woman was integral to Caroline's self-esteem. Competence and autonomy were balanced with connection and intimacy. She did not want to isolate herself from friends nor Tom to drop out of the glider group. However, she wanted their emotional bond to be a priority. Caroline was willing to give up the dream of a best friend couple style, but needed a viable bond of respect, trust, and intimacy. Their marriage was on solid footing with a complementary couple style.

Sex was a positive, energizing marital force. They enjoyed a range of experiences—sex as play, intimate sex, passionate sex, sex as a way to feel close, sex as a tension reducer, romantic sex, sex to connect after feeling frustrated or angry, sex bringing them together. Sexually, they enjoyed flexibility instead of being tied to traditional female-male roles. Caroline would initiate as often as Tom and valued eroticism and passion. An enthusiastic, giving partner enhances sexuality. Intimate and playful experiences were as important for Tom as for Caroline. Emotional intimacy nurtured their marital bond and sexual intimacy energized it.

Caroline and Tom felt committed to each other and their marriage. They realized there would be difficulties, disappointments, conflicts, and hard times, which they would survive as long as they remained respectful, trusting friends. They could and would work it out. This was a spouse and marriage to be valued.

The Trap of "Let It Be"

Marriage cannot be treated with benign neglect, certainly not in the first 2 years. Of course, there is the danger of going to the extreme of overanalyzing every marital interaction so neither the individual nor the marriage has time and space to breathe and grow.

The common trap is not devoting enough time or energy to your marital bond. Our culture puts inordinate importance on romantic love and choosing the right spouse, but once a couple marry, the relationship is treated as a "done deal." The message is get on with life, let the marriage alone with the hope time will work things out. Marriage is not about wishing and hoping, it is about communicating and working together to develop a vital, secure bond. Even after 10 or 50 years of successful marriage, you cannot just "let it be." It is tempting to rest on your laurels. Tempting, but self-defeating. Marriage is an active process, not a finished piece of work to put on the shelf like a trophy.

Invest time and psychological energy throughout your marriage, especially in your first 2 years. A prime reason for waiting at least 2 years before having a baby is so you can develop a marital style and strengthen your marital bond. Ideally, a planned, wanted child is an affirmation of marital vitality and stability. Contrary to cultural myth, a child cannot save a marginal marriage. A planned, wanted baby affirms the family but stresses the couple. There is less time and energy for adult concerns. If the marriage is not solid, a new baby can overwhelm the couple. A baby's needs are immediate. You cannot put a baby off for an hour—when her diapers need changing or she is hungry, she needs it now. You cannot say, "Let the baby be." Your marital bond needs to be solid before bringing a child into the family.

Exercise—Strengthening Your Marital Bond

Respect, trust, and intimacy are the core elements in marriage. This exercise focuses on concrete, personal strategies and techniques to strengthen your marital bond. There are two time focuses: the present and 2 years in the future.

Identify as specifically as possible personal and marital characteristics you respect; just as specifically, personal and couple characteristics you feel are problematic. Write these down and talk to your spouse about them. Be sure there are at least as many positive characteristics as negative, and hopefully many more. If there is a majority of disrespectful, negative characteristics about the spouse or marriage, this indicates a need for marital therapy, not a self-help book. When there is a lack of respect for your spouse and/or marriage, you are facing big trouble. This is the time to address these core marital issues.

Be clear about personal and marital strengths. It is equally important to specifically identify individual and couple weaknesses and problems that diminish respect. This is not to put down or humiliate the spouse, but to increase each person's awareness of problem characteristics so they can be discussed and addressed. Ideally, this allows problem resolution or at least reduced power to the problematic characteristics. Some of these can be dramatically changed, most can be significantly modified, and some have to be accepted and worked around.

What promotes trust for your spouse and marital bond? Be specific in affirming what you value and trust about each other and your marriage. Conversely, be specific about what you worry about or do not trust. Usually, the issue involves the partner's motivations and/or intentions. What needs to be clarified and reinforced in order to strengthen your trust bond?

What strengths and problems are associated with emotional and sexual intimacy? This is the hardest area to discuss honestly. Be clear about what you value emotionally—how is this felt and communicated? What causes emotional distance and alienation? Sexual intimacy energizes your bond—what aspects of touching, eroticism, and intercourse do you value? Sexual dysfunction and dissatisfaction subvert your marital bond—do you experience sexual dysfunction or inhibited desire? Remember, the motivation to confront problems and complaints is to promote change, not to put-down your spouse or get defensive.

How satisfied are you with your marriage? Is your bond vital and growing? Or is it vulnerable and diminishing? How can you increase respect, trust, and intimacy?

The second phase of this exercise is how to strengthen your marital bond in the next 2 years. Identify at least three individual and three couple characteristics that enhance respect and that you want to reinforce. Then identify two individual and two relationship areas to improve in the next 2 years so respect will grow. Respect is the core element in maintaining a viable marriage.

How can you build and strengthen marital trust? One strategy is to share with your spouse a sensitive or secret incident from your past. Before you do so, tell the spouse your motivation. Healthy motivations are to help you process the incident and to confront guilt or shame. Be sure your motivation is not unhealthy, that is, to elicit the spouse's sympathy or as a means of expressing hostility. In sharing a secret, the focus is to invite the spouse to be a "partner is healing" so that the past incident does not control your self-esteem or inhibit couple growth. How can you strengthen trust in the next 2 years? Understandings and agreements that promote personal and marital trust are key.

Sharing sensitive or secret material in the present or concerns about the future is even more sensitive than sharing issues from the past, yet it can increase marital trust. Whether the issue is a concern about gambling or drinking, desire for an affair or attraction to a coworker, fantasy about making a "killing" in the stock market or a high-risk business, or a perceived need to prove something to a parent or keep up with the success of a sibling, sharing these vulnerabilities or fears with your spouse and processing their meaning and possible consequences can bring you closer and increase trust.

A highly recommended strategy to enhance emotional and sexual intimacy is to set aside quality couple time. Couples spend time cooking, cleaning, watching TV, doing the mundane tasks of married life, which are important but do not build intimacy. In our marriage, we use walks to share feelings and to talk. Sometimes the walk is to connect, other times to make plans, to argue an issue, to feel close, a bridge to sexual desire, a form of afterplay following a sexual encounter. Develop your couple equivalent to our walks that maintains and reinforces emotional intimacy.

Sexuality will not remain vital if sex is a late-night routine that follows a stereotypic, predictable pattern. The prescription for marital sexuality is integrating emotional intimacy, nondemand pleasuring, and erotic scenarios and techniques. Set aside time for couple dates as well as be open to spontaneous encounters. Touching both inside and outside the bedroom and not all touch leads to intercourse are important guidelines. Request erotic scenarios and techniques that keep desire, arousal, and satisfaction high.

The commitment now and in the next 2 years is keeping your marital bond vital, growing, and satisfying.

If Your Marital Bond Remains Brittle

If your marital bond remains brittle, we strongly suggest seeking professional help. Marital therapy is not a sign of weakness or failure. It is a sign of good judgment. You value this marriage and are concerned it is not developing in a healthy manner. The adage among marital therapists is couples come to therapy at least 3 years after they should have. The therapist has to deal with layers of disappointment, resentment, anger, and blaming before addressing core marital issues and conflicts.

Early intervention is the healthiest strategy. If the problem has not spontaneously remitted after 6 months, we urge you to seek marital therapy. Learning communication and problem-solving skills can help not just by alleviating the immediate problems, but promoting positive attitudes and experiences that inoculate your marriage against future problems. Appendix A offers guidelines for choosing a marital therapist.

Closing Thoughts

Strengthening your marital bond of respect, trust, and intimacy is a vital task in the first 2 years. At its core, marriage is a respectful, trusting friendship. Emotional and sexual intimacy provides special feelings and energizes your marital bond. You owe it to yourself, the spouse, and your marriage to devote the time and energy to build and reinforce a strong, secure marital bond.

CHAPTER 3

Developing a Couple Style

Marriage is a balance of needs—his, hers, and ours. Traditional self-help books espouse achieving a "happy marriage" as if all marriages should strive to follow the "perfect" model. In truth, there is *no* perfect marital model, nor should there be. Marriage is not a cookie-cutter pattern; one size does not fit all. Each individual and couple is unique. Develop a couple style that fits your uniqueness as people and reflects what you value as a couple.

We encourage newly married couples to consciously think about and discuss the marital style that best fits their personalities and needs. There are four marital styles that have empirically been shown to promote a healthy marriage: complementary, conflict minimizing, best friend, and emotionally expressive. This chapter provides information, guidelines, and two exercises to help you adopt a marital style that is comfortable and functional for you. Each style has advantages and potential traps. Discuss which couple style best fits your needs, values, and situation.

The previous chapter emphasized creating a marital bond of respect, trust, and intimacy. These are expressed differently in each marital style. It takes most people at least 6 months to develop a couple style, and few couples have a "pure" style. Your couple style is not set in concrete, but it does provide a foundation so your marriage meets needs for intimacy and security. Like a house, a marriage needs a solid foundation. A house involves preventative maintenance, remodeling, and additions. Your marital style requires continual time, energy, inputs, and modifications.

Empirically for the majority of couples, satisfaction goes down during the first year of marriage. The unrealistic romantic love idealization is confronted by reality. Many couples do not replace romantic love with mature intimacy and realistic expectations, causing the spouse to withdraw, feel disappointment, with increased resentment. The hope of being a perfect couple with the spouse meeting all your needs is neither realistic nor healthy. Romantic love couples are vulnerable to eroding respect, trust, and intimacy. You can prevent this by developing a couple style based on an understanding of each other, mature intimacy, and realistic expectations.

Common Marital Styles

The most common marital style is complementary, followed by conflict minimizing, best friend, and emotionally expressive. The most stable is conflict minimizing; both best friend and emotionally expressive can be vulnerable to disappointment, resentment, marital disruptions, and divorce.

The complementary couple style is most frequent because it offers both satisfaction and security. There is less emotional closeness than in the best friend marital style, but that is preferred. This style gives both the man and the woman freedom to value his/her autonomy and pursue individual interests. Each spouse has his/her domains of competence and influence. Validation and reinforcement meet the guideline of 5-to-1 positive to negative experiences and feelings. The danger is that the couple becomes complacent and takes each other and their relationship for granted.

Conflict-minimizing couples enjoy the stability and security of marriage and family. Often, these couples follow traditional religious and gender norms so there is less conflict and need for negotiation. The couple must remain aware of the need to stay connected and value emotional aspects of their marriage. The danger is that security comes at the expense of personal and couple growth and satisfaction. When there is a major conflict, they are not prepared to meet it.

Best friend marriages are seen as ideal in terms of high levels of closeness and caring, sharing their lives and feelings. Our chosen couple style is best friend, but we are aware of the dangers of this style. The trap is losing a sense of autonomy and becoming dependent. Disappointment and resentment can lead to a bitter, alienated relationship. Best friend couples need to be especially aware of balancing autonomy with coupleness and have realistic expectations about the spouse and marriage.

Emotionally expressive marriages are the most volatile, vibrant yet potentially insecure. These are not dull, "vanilla" relationships. If they are to succeed, both people need to be willing to deal with the range and intensity of emotions. If these marriages are to remain secure, the commitment to the marital bond must remain strong through angry and painful times.

The Complementary Couple Style

The complementary couple is the most common marital style. This style emphasizes continuity and security.

Many, but not all, complementary couples organize their lives in a traditional manner. The male is the main worker, so he devotes time and attention to promoting his business or career. He takes pride in the role of prime money producer for the family. The woman has freedom to organize her life, career, house, and children in a way that pleases her rather than feeling scattered among conflicting roles and responsibilities. Both value their complementary roles and the balance of autonomy and interdependence. There is little competitiveness; instead there is support and appreciation.

A major strength is respect for each spouse's contribution. The communication pattern is inquiring into each other's day and experiences, listening and providing emotional support, and offering help when asked. There are few demands or ultimatums; the focus is on working together and maintaining a compatible, functional marriage. Arguments and conflicts are addressed and dealt with, but are not dominant. The couple is eager to reach understandings and agreements. Since there are individual domains, the spouse in whose domain the problem is usually suggests the resolution. Sexuality is an important part of this marital style. Sexuality is positive and functional, but not a big production. They joke about the extreme way sex is portrayed in the media. They are an affectionate couple, both at home and in public. They have couple and family friends, feel part of the community, and are often religiously and/or socially active. Each spouse maintains contact with same-sex friends.

There are potential traps with this marital style. The predominant one is that the marriage becomes routine and the couple feel stagnant. Other traps include growing apart, being less involved in each other's lives, roles becoming rigid. A particular poisonous trap is feeling you are carrying more of the burden and your contributions are not appreciated. Sex can become mechanical and stagnant, with decreased frequency and quality. Complementary couples are vulnerable to crises because they do not expect them and lack confidence in their coping skills. Whether an extramarital affair, illness of a child, or loss of a job, the problem disrupts the marital balance. When one spouse wants to change her life, he feels threatened. Change can be hard to integrate into this marital style, especially when it is unilateral.

The Conflict-Minimizing Couple Style

Conflict-minimizing couples would rather maintain a positive exterior than deal with difficult issues. The advantages of this marital style are cordiality, predictability, and security. The couple view themselves and are viewed by the community as a "nice, normal couple." They share activities with couples and families, especially extended family. A prime benefit is an abundance of social, friendship, family, and religious support for the marriage. Communication is supportive and nonadversarial; they are compatible on most dimensions.

Conflict is mild and short-lived. In the conflict resolution style, one person gets to do things his way or there is a compromise. Each spouse has her/his domains of control with little conflict over "turf." Sources of frustration are shared with same-sex friends or family. Humor and gender jokes are used to smooth things over. There is not an emphasis on sexual experimentation, but affection and sex are valued. The couple typically follow traditional sex roles, with the woman initiating affection and the man initiating intercourse. They emphasize positives, especially enjoying home, family, and friends. They think of themselves and their lives as busy, full, and satisfying.

The major trap for conflict-minimizing couples are problems and conflicts that cannot be avoided. There are hard issues that have to be dealt with—a job loss, one spouse experiencing a depressive episode, a fertility problem, attraction to another person, illness or death of a parent, or a financial crisis. The couple is so intent on avoiding problems that by the time the problem is addressed, there is an impending disaster or the problem has become chronic. It is easier to deal with acute problems—not addressing problems in an efficient, effective manner can subvert the marriage. Joy, excitement, and sexuality can atrophy if there is little emotional contact. Personal growth is inhibited because of fear that any change could negatively affect the marriage. When they live parallel lives with little genuine connection, the marriage can degenerate into a mediocre, boring pattern.

For conflict-minimizing marriages to remain satisfying, the couple needs to stay involved and reaffirm what each values about the other. Enjoy the process of your lives and marriage. Do not be complacent.

The Best Friend Couple Style

The best friend marital style is the one we adopted, but we do not recommend it for most couples. The core is a respectful, trusting, close friendship. Best friend couples feel like an intimate team who share their lives and have no secrets. They listen to and support each other—respectful, empathic, and caring communication predominates. They try to address differences, problems, and conflicts at the time rather than pretending everything is fine. The "positive influence" model of conflict resolution is utilized.

Emotional and sexual intimacy provide special feelings that energize the marital bond. Each person is free to initiate and make requests. They are comfortable with a variety of pleasuring and intercourse scenarios and techniques. Sexual expression is creative: It can be tender, erotic, or both. A respectful, trusting friendship is the base—emotional intimacy nurtures the bond while sexual intimacy energizes it.

Best friend marriage involves sharing your lives—house, money, parenting, jobs, bills, cooking, cleaning, and helping each other. Even more important is sharing experiences, and feelings, enjoying each other, caring and feeling cared for, and celebrating special times. The spouse is your best friend, your "soul mate." Couples share many activities and interests (hiking, community action projects, the theater, listening to or playing music, travel, political activities, religious involvement, coed sports teams, remodeling their house, playing volleyball or attending aerobic classes, watching TV or renting videos, or a shared hobby such as sailing or bike riding). A special resource is couple friends who like you individually and are supportive of your marriage. Couple friends who share your lifestyle (having or not having children, joy of outdoor activities, or working hard and playing hard) are particularly valuable.

The best friend marital style is inviting, but has major traps to be aware of and monitor. The most significant trap is thwarting individuality and autonomy for the sake of "coupleness." Another potentially fatal trap is feeling disappointed in the spouse, which evolves to resentment of the marriage. Other traps include not valuing or enjoying such a high degree of intimacy. Most people find marriage is healthier when there are personal and emotional boundaries. A common trap is that one spouse becomes dependent or passive. Couples become complacent. They stop growing as individuals, and the relationship stagnates. Best friend couples often do not make healthy individual or couple changes, settling for lukewarm compromises. Another trap is being so close you lose erotic attraction and experience inhibited sexual desire. Best friend couples are destabilized by an affair, which breaks the trust bond.

The Emotionally Expressive Couple Style

This marital style is the most interesting and engaging, but the least secure. The couple readily express feelings and wants, many times at high velocity. Life is seldom dull for an emotionally expressive couple. A prime strength is being highly engaged and sharing a range of feelings from joy to anger. They are a playful and erotic couple—the emotional charge carries over to the sexual charge. Unlike the complementary or the best friend couple, empathic listening and support are not highly valued. Expressing feelings, perceptions, and opinions is mixed with trying to convince the spouse to see it your way and act as you want. Conflicts and lobbying become quite heated. Healthy emotionally expressive couples do not "hit below the belt" nor threaten retaliation. Making up after an argument generates positive emotions and sexuality. These are vital marriages, with little complacency. Another hallmark is change; routine and security have low value. Both individual and couple changes are promoted. Personal expression is highly valued, not lukewarm compromises. There is a great deal of energy.

The biggest trap is that conflicts can get out of control and the marriage becomes the "War of the Roses," culminating in divorce. Other traps include too many ultimatums—"going to the mat"—so the relationship is under high stress. There is too much "drama." Conflicts become power struggles resulting in unilateral, self-defeating decisions. Bitterness and resentment over fights and bad decisions lead to alienation. A major trap is impulsively entering into an affair that throws the marriage into crisis. Arguments about parenting, especially with adolescent children, disrupt the marital bond.

If the marriage is to remain healthy, emotionally expressive couples do not cross the line of humiliation or betrayal. You need to maintain appropriate parameters of emotional conflict; do not use personal put-downs or threats or be abusive.

Organizing Your Relationship

When people talk about organizing their lives, they refer to where they work and live. Practical dimensions are important, but are not the essence of marriage. A critical factor is the quality and amount of intimacy. The best friend couple style emphasizes a close, intimate relationship while the conflict-minimizing style emphasizes personal boundaries. Marriage books and popular culture advocate the more intimacy the better. Empirical research finds this is not true. The crucial factor is reaching a mutually comfortable level of intimacy.

A common marital pattern is the pursuer-distancer dance. Typically the wife pushes for closeness, while the husband protects his autonomy. In truth, both women and men have needs for autonomy and for intimacy. It is not a good-bad conflict; both autonomy and intimacy are healthy. The issue is reaching a balance that meets his-her-our needs.

Best friend couples share a great deal of intimacy, discuss a range of feelings and experiences, have no secrets, and value their affectionate and sexual relationship. They discuss plans and fears, and are aware of each other on a day-to-day basis. The main traps for the best friend style are compromising autonomy, surrendering friendships and interests, and if the high expectations are not met, feeling disappointed and resentful toward the spouse and marriage.

The conflict-minimizing couple maintain strong personal boundaries, devote energy to work and friendships, use others to discuss plans and feelings, are involved in church, community, sports, or political realms, and value practical and stable aspects of marriage and family. The traps are taking the spouse for granted and allowing emotional and sexual intimacy to erode. The dangers are not enough emotional connection and an inability to deal with unexpected conflicts or crises.

Complementary couples enjoy a moderate degree of intimacy while maintaining individuality. One reason this is the most popular couple style is it blends autonomy and coupleness. Being validated and acknowledged by the spouse builds self-esteem and reinforces the marital bond. The traps are taking each other and the marriage for granted, feeling burdened by responsibilities, feeling the marriage is no longer equitable, and losing an intimate connection.

Emotionally expressive couples intensely value both individuality and coupleness. The interplay is like an accordion, sometimes very close, other times very distant. This is the most exciting and challenging marital style. The sense of aliveness and emotional responsiveness is great; sexuality is a vital component. The traps of this style are that limits are stretched and broken, anger and vindictiveness prevail, and the trust bond is broken. This is the most volatile marital style with a high divorce rate. For this style to succeed, each spouse has to trust their commitment to deal with difficult emotional issues, not betray the spouse, and survive hard times.

An important issue for couples is how the tasks of living are shared. Who pays bills, does the cooking, vacuums, mows the lawn, sews on buttons, does dishes, shops for groceries? This includes how "scut" jobs are allocated—cleaning the bathroom, staying home to wait for the repairman, deal with the overdue bill, follow up with the disappearing contractor. Some couples divide tasks on the basis of gender (men mow, women cook), others divide all chores fifty-fifty (each person cooks three meals and they go out the seventh night), other couples try to design an equitable system, many settle for a haphazard approach.

We advocate the equity alternative, organizing marital tasks on the basis of interests and skills. This is the hardest to develop, requires the most communication, and has to be monitored so it remains equitable, that is, one spouse does not feel taken advantage of. In our marriage, we have tried all four systems. Traditional gender roles did not work because Emily is competent at mechanical and outside work while Barry is good at doing dishes, driving carpools, and grocery shopping. The fifty-fifty system is politically correct, but breaks down in practice. People are not equally skilled or interested in tasks. In our marriage, some tasks are done along traditional gender roles—Emily does the cooking and Barry manages the money. Other roles are reversed—Emily does home restoration and Barry mops the floors. As in the complementary marital style, each expresses appreciation for the other's contributions. What system of dividing tasks fits your preferences and situation?

An important dimension involves friendships and group activities. Do you maintain individual friends or develop couple friends? If one spouse does not like your close friends, do you maintain these friendships, pretend everything is fine and do things as a couple, or drop the friendship? If one spouse is very involved with sports or a religious group the partner does not like or feels is interfering with the marriage, what do you do?

We advocate developing couple friends who like both of you and are supportive of your marriage. Good couple friends are an invaluable marital resource. However, couples in conflict can be a strain on your marriage. Avoid getting caught in the middle of another couple's problems, especially if they are separating or divorcing. Your new marriage does not need that stress.

Maintain individual friendships; there is no reason everyone has to be a couple friend. Maintaining "his" and "her" friends is healthy. People worry about opposite-sex friends as a potential for an affair. If there is a potential risk, introduce the friend to the spouse; this is a concrete symbol you are a committed couple and will not tolerate a hidden agenda. If there is sexual attraction or risk of an affair, whether with a friend or work colleague, you need to discuss with your spouse ways to deeroticize that relationship. If that is not possible, terminating the friendship, switching work assignments, or getting a different job is the healthy alternative. Secretive friendships pose a high risk for your marriage. A helpful analogy is that of walls and windows. In secretive relationships, the other person has a window on your life and the spouse is walled off. In healthy marriages, there are clear windows with the spouse, high-risk people and groups are walled off.

How do you socialize at dinner parties, family gatherings, formal events? Do you prefer to mingle as a couple, or would you rather interact individually? Are you socially comfortable, or do you feel dependent on your spouse? In situations where you do not know people, what can you ask of the spouse and what can the spouse offer? Some people prefer socializing with one other couple or in small gatherings. Other couples thrive with large parties or family gatherings of 30 people.

Develop a comfortable social style, and be helpful to each other in stressful situations. You want to see your spouse and have others see him as interpersonally attractive, a good person to be with. If there are sources of discomfort (spouse is too loud, drinks too much, is judgmental or rude, tells stories that go on forever, one-ups people), confront this problem. Do so in a supportive, not critical or blaming, manner. Each couple has interpersonal strengths and weaknesses. This was an issue early in our marriage. Neither of us enjoys large formal events. Barry has a fondness for listening to folk music in smoky bars, a setting Emily disliked. We discussed these differences, and over the years reached agreements, that is, we listen to music at open-air concerts and/or sit in the nonsmoking section. We skip cocktail parties or if attendance is required, leave after a socially appropriate period. We accept each other's foibles— sometimes acceptance is more realistic than change. Each spouse is an individual; you are not clones of each other.

Couples develop their own traditions and symbols. You come from different backgrounds—how your family celebrated Thanksgiving and birthdays, the importance of a greeting in the morning, whether people hugged or kissed when leaving, how conflict and anger were managed, religious traditions. These are not right-wrong issues, but differences in what is valued and how it is expressed. There are gender differences in the meaning of symbols. Males traditionally value concrete symbols—buying a gift or setting up a computer for the spouse. Females traditionally value emotional symbols—flowers, staying in touch when out of town, calling when you will be late. There is a strong tendency to want from the spouse what you are used to giving rather than to accept what your spouse gives. You are different people, be aware of and honor each person's symbols. One husband learned to value his wife's symbol of caring, writing notes and placing them in an article of clothing he would find when unpacking. She came to appreciate his symbols of caring, bringing her a muffin and coffee in bed and repairing equipment at her office.

Couples develop mutual symbols and traditions. A couple who is saving money for a house down payment adopted a tradition of designing personalized birthday and holiday cards instead of buying presents. Other examples are couples who for their anniversary return to the hotel where they spent their wedding night, lighting candles and saying prayers to celebrate religious holidays, hosting a neighborhood pot luck dinner each spring, on New Year's Day hiking in the mountains and setting goals for the year, visiting in-laws and adding to family genealogy, cutting down a Christmas tree and decorating it with a new ornament each year. Traditions and symbols bond your marriage.

Exercise—His and Hers:
Personal Characteristics and Styles

Awareness of and respect for individual differences and autonomy is crucial in developing your couple style. Each spouse draws up a list of at least five personal characteristics in which she is different from him. People point out funny little things like what you put in your coffee, jokes you laugh at, how much time you spend in the bathroom. Be aware of substantive differences—political or social values, desire to travel or live in another country, pursuing a hobby or sport, religious beliefs, maintaining close relationships with siblings, living in the city instead of the suburbs, performing music for friends, or different levels of expertise in investments. Be especially aware of characteristics around emotional intimacy, sexual preferences, ways to address conflict, and social preferences. Exchange lists and discuss these characteristics, acknowledge them, do not minimize. Be sure you know what your spouse is referring to and how she views this difference. Listen carefully. Listening is different from agreeing. When there are areas of difference, state your feelings and perceptions, be sure it is not a criticism or put-down. Your spouse does not need your stamp of approval; he does want to be aware of your concerns. For example, state how much you admire her skill in dealing with difficult situations while expressing concern that her attempts to maintain positive relationships with every friend and family member is unrealistic and could backfire. Do not try to one-up your spouse; share differences with the intention of increasing awareness and acceptance.

Acknowledge and validate differences. Ideally, each spouse values differences and these can complement your marriage. At a minimum, the spouse accepts differences, even if she does not like them.

Autonomy and Intimacy

This is a "both-and" not an "either-or" issue. Marriage needs both autonomy and intimacy. The marriage is healthier when each person is a fully functioning human being, able to take care of him or herself. Avoid extremes of being totally dependent or two people who share the same house but little else. Share your lives in an interdependent manner. Although it might sound easy, maintaining a balance of autonomy and intimacy is a challenge.

Marriage makes a major contribution to psychological well-being. Yet, marriage should not contribute more than 25 percent. Love songs and movies celebrate the myth of the person who is so in love that she gives up everything, even her life. That has nothing to do with mature intimacy: it is a dependent, self-negating view of marriage. We chose a best friend couple style and maintain high levels of respect, trust, and intimacy. In addition, we value autonomy and individuality. If one of us died next year, it would be a devastating loss, yet neither doubts the spouse would survive, deal with the grieving process, and reorganize his/her life. This is not a negation of our spouse or marriage, but a recognition of two people valuing a close marital bond.

Autonomy and respect for individual differences promote marital respect and trust. However, the spouse who hides behind individual differences subverts the marriage. For example, the spouse who goes drinking with friends three times a week or watches sports on TV 8 hours a day is doing something other than engaging in individual enjoyment. The person who says it is my right to compulsively gamble, switches jobs every 6 to 18 months, or avoids kissing, is hiding behind the individual differences rationale. It is an excuse to avoid dealing with a problem. Individual differences reflect personal strengths and preferences. Do not use individual differences to cover up individual problems, maintain secrets, or have hidden agendas.

Ideally, marriage is based on a positive influence process. A healthy marriage brings out the best in each person. The spouse respects differences and strengths. Individual problems are addressed, and your partner is supportive of the change process. Marriage is not about molding your spouse to your ideal image, but respecting and loving him with weaknesses as well as stellar characteristics. Change is his responsibility; the spouse supports and reinforces change.

Identify a healthy balance between autonomy and intimacy in establishing your couple style.

Exercise 2—Developing "Ours"

This exercise asks you to closely examine four couple styles—complementary, conflict minimizing, best friend, emotionally expressive—and agree on and refine the couple style that fits your needs and preferences. Few couples have a "pure" style. For example, Barry and Emily's predominant style is best friend, but in some areas, we use conflict minimizing and in others the complementary couple style.

Discuss the process areas of marriage:
1. Communication and support.
2. Intimacy and sexuality.
3. Problem solving and conflict resolution.
4. Sharing time and having fun.

Look at specific content areas:
1. Children.
2. Careers.

3. Money management.
4. House and household chores.
5. Social and sports activities.
6. Family, religious and community involvement.

How do you discuss and handle process and content issues? Which couple style best reflects your values and how you want to organize your lives? Be honest: Do not give the socially desirable response or what you think your spouse wants to hear.

The two core components in your couple style are the degree of intimacy and your approach to conflict management. As individuals and a couple, how much intimacy and what quality of intimacy fits you emotionally and sexually? What are your preferences for dealing with differences and conflicts? Do you enjoy talking about these and reaching understandings/agreements, or would you prefer to minimize them?

One couple said they valued an emotionally expressive style and gave examples of highly emotional talks, exciting sex, and vigorous arguments. However, when they carefully assessed marital roles and domains, they realized their primary couple style was complementary. Another couple viewed themselves as following the best friend model, but when they examined how they handled content areas, they realized they had become a conflict-minimizing couple. This was not what they wanted, and they agreed to take specific steps to increase intimacy, share tasks, and confront difficult issues.

How do you deal with process issues? How do you manage content issues? Are these congruent with your preferred couple style? Reach a mutually agreed upon couple style that fits your values and situation.

Be aware of the advantages of your chosen style. For example, a major strength of the conflict-minimizing style is stability: These couples have the lowest divorce rate. A major strength of the emotionally expressive style is a vital, lively relationship. A major strength of the complementary style is well-defined roles where each person's contributions are acknowledged. A major strength of the best friend style is high levels of sharing and intimacy. Play to the strengths of your marital style. Contrary to the media myth, you cannot have it all. Enjoy what you have, and acknowledge its value.

The flip side is to be aware of traps in each couple style—be sure these do not subvert your lives and marriage. The main trap for the best friend style is stifling individuality and being disappointed in the spouse and marriage. For the complementary style, it is slipping into rigid roles that are not functional and feeling burdened by responsibilities. For the emotionally expressive style, it is breaking the couple bond, emotional outbursts that weaken respect and trust—you "go to the mat" too often. For the conflict-minimizing style, it is a lack of emotional connection and denying a problem exists until it becomes a marriage-threatening crisis. Write out potential traps and review them at least once a year to be sure your marriage remains free of traps and poisons.

Integrate your chosen couple style into your lives so it promotes the well-being of him, her, and us.

Change and Stability

The balance between change and stability is important. Both individuals and their relationship change with time and life events (birth of a child, buying a house, job change, societal changes). Marriage fulfills needs for security better than any other relationship. Like intimacy, change/stability is not a dichotomy but a continuum. You need to establish where you feel most comfortable, fitting the reality of your lives.

Conflict-minimizing couples value stability; emotionally expressive couples value change. Marriages have to be adaptable enough to integrate individual and couple changes while maintaining security. Change is easier when planned and chosen—for example, the couple who move to a lower-cost, lower-stress city where there are good job opportunities. Change precipitated by a job termination or one spouse diagnosed with a chronic illness requires a different coping strategy.

Traditional marital vows are "for better or worse." Any marriage will succeed when everything goes well. The test of marital viability is dealing with difficult or sad events. Each spouse has his or her style of coping with crisis and loss. Differences are acknowledged as the couple struggle with stressful changes. We advise couples not to deny the reality nor allow the problem to dominate their marriage. A particularly painful example is the death of an infant or the less traumatic, but extremely sad, miscarriage. You cannot expect your spouse to react emotionally the same way as you, but you do deserve your spouse's understanding and support. People grieve differently. For one spouse, religious symbols and prayers are a great help; for the partner, looking to the future and another pregnancy is most helpful. Do not argue which coping mechanism is best. Realize each person has different emotional needs and ways to express them. Accepting the sad or traumatic experience and regaining equilibrium is crucial for your marriage.

Change is a given of the human condition, whether planned or a reaction to circumstances, whether positive or problem driven. Some people are risk takers who enjoy the challenge—for example, the entrepreneur who starts a new business every 3 or 4 years. A spouse may choose an organization that offers tenure or job security because that fits his personality style. Some couples buy a house with a 30-year mortgage with the intention of paying off the mortgage and staying until retirement. Other couples buy homes every 3 to 5 years or rent and move every 1 to 2 years. This is not a "right-wrong" choice but a matter of reaching agreements that meet his-her-our needs and personality characteristics.

Agreements versus Compromises

The traditional marital advice was to "compromise." Although it is not always possible to meet his, her, and our needs, agreements are more likely to succeed than compromises. In a compromise, no one's needs are met. The classic example is going out to eat. He wants to go to an Italian restaurant, she wants to eat Chinese; they "compromise" on a mediocre Continental restaurant neither enjoys. In striving to reach agreements that meet the needs of both individuals, clearly state feelings and preferences, what you are unwilling to do, and what you can live with. Examine a range of alternatives, and reach a resolution that successfully addresses the issue. Ideally, the agreement would be a win-win situation that meets each spouse's needs, is good for the couple, and resolves the conflict. Most agreements are not this successful, but at a minimum both can live with the agreement and it reduces or ends the conflict. Using the dining out example, a couple might decide to eat at a French-Vietnamese restaurant, go to the Italian restaurant with the spouse choosing the wine, or go to the Chinese restaurant that night and the Italian restaurant the next time.

Agreements require more thought and discussion than compromises and are more complex. In other words, agreements demand time and energy. It is worthwhile to create a resolution that meets individual and couple needs. This is not necessary for all conflicts—it makes no sense to have a prolonged discussion over whether to take the highway or a back road on a one-time excursion. It does make sense to discuss and reach an agreement about who washes the dishes and who takes out the garbage. If the problem causes stress or discomfort for one spouse, it deserves the attention of the couple. Devoting time and energy to reach a satisfactory agreement is a worthwhile emotional investment.

Making good agreements sounds easier in theory than it is to implement in reality. The agreement process involves a series of component skills:

1. Listen to each spouse's feelings, needs, and perceptions in a respectful, caring manner. Listening and validating are different than agreeing but are a necessary step.
2. Creatively generate alternatives that address the issue.
3. Do a cost-benefit assessment of alternatives and reach an agreement that best meets individual and couple needs.
4. Develop a system to monitor, alter if necessary, and successfully implement the agreement.

Not all agreements work or are satisfactory, but agreements are more likely to promote couple functioning than lukewarm compromises. Even if it is a poor decision or an unsuccessful agreement, you made a good faith effort and are less likely to blame or harbor resentment.

Barry and Emily continually make and modify agreements about budgeting and money management. Money has been a consistent source of difficulty and stress in our marriage. Although we have implemented a number of agreements that resolved specific problems, other agreements have not been successful despite our best efforts. Sometimes you just cannot resolve the problem. This is not a reason to give up on the positive influence and agreement process—that makes a difficult situation much worse. In reality, some problems do not have a satisfactory resolution. As long as there is an ongoing dialogue, resentment, frustration, and blaming will not subvert your marital bond.

Playing to Each Spouse's Strengths

Each person has strengths and weaknesses. Learning to play to and emphasize strengths is a prime marital task. For example, one spouse enjoys planning weekend activities and makes the phone calls to reserve camping facilities. She takes this as her task rather than taking turns. The spouse who is interested and good at a content domain takes the lead. This system is easier to implement for complementary and conflict-minimizing couples. Sometimes, the division of tasks follows traditional gender roles and other times reverses it. The husband might enjoy managing investments (traditional gender role) and also be the one who plans and cooks a gourmet dinner for six (reverse gender role). The wife might enjoy and be in charge of car upkeep and also be the one who organizes housekeeping chores and does laundry. If both are good at something, it can be fun to do it in tandem.

The spouse need not be good at everything. Accept her strengths, reinforce and enhance those. Be aware of weaknesses and vulnerabilities, accept these as part of her. In couple agreements, each plays to strengths and works around weaknesses.

Acknowledge and reinforce each person's marital and family contributions. Competitiveness and envy are downplayed, support and praise emphasized. You are a team with each spouse playing to strengths. As a couple you have a better quality life than you would as individuals.

MICHELLE AND CARTER

Michelle and Carter were alumni who met at a college homecoming football game. Michelle was 28 and Carter 26. They had not known each other in school, and their postcollege paths were quite different. Michelle moved to Boston as a financial analyst (her college major was finance). Carter moved to a small town on the water 50 miles east of Washington, DC, and began a home restoration company, specializing in historic preservation (his major was history). They had in common loyalty to the alma mater and a love of college football.

Two months later Carter was in Boston for a professional meeting and called Michelle. Saturday afternoon they took a long walk through the Back Bay section commenting on good and bad examples of historic restoration. Carter was surprised to learn Michelle knew a great deal about historic architecture, but even more surprised to find she had a number of creative ideas about financing home restorations. The walk extended to a romantic dinner at a historic restaurant and Carter's suggestion they spend the night together. Michelle was attracted and intrigued, but had a rule against a long distance relationship. Carter gracefully accepted this and invited her to Sunday brunch. Afterward they walked through an unrestored part of Boston.

Carter invited Michelle to visit his small town when she wanted a break from the city. He assured her there would be no sexual pressure. They corresponded via e-mail and talked on the phone. Two months later, she flew to the area for a long weekend. Carter proudly showed her house restoration projects. His pride and joy was his home, a 95-year-old Victorian a block from the water. Michelle fell in love with the small town and Carter.

The ensuing romance evolved over an 8-month period with travel back and forth. Michelle was the methodical planner, Carter the optimistic romantic. Michelle secured a job, although at a substantial pay cut, two miles from Carter's home. Before she moved, she insisted on a room of her own in the house for an office as well as for her favorite hobby, quilting (which she had learned from her grandmother). Michelle and Carter agreed they would live together at least 6 months and not longer than a year to determine whether they would be a viable marital couple. Carter was optimistic, but Michelle had seen her parents' marriage end in divorce (and her father's second marriage fail). A brother was divorced, and her best friend's marriage lasted less than a year. Michelle wanted an intimate, stable marriage and children. She was willing to try but wanted to be sure they shared the same expectations and values. Michelle would not accept a marginal marriage. She wanted a committed, satisfying, stable marriage.

In deciding to marry and discussing their couple style, Carter and Michelle found the best place to talk about serious issues was while sitting on a broad comfortable rock looking over the water. The complementary couple style fit their needs best. Both enjoyed individual time, interests, and friends too much to embrace the best friend style. Michelle was too reserved to enjoy the emotionally expressive style, and Carter did not respect the "let all your emotions out" ethic. They were disclosers and problem solvers, so conflict minimizing was antithetical for them.

Carter loved the freedom to take risks and grow his business. He enjoyed being his own boss and carrying a project through to completion. Michelle found working in a decision-making role in a large organization with perks, health benefits, and secure pay fit her needs. Although she loved small town living and a milder climate, she missed the excitement and financial rewards of Boston. Carter enjoyed traditional male activities of hunting, fishing, sailing, and golf. Michelle enjoyed the latter two; they would sail and golf with couple friends. Michelle joined a quilters group that was a highly reinforcing activity and developed close friendships, including two women who were considerably older.

Couple tasks were divided on the basis of strengths and interests, not traditional gender roles. Michelle was in charge of finances and investments, organized couple activities, and dealt with extended family. She bought clothes for both of them, did interior furnishing and decorating, and encouraged religious and community involvement. Carter appreciated her skills and effectiveness. He did outside house and lawn work, was the cook and cleaner, organized vacations, encouraged exercise and keeping fit, and did nitty-gritty chores like going to the cleaners and arranging for contractors. They had a list of "scut" chores—cleaning bathrooms, washing windows, calling about disputed bills. These were put in a "junk job jar" and pulled randomly.

At least once a month, Michelle and Carter would sit on the rock and discuss issues and concerns. Michelle wanted a child but was afraid they would revert to traditional roles and marital vitality would be drained. She wanted to wait at least a year so she would have a solid niche in her job and could negotiate two-thirds time with the ability to do some work at home via computer. Carter was eager to have a child and committed to be an involved father.

They attended prepared childbirth classes and enjoyed parenting their infant son. Many fathers he knew did not tune into parenting until the child was 2 or 3; mother was the prime parent. Carter was an active father from the beginning. He did not make the unrealistic promise that everything would be split fifty-fifty, but did promise to be involved and caring, not a backup parent.

Carter and Michelle realized marriage is a complicated balance of his-her-our needs and is even more complex with a baby. They vowed to bring the baby to their rock and continue to share feelings, problem-solve, and value their marital bond and couple style.

Dealing with His-Her-Our Weaknesses

Marriage books talk much more about strengths than weaknesses. In truth, each spouse and each marriage has weaknesses. Being loved and accepted with your weaknesses and vulnerabilities is a special resource for a marriage. In a healthy marriage, the spouse is motivated and receives support to address weaknesses and change what is changeable. Often, it means accepting weaknesses and vulnerabilities and working around them. Certainly, it means not using weaknesses or vulnerabilities against your spouse. For example, Barry is incompetent mechanically, Emily is incompetent in financial matters, and we are uncomfortable in formal social settings. We accept these weaknesses and compensate by having Emily be in charge of mechanical repairs and developing a working relationship with plumbers, electricians, and auto mechanics. Barry tries to do financial management with the help of a professional financial adviser. We enjoy small informal gatherings with friends and do not attend formal events. When we have to attend these events, we are supportive and reinforce ourselves afterward by doing something enjoyable. We are not proud of these weaknesses but accept them, cope with them, and do not allow them to control self-esteem or our marriage.

Closing Thoughts

A healthy, stable marriage requires balancing his, her, and our needs. Respect individual differences and the autonomy of each person. Do not sacrifice yourself for the marriage. A healthy marriage is a major factor in psychological well-being, but marriage contributes only one quarter to self-esteem. Respecting and accepting individuality and seeing the spouse as a fully functioning person is a solid foundation for life and marriage. A good marriage brings out the healthiest parts of each person.

Develop a couple style that fits individual needs, preferences, and values. Agree on the couple style that is best for you and individualize it so it meets your emotional needs while fitting the reality of your lives. A couple style that balances individuality and coupleness promotes intimacy, satisfaction, and stability.

CHAPTER 4

You Are Not Clones:
Dealing with Differences

A healthy marriage involves two individuals who are committed to sharing their lives. Marriage does *not* mean being joined at the hip. Couples who value autonomy and accept individual differences are more likely to have a satisfying, secure marriage. A healthy marriage, regardless of preferred marital style, acknowledges individual differences.

A vital marital task is to reach a balance between individuality and coupleness—between "me-ness" and "we-ness." There is *not* one right balance; it depends on the feelings, needs, and preferences of each person and couple. This balance is not set in concrete; it is affected by situational factors and changes over the course of your marriage. For example, the couple who works together as opposed to living in separate cities because of work. The balance is altered when children are born and altered again when the last child leaves home and you are a couple again.

Some people strongly emphasize individuality, others interdependence. Find a comfortable balance on the continuum; we advise against extremes. The spouse who has been "a rock and an island" moves toward greater connection with shared vulnerability. The spouse who clings or feels empty when alone learns to emphasize personal worth and autonomy. Extreme positions make it difficult to integrate coupleness and individuality.

A healthy marriage facilitates individual growth. Change is welcomed, not feared. Change is not at the expense of the marriage. Individuality affirms, not negates, your marital bond. For example, the spouse who pursues her interest in classical music, takes lessons, and attends concerts is a happier person. Individual well-being facilitates marital satisfaction. The husband who maintains involvement with the community church or social action group brings a source of activity and people into his life and marriage. Individual interests and growth can have a positive, reciprocal relationship with couple interests and growth.

Accepting Differences

Couples who share core interests, values, traditions, and ways to organize their lives have easier marriages. Our culture loves stories about the magical attraction of people with totally different backgrounds and values. The "opposites attract" theme makes great stories in movies and talk shows, but empirical studies strongly support the shared similarities approach to mate choice, especially core personality factors and values. The more important the factor—desire for children, wanting to stay in the community versus travel the world, ambitious about career versus laid-back—the more similarities matter. These are critical for compatibility and satisfaction.

Even the most intimate couples have individual differences. One spouse enjoys hiking and backpacking, which the partner has not tried. Perhaps she finds she enjoys it and this becomes a joint activity, or she likes hiking but not backpacking, or neither. If the latter, the spouse does this activity with friends or by himself. What works for you as a couple? Trouble ensues if he demands she does it his way or she demands he give up a valued activity as a "symbol of love." Giving up something that is healthy for you is not a sign of love, it is a sign of dependence.

We have a variety of shared interests and activities, including writing. Our best friend marital style promotes shared experiences and activities. Just as important are individual interests and activities. Emily is artistic, enjoys quilting, gardening, antiquing, tole painting, and home restoration. Barry has increased appreciation for those activities and accompanies her and provides labor for projects. Yet, they are clearly hers, not his. Barry enjoys travel, folk music, ethnic restaurants, and biking. Emily enjoys some of these activities and takes a pass on others. Individual interests spice up our lives and marriage. Because of Emily, Barry has come to appreciate classical music, historic architecture, and small town living. Emily's life has been enriched by travel, exploring cities, and interacting with a range of people.

Individual differences can be a source of tension and conflict. Examples include the "golf widow," he complains about being dragged on shopping trips, she feels he is addicted to TV sports, he complains there is no time because she is always on the phone planning an extended-family gathering or getting stuck in family conflicts. What happens when this activity is bad for the person (gambling, drinking, staying up all night watching TV, compulsively playing computer games)? Under the guise of an individual activity, he avoids the spouse and marriage. Is going to flea markets or dance workshops every weekend a passion or an excuse to avoid?

Motivations and intentions are crucial to understanding the function of a behavior. The same behavior positively motivated has a facilitative effect on your marriage, but if negatively motivated can subvert the marriage. For example, the spouse who volunteers to lead a church social action project and sings in the choir feels good and involves the couple with the church community. Negatively motivated, it is a way to avoid dealing with conflicts and marital issues under the guise of religious devoutness. An activity can hide anything from a fear of intimacy to a covert expression of hostility. Behavior is multicausal and multidimensional. You need to understand the person, your marriage, and the situation. Most of all you need to be aware of the motivations and intentions.

To understand individual differences, it is important to disclose and process feelings, preferences, desires, and intentions. Share what is important to you; this allows the spouse to understand and react to differences. Communication and empathy are necessary but not sufficient. It is very difficult, if not impossible, to integrate individual differences into your marriage if the spouse does not understand your meaning and motivation.

A couple argued incessantly over the wife's coed soccer team. He felt this was a singles activity she should give up now that they were married. She counterattacked saying he had no right to boss her around. She then explained she had a poor body image until beginning soccer at age 10 and being on a competitive team improved her body image and confidence. Winning the award in senior year as best female athlete was a highlight of an otherwise difficult high school experience. Now he understood her motivation. When they have children, she plans to coach soccer. She assured him the guys she met through soccer were in the "buddy" category—he had no reason to fear an emotional or sexual involvement. She asked him to participate in one-on-one soccer drills (which would be fun) and occasionally come to the games. Her father and brothers initially made fun of soccer, but eventually all but one saw her play. In fact, her father became quite a fan. This put the soccer team in a totally different light for the husband. He was a runner and swimmer who had little interest in team sports, but he learned to appreciate her interests. They made two couple friends through the soccer team.

Often, individual interests are idiosyncratic and not shareable. One husband had a fascination with model trains, which his wife found uninteresting. She was surprised at how consuming and expensive this hobby was, but since it filled healthy needs for him, she accepted it. They coordinated schedules so train outings and meetings did not interfere with couple plans. He was passionate about this hobby but did not hide behind it nor allow it to subvert couple time. He knew club members who used the hobby as a wall to block out the spouse.

A wife was a computer whiz and used these skills to pursue her passion, to make money in the stock market. She purchased sophisticated software that allowed her to chart stock trends. She lobbied the spouse to give her discretion over their savings and retirement investments. They reached an agreement whereby she managed all retirement investments and half of their savings. In addition, she used the software to do their taxes. Although he was fiscally conservative, he appreciated her competence. He felt lucky to have such a talented spouse.

Nitty-Gritty Differences

Couples experience more stress and conflict over nitty-gritty differences than major life issues. Little things count in marriage.

Differences can work to good advantage, especially for complementary couples. For example, the spouse who likes detail work is in charge of balancing the checkbook, the extroverted spouse organizes their social calendar, the spouse who likes the outdoors designs and plants the garden. Nitty-gritty differences can be problematic: One spouse likes order, the other is messy and disorganized; one is active and athletic, the other sits around listening to music; one loves talking on the phone, the other abhors the phone.

Some nitty-gritty differences are easily accepted, others have to be negotiated. A spouse who reads the paper from back to front might be unusual but does not cause relationship difficulties. The spouse who rinses dishes and pans rather than washing them could cause disease; this is unacceptable. Conflict escalates from a minor irritant to a major source of distress. This must be addressed and negotiated and an agreement reached. Couples treat nitty-gritty conflicts with benign neglect until they become a source of chronic problems. The time to address a conflict is in the acute stage, before resentment builds.

A key to resolving nitty-gritty differences is realizating that it is not a matter of right-wrong but of different preferences and styles. A couple had a continual argument over the right way to load a dishwasher—there is *not* one right way. The agreement was to put cups on the upper section so they would not get chipped because they were family heirlooms. Although she did not agree, she was willing to carefully stack the cups. Some couples establish "turf," his or her domain. They do things her way in her domain and his way in his domain. The details of the resolution are less important than reaching an agreement both can live with.

What if your spouse's habits upset you? Perhaps he uses "uh" five times a minute, she becomes embarrassed and avoids eye contact, he compulsively touches his beard, she gives money to each street person you pass. Instead of attacking your spouse's personality or issuing ultimatums, view this as an irritating habit and make specific suggestions for change. For example, reduce the "uhs" to one a minute, practice eye contact one-on-one and then in a small group, have him keep his hand in his pocket, give money to a food kitchen instead of street people. Support your spouse and facilitate change. Do not be her worst critic.

LIZ AND DICK

This was 24-year-old Liz's first marriage and 27-year-old Dick's second. They met at a party hosted by a friend. Ten months before, Dick's ex-wife decided to move out of state for a job and leave the marriage. Friends said it was good there were no children, but Dick felt depressed that the marriage had been such a waste.

Dick had been a shy teenager who fell in love with the ex-wife at seventeen. Being divorced at 27 was not easy. Liz had withdrawn from college for 2 years to live and work in France and was now in her final semester. She was an adventurous person interested in new people and experiences. At the initial meeting Dick was attracted, but it had not been mutual. Liz was dating a graduate student from Kuwait and enjoyed the international community.

Dick was an avid soccer player. His team played a team with Kuwaiti players, a game that Liz attended. Dick was the goalkeeper and allowed no scores, making two spectacular saves. Liz was athletic, a golfer and tennis player, but knew little about soccer. She was struck by how self-confident and in control Dick was on the field as opposed to his hesitancy and awkwardness in social situations. Liz majored in computer systems information. Dick was an economist knowledgeable about computer applications. As they talked over postgame pizza and beer, Liz asked him to set up an information interview. Dick prided himself in helping, and was pleased to talk with her the following week. He introduced her to people in the computer division. After college, Liz was hired by this company.

Over the next few months, Liz and Dick would see each other informally at work and soccer games. In the spring, both joined the company coed softball team. Liz had recently ended her dating relationship, which gave Dick the courage to ask her to a movie. Afterward, they went for a long walk, one of Dick's favorite activities. Liz was used to bars, dancing, and socializing. This date was much more personal and pleasant. She began thinking of Dick in a romantic way, the way he had viewed her for months. There are significant advantages for a relationship developing out of a friendship (as long as there is genuine attraction). The attraction had always been there for Dick, and it was growing for Liz.

Liz was a romanticist; once involved she put all of herself into the relationship. She told Dick what a great guy he was, cheered at soccer games, bragged about him to friends, brought him home to meet her family, and introduced him to her social circle. Although Dick enjoyed parts of this, it was not his style. He is interpersonally discriminating rather than extroverted, but he went along to please Liz. This was to haunt him after marriage, when Liz angrily attacked Dick for pretending to be something he was not.

They had known each other 2 years and been a couple 9 months when they married. This gave them ample time to discuss life plans, psychological issues, and personal vulnerabilities. However, like most premarital couples, these crucial conversations did not take place or occurred in a cursory manner. Liz idealized Dick and the relationship, assuming he valued what she valued and there were few differences. Dick reveled in Liz's love and did not want to spoil it by raising concerns and vulnerabilities. He hoped these would work out in time or be dealt with after marriage. The road to disappointment and resentment is paved with naive high hopes.

Romantic idealism did not even last until the marriage. Liz planned a wedding full of symbolism and a major social event. As it got closer, Dick's anxiety and discomfort increased. He did not like being the center of attention. His parents were being difficult, feeling they had already done this for the first wedding. Relatives were put off by how elaborate the wedding was.

Dick felt caught in the middle but was emotionally paralyzed and unable to communicate his discomfort and concerns. Noncommunication is the milieu in which minor problems turn into major crises. A week before the wedding there was a blow-up about arrangements for the rehearsal dinner to be hosted by Dick's parents. It did not meet Liz's criterion for festiveness. She had a screaming match with her future mother-in-law with name-calling and counteraccusations. Liz felt the wedding was ruined and if not for social embarrassment would have canceled it. Dick felt panicky; he was frightened this marriage would be a repeat of his first. The love, optimism, and energy that attracted him to Liz now felt like emotional volatility that could blow up at any time. When the person is on a pedestal, the fall is hard and devastating. Dick was no longer viewed as a warm, caring man but a socially awkward wimp who would not stand up for Liz. The wedding did not get their marriage off to a healthy start.

Their employer had an EAP (employment assistance program) counselor whom Liz consulted two weeks after the wedding. The counselor was a concerned, competent professional. Rather than focusing on pathology, the counselor framed this as a crisis intervention case, with a focus on realistically dealing with differences. Liz left the meeting feeling hopeful and agreed to bring Dick the next time. Dick was fearful, especially of the stigma of being twice divorced. He was willing to do anything to win back Liz and save the marriage, but he felt stymied. He could not be the miracle man she hoped for nor did he want to attack his parents to prove he was not a wimp. The counselor suggested a four-session contract to address individual differences and marital issues. If more was needed, she would make a referral for marriage therapy. Liz and Dick committed to doing written and verbal communication exercises at home between sessions.

The first exercise focused on affirming individual worth. Each was asked to tell the spouse the psychological, physical, interpersonal, sexual, and career characteristics they admired and liked about him or her. This was the opposite of the premarital pattern of exaggerating, overpromising, and idealizing. It was a positive, realistic, specific acknowledgment of personal strengths. Dick went first. Liz was impressed how he had prepared, writing out a list of 14 characteristics he admired and sharing how he felt about her. Dick might not be Prince Charming, but he was thoughtful, solid, and genuine. Liz resented what happened before and during the wedding but opened herself to a respectful, trusting, intimate marriage. Liz was not a structured person; she did not list characteristics, she expressed feelings. This was not right-wrong, but an example of individual differences that each could accept and appreciate. Dick's loyalty to his parents changed from a source of contention to a symbol of solidness, indicating his ability to provide a nurturing, stable marriage. Liz wanted Dick to realize emotional expression would enhance their complementary marital style and not view it as a source of fear. Emotional expression within the context of an intimate, committed marriage is energizing. Dick learned to trust that Liz's intention was to enhance, not disrupt, their marital bond. Liz trusted Dick was willing to express feelings, deal with differences, and confront conflicts rather than "faking good." As they shared strengths, vulnerabilities, and differences, trust increased.

The EAP counselor suggested each make three specific requests for changes that would increase respect for the spouse. These were requests, not demands, about characteristics the spouse could change (i.e., the spouse can act responsibly in managing health or financial concerns but cannot change her height). Dick's requests were specific and written. Liz's were verbal and emotional. Liz was not trying to remake Dick, but did want him to stop apologizing for himself and take emotional risks with her and others.

A major difference was that Liz was energized by people contact. She relished parties and large events. They reached an understanding about which events Liz wanted Dick at and which he could skip. Dick interacted, he did not hide in a corner. Dick planned events with one or two couples, his preferred social milieu. An irritating difference was that Dick liked things picked up and in order at night; he hated dirty dishes in the sink in the morning. Liz's tolerance for disorder was considerably higher, although she felt he exaggerated her messiness. Again, they needed to recognize and validate differences. Liz agreed not to let dishes go for more than 2 days. They usually worked in tandem to clean up the kitchen.

At the end of the four sessions, they agreed the marriage was on track. Liz and Dick were developing a respectful, trusting relationship in which individual differences were acknowledged, accepted, and integrated. The counselor suggested they take a 10-session church-sponsored class about marriage and spirituality. They enthusiastically agreed to do so.

Individual Differences and Marital Style

The four marital styles meet the challenge of individual differences in different ways. The best friend style accepts autonomy, but not at the expense of coupleness. Marriage involves two people who are well bonded. Individual differences are respected and enhance the couple's life. Problematic differences are discussed, some changed, others accepted. The complementary couple style advocates each spouse playing to strengths by establishing his or her domain and manner of doing things. Complementary couples have the freedom to express differences. Emotionally expressive couples are aware of differences but try to talk the partner into changing. There is less acceptance or tolerance—why not do it my way? Conflict-minimizing couples downplay individual differences. Irritating differences are sources of complaints to others, not directly to the spouse. Differences are avoided, not confronted. Best friend couples find it hardest to accept individual differences, yet that is crucial for a successful best friend marriage.

Each couple decides how best to deal with differences. There is not a right balance between autonomy and intimacy. What fits your comfort level and marital style? Each couple establishes their unique balance.

Use differences to affirm individuality and add new, interesting dimensions to your marriage. Our guideline is to accept differences as long as they do not threaten or negate our couple bond. An example is Emily wakes up slowly and enjoys coffee in bed or sitting on the porch. Barry wakes up quickly and is ready to begin writing or take a walk. He writes downstairs and brings her a cup of coffee when she wakes. We try to accept and integrate differences. Other idiosyncrasies need to be changed. For example, Barry would often talk to Emily while at the same time reading, which she found irritating. He likes doing two things at once, so we talk while doing a chore like folding clothes or raking leaves.

Exercise—Valued Differences and Irritating Differences

This exercise can be verbal or written but needs to be a serious thought-out process, not a venue for offhanded comments. Writing a list and discussion facilitate a thoughtful approach. This is an example of individual differences: One spouse might prefer writing, the other speaking. What is your most comfortable way to communicate?

Note at least three of your spouse's characteristics (not shared by you) that you admire and value. These could be major characteristics or personal idiosyncrasies. Examples include ability to play multiple musical instruments, follow mechanical directions, knowledge of social protocol, drive a stick shift car, be an excellent photographer, make creative appetizers, stay up all night and function the next day, be detail-oriented and so keep track of paperwork, cry at a movie, have the discipline to stop smoking, be bilingual, tell jokes. The spouse listens and accepts these without "yes, but" or minimizing the characteristic. How can positive differences be integrated into your marriage so they enhance the bond and add spice to your lives?

Choose three irritating characteristics for which you request changes or modifications. Focus on specific attitudes, behaviors, or emotional responses; this is not a criticism of the spouse's personality. Examples include reduce snoring, not smoking (or at least not in the house), not spend an hour a day on the phone with her mother, not walk away if a sensitive topic comes up, break the cycle of 3 hours of TV every night, confront fear of driving over bridges, not control all aspects of the couple's social life, not drink by himself, stop going with friends to events without asking the spouse, stop being arrogant when talking to neighbors, stop avoiding family functions, curb compulsive hand washing, not stay up until 2:00 in the morning in computer chat rooms, follow through on chores. The spouse listens, rather than reacts defensively, to the requests. He has three options:

1. Agree to change and develop a change plan.
2. Modify the irritating behavior.
3. Say he cannot change, but discuss how to limit the negative impact.

For example, if the irritating behavior was smoking, Option 1 is to join a stop-smoking program and ask the spouse's help in monitoring and implementing the program. Option 2 is to reduce smoking by half and not smoke in the house. Option 3 is to not smoke in front of the spouse and use a special toothpaste and mouthwash to reduce smoking odor.

In discussing individual differences and negotiating changes stay away from right-wrong power struggles, tit-for-tat agreements, threats, or ultimatums. Affirm the spouse's autonomy and right to her individuality but reduce the negative impact of irritating differences.

Individuality and Intimacy

In our culture male individuality is acceptable, female individuality less so. Her self-esteem increases as she values individuality and autonomy. Traditionally, it is the woman who values the marriage and nurtures the bond. This is another example of pre-marital and gender learnings subverting the marriage, resulting in lowered satisfaction. Ideally, both spouses are invested in their marriage. A fully functioning marriage involves two autonomous people who share their lives in a satisfying manner but not at the expense of individual desires and needs. Healthy marriages are composed of two fully functioning human beings. An intimate marriage brings out the best in each person. The unit is stronger than its component parts.

This requires women to value autonomy and individuality and men to value intimacy and marital involvement. Even with the best friend marital style, people are not clones, individual differences are honored and valued. This facilitates growth, spice, and change.

Intimacy promotes, rather than hinders, change. Intimacy invites honesty and sharing, balancing hopes and dreams with reality. Marriage cannot rest on its laurels. Each individual and the relationship can and should change. This entails a continual process of sharing feelings, desires, and concerns; examining individual and couple alternatives, assessing potential benefits and downsides, reaching an agreement that at a minimum both can live with and optimally would be good for both individuals and their marriage, and a plan to successfully implement and monitor the agreement. This is a vital, dynamic process, not a sterile formula. Differences are honestly shared, not kept secret or minimized. Conflicts are dealt with, not allowed to fester and poison respect. This process increases trust in your spouse and marital bond.

Individuality and intimacy not only coexist but they promote a satisfying marriage. Differences are a source of vitality. Couples in conflict-minimizing marriages are most wary of individual differences, but this is a misplaced fear. The spouse who returns to school increases her competence, and the intellectual stimulation enhances their marriage. Spouses applaud each other's personal growth.

The fear is that there is a hidden agenda or acting out a dissatisfaction. For example, a husband who wants to build an addition to the house or remodel the basement so he has a workroom or office that, for a spouse, is problematic if his motivation is to avoid the partner or marital issues. There is also the woman who returns to school for a degree or a career change with the hidden agenda of becoming financially independent so she can leave the marriage.

As in other areas of life, motivation is key. The same behavior positively motivated promotes individual and couple growth. You need to understand your spouse's motivations and intentions. Establishing this dialogue process early in the marriage inoculates against problems as your lives and marriage evolve.

Respect and trust are crucial in integrating individual differences. Many marriages begin with an unrealistic romantic love idealization of the person and relationship. Disappointment and resentment increase until the marriage is devitalized. Respect and trust grow not because everything is perfect, but because you deal with differences and conflicts. Acceptance of the person you are, with strengths and weaknesses, is validating. Even more so is the positive influence process, being open to feedback and requests of your spouse. Marriage brings out the best in you. Honor your spouse's individuality, accept differences, reach understandings, and positively influence each other.

Closing Thoughts

A healthy, satisfying, and stable marriage involves two autonomous individuals who are committed to sharing their lives. Autonomy and individual differences are honored and valued; there is not pressure (overt or covert) to give up who you are for the sake of the marriage. You do not deny or minimize differences. Differences are accepted and integrated in your marriage, which promotes individual and couple growth. Positively influence each other: The marriage brings out the healthiest characteristics of each person.

CHAPTER 5

Love Does *Not* Mean Never Having to Say You're Sorry: Positive, Realistic Expectations

The romantic love model espoused in novels, songs, and movies is seductive, but poisonous for your marriage. The assumption is that as long as you love each other, everything will be fine. The classic movie *Love Story* promised "love means never having to say you're sorry." That sounds and feels loving, but in reality it is untrue and self-defeating. Love is *not* enough to maintain a healthy, secure marriage. The road to alienation and divorce is paved with romantic love myths and unrealistic expectations.

Intimacy is a crucial component of your marital bond. Intimacy energizes your bond and builds special feelings about your spouse and marriage. However, emotional and sexual intimacy cannot compensate for lack of respect or trust. The essence of a healthy marriage is a respectful, trusting friendship. Positive, realistic expectations, including understandings and agreements that facilitate marital communication, are crucial.

What is the difference between (a) unrealistic hopes, (b) positive, realistic expectations, and (c) settling for whatever you get? We suggest an exercise to make these distinctions personal and concrete. Each spouse responds separately to the following four vignettes. Write responses independently and then discuss them. For each vignette place your expectations in one of three categories: "unrealistic hopes," "positive, realistic expectations," or "settling." A simple example illustrates this.

A husband heard of a scheme to generate income quickly and easily by distributing marketing materials on weekends. His wife feels since they both work hard Monday through Friday, weekends should be for couple time and leisure. In addition, she questioned the ethics of this marketing scheme. The "unrealistic hope" is that this is a perfect couple project; it will be lucrative and fun. A "positive, realistic outcome" involves their fully discussing this opportunity: he researches the ethics, time, and feasibility; they reach an agreement both can live with that allows him to try the opportunity while preserving couple time. "Settling" expectations are that the husband pursues his plan, the wife is frustrated and hurt, and when the plan does not work she says, "I told you so."

Respond to the following four vignettes by writing and then talking. The three categories are unrealistic hopes; positive, realistic expectations; settling.

Vignette 1. Sarah's widowed mother is diagnosed with cancer 7 months after Sarah marries Josh. Her mother lives by herself 200 miles away. Sarah invites her to live with them since there are better oncologists and a cancer unit nearby. Sarah promises Josh this will not affect their lives or marriage.

Vignette 2. Eight months after marriage, Mary discovers Steve has two outstanding credit card balances totaling $4,000. Mary feels Steve intentionally kept this from her and worries he has a gambling problem, which he vehemently denies. Steve wants Mary to co-sign a $5,000 line of credit.

Vignette 3. Robert is a very organized person both at work and home. He makes a weekly list of chores, and each weekend they plan a major housecleaning or repair project. Robert chides Susan for bringing work home, saying she is not efficient from 9 to 5. He brags how involved he is in housework in comparison to other husbands and how lucky Susan is. She feels he is subtly undermining her competence, but she enjoys the fact that they are making progress at the house.

Vignette 4. Karen and her female friends read sex surveys, feeling validated that their experiences are in the normal range. Rex and his friends read the same reports and feel their wives are cheating them sexually. Rather than prompting a sharing of feelings and perceptions, this conflict becomes a battleground with Rex pushing sex each night and Karen feeling harassed and forced to say no.

What do your responses to these vignettes say about your marital expectations? Are one or both of you too willing to settle? Are you naively hopeful, becoming bitter if expectations are not met? What are positive, realistic expectations? Do you positively influence each other and reach healthy agreements? Are your expectations realistic? Can you accept nonperfect solutions, aware that some problems are not resolvable? The key is to be both positive and realistic.

Why Love Is Not Enough

Why is love not enough to carry the marriage and bypass hard times? Why the emphasis on realism rather than love? We are not antilove, although we prefer the concept of mature intimacy.

There are two problems with romantic love that subvert and can even destroy the marital bond. The first is putting the spouse on a pedestal as the all-loving, all-good person. Respecting and caring for the spouse is healthy; idealizing him and putting him on a pedestal is harmful. The spouse is respected and loved for strengths and weaknesses, not as a romantic fantasy. The second problem is that romantic love idealizes the relationship and promises love will keep everything golden. People naively hope love will overcome any and all problems. Love does motivate the couple to deal with disagreements and hard issues, but it cannot deliver on the promise of a perfect life and marriage.

Any couple can be happy as long as everything goes well. The measure of marital viability is the ability to deal with conflicts and hard times. Loving feelings provide motivation, but love alone will not conquer problems. The couple need to learn conflict resolution skills—the ability to discuss feelings, examine alternatives, and reach a reasonable agreement. If you believe romantic love will protect you from conflict, you are setting yourself up for disappointment and alienation. Loving feelings are necessary, but not sufficient, for coping with differences, disappointments, and hard times.

Positive, realistic marital expectations and romantic love are in conflict. Romantic love sells movies, records, and novels but does not promote a healthy marriage. Realistic expectations are not a media hit but do facilitate viable, stable marriages that promote thriving in good times and help you survive hard times.

People complain that realistic expectations seem uninviting and unsexy—a second-class, boring marriage. Theoretically, clinically, and personally, we could not disagree more. There is nothing second class about realistic expectations: They provide a solid marital foundation. Idealizing a marriage by saying you will love each other no matter what results in disappointment and resentment (and perhaps divorce). Accepting and loving the spouse is crucial, and, in addition, you need to deal with conflicts, disappointments, and hard issues. Realistic expectations and a satisfying marriage are complementary. Respect for the spouse increases when you realize she can handle a conflict with a painting contractor or an obnoxious neighbor. Trust increases when she sees you rebound after losing an important sale rather than give up and get drunk. Life has disappointments and hard times, and so does marriage. It is naive to think otherwise. Knowing you can deal with and survive painful, difficult experiences strengthens your marital bond. Realistic expectations promote a vital, secure marriage.

DANIELLE AND ADAM

Danielle married at 18 because she was pregnant. Her parents discouraged the marriage, but Danielle believed love would overcome all. When her husband left 2 weeks after her son was born, Danielle was devastated. She considered placing the baby for adoption (there is a long waiting list to adopt healthy infants), but after a month she felt bonded and could not proceed with adoption. Danielle realized the baby's father was irresponsible and did not want to be a husband or father. She needed to be a responsible single parent. Danielle earned her general equivalency diploma, obtained financial aid, and enrolled in a 1-year course as a licensed practical nurse. Her parents and friends were supportive, practically and emotionally. Over the next 8 years Danielle followed realistic plans for her life and child.

Danielle was 26 when she met 29-year-old Adam, the roommate of a cousin, at a family picnic. Adam was a master's degree economist working for the state government. In his professional life Adam was goal-oriented, but personally he was a romanticist. Adam was quite attracted and followed up with phone calls for the next 3 weeks until Danielle said yes to dinner and a movie. Danielle's experience was men began as romantic and enthusiastic, but faded out. Danielle was cautious; she had worked hard to establish her life and was reluctant to risk it with a new relationship.

Danielle worked as an aide at a nursing home, a job she enjoyed, but she bridled at the poor management. She took training classes with the goal of completing a college degree and working in nursing home administration. She realized it would be a long, slow road. Not surprisingly, Adam's knowledge of economics and administration fascinated Danielle.

Terry, who was now 8 years old, got along with Adam, although Danielle made a point of not having a boyfriend heavily involved with her son. Terry had an excellent relationship with Danielle's father and brother, so she did not worry about a male model in Terry's life. Adam wanted more contact, but Danielle's strategy of gradual involvement was best. Adam's relationship with Terry continued to improve, especially after the marriage.

At Danielle's insistence, the crucial yet difficult discussions about their lives occurred before marriage. Adam promised the world (and meant it). He offered to pay for college, adopt Terry, have a baby, buy a house, and plan two couple vacations a year. Danielle asked what would happen when they encountered stress and problems—would he resent her and the marriage? Danielle admired Adam's optimism but worried about his ability to deal with frustrations and hard choices. Adam felt Danielle was afraid to act on her dreams and hopes. This was a source of argument and distress.

The minister who conducted premarital counseling observed how aware they were of each other's fears and vulnerabilities. However, they had poor conflict-resolution and problem-solving skills. He encouraged them to focus on specific issues rather than argue abstract principles. Danielle found this a helpful guideline. She agreed to focus on change and optimism if Adam agreed to be practical and prioritize hopes and plans.

Danielle signed up for two courses a semester and reduced her work commitment. She remained on the birth control pill, and Adam agreed they would not have a child until Danielle finished her degree. Danielle wanted to be married at least 2 years before beginning the process of Adam's adopting Terry. She wanted to be sure the marriage would be viable and stable.

Adam agreed to share information about career successes and failures with Danielle, as well as reviewing income and expenditures on a monthly basis. Adam wanted Danielle to trust him, not because of naive love, but based on his good intentions, judgment, and follow-through. He was not the "knight rescuing the poor damsel." Adam saw Danielle as a strong, resilient person who should take advantage of opportunities to improve her educational, professional, and financial situation. Adam did not need a wife who was dependent but a spouse to share life and develop a healthy interdependent relationship.

Danielle was an aware, liberated woman. She could maintain autonomy while sharing feelings, sexuality, parenting, and life with Adam. He held a number of traditional gender assumptions, which Danielle challenged. Adam accepted her insights and was open to her influence. He was adamant about the practical and financial advantages of marriage and Danielle's completing her degree. Danielle agreed with Adam on content but challenged him on process issues, seeing him as "controlling," using facts as a rationale for doing things his way. This was not Adam's intent, but he valued content over process in both his personal and professional life.

Adam felt Danielle was overly cautious and fearful of change. Although she initially resisted this observation, Danielle realized it was true. Disappointments caused by the first marriage and being a single parent had too much control over her present decisions. After two semesters of college with excellent grades, she enrolled as a full-time student. During a summer internship in hospital administration she learned concepts and skills that could be transferred to the nursing home. Adam used flextime to be home for Terry. Adam was not a passive baby-sitter; he helped with homework and car pools and taught Terry fundamentals of cooking.

A hard issue for most couples is time. Marriage is a balancing act: individual, couple, work, parenting, household, friends, extended family, sports, and hobbies. There is never enough time. Adam was an avid TV sports watcher on weekends. For Danielle, this was a major irritation. She wanted time to socialize with friends, do chores, engage in outdoor activities as a three-person family, have couple time, and share sexual intimacy. Adam tried to placate Danielle, but to no avail. They agreed he would watch a maximum of 5 hours of sports per weekend day. Danielle scheduled her individual activities around these times. Danielle accepted Adam's preferences, even though she did not value watching sports on TV. She was not happy, but at least both knew the parameters. In an interesting side effect Danielle and Terry began attending football and baseball games with Adam. He became an assistant coach for Terry's baseball team.

As an economist and the major wage earner, Adam assumed the role of family money manager. Danielle admired Adam's expertise but felt he had extravagant spending habits. Adam had a regular savings and investment program and was willing to spend surplus money on Danielle, Terry, and leisure activities. Danielle felt they could save an additional $250 per month for an emergency fund rather than borrow on credit cards (this was Adam's backup). She had the facts on her side, and Adam reluctantly agreed but set the amount at $200 a month.

Danielle's increasing respect and trust for Adam translated into increased sexual desire. This was a pleasant surprise for Adam, whose desire had been high premaritally, decreased after marriage, and increased again in response to Danielle's interest. Danielle had realistic expectations of sexuality. She realized some experiences would be fabulous, either because there was a great deal of intimacy or because one or both felt lustful. Most times sex was pleasurable and satisfying. Often, sex was better for Adam than Danielle—she accepted this. Other times sex was mediocre or disappointing; Adam found this harder to accept. When she was more into the sex than he, Adam felt a bit intimidated, although responsive. Danielle assured him sex was not a competition, he did not have to match her. Danielle was aware it was normal for males over 35 to occasionally not have an erection sufficient for intercourse. Danielle wanted Adam to enjoy variable, flexible sexual expression. Being comfortable with erotic, nonintercourse sex inoculated Adam against erectile problems with aging. Sexuality was a special experience, which energized their marital bond.

They needed to establish realistic expectations about parenting before Danielle considered having a baby. Adam played an important role in Terry's life, but Terry was not looking for a substitute father. Adam strove to establish a "favorite uncle" relationship similar to what Terry had with Danielle's brother. Adam was pleased but wanted an "our" child.

Adam and Danielle agreed to review short- and long-term goals every 4 months. This was Adam's idea, but Danielle was receptive. Danielle was committed to a respectful, trusting, intimate marriage, wanting to be sure they remained both optimistic and realistic. Adam appreciated the specific, realistic focus. He wanted to be sure they continued to grow and not become bogged down. Their goals were a satisfying marriage, a baby, and two successful careers. Adam was pleased with his contribution to Danielle's optimism and risk-taking. He no longer believed in romantic love or having everything they dreamed of, but wanted a vital and satisfying marital and family life. They did not have to settle for a "humdrum" existence. Danielle appreciated his enthusiasm as long as he remained realistic. Her confidence in Adam and their marriage was reinforced.

Dealing with Disappointments and Problems

A test of marital viability is the ability to deal with disappointments and problems. Major problems include one spouse being fired, infertility, being sued, a chronic illness, estrangement from extended family. Disappointments and setbacks are less dramatic, but are impactful. Examples include not developing couple friends, structural problems in the condominium you bought, not receiving a promotion, tension with a brother-in-law, irritation at spouse's eating habits or political views, finding spouse is a poor driver or repair person.

If the spouse was viewed as perfect and on a pedestal, this results in a devastating fall. You are equitable partners; neither belongs on a pedestal. Awareness of your spouse's vulnerabilities and weaknesses is integral to a respectful, loving marriage. This cushions your emotional response to disappointments and setbacks. For example, one woman married knowing her husband was a bright, hardworking systems analyst. She did not realize he was not interested in nor good at managerial tasks. He enjoyed challenging technical jobs, but these entailed a good deal of travel, which she found stressful. To make a good salary he either had to do technical work requiring travel or do administration, which he detested. They agreed he would switch jobs to a smaller company where he had challenging technical work with a minimum of travel. She continued full-time employment so their combined income provided a reasonable standard of living. She hoped for a traditional marriage where her income would be supplemental, not necessary. The trade-off of her being a higher income producer in order to have an involved marriage with him at home more was worthwhile.

Realistic expectations involve agreements about life organization that decrease disappointments. When conflicts occur they are dealt with and problem-solved so resentment does not control your marriage.

One of the most painful disappointments involves sexuality. Initial sexual encounters, driven by romantic love, newness, and passion, are impossible to maintain. Too often, romance and passionate sex give way to routine, low-quality sex. Attempts to replicate romantic love/passionate sex are a major reason for affairs, putting the marriage in jeopardy. Contrary to popular myth, extramarital affairs are most common in the first 2 years of marriage. Sexual problems are the major cause of divorce during the first 2 years. Are sexual disappointments and setbacks inevitable? No. But romantic love and passion do not endure, seldom even lasting until marriage. This is normal and need not be a source of disillusion or resentment.

The issue is whether romantic love will transition to mature intimacy with passionate sex replaced by high-quality sexuality, which integrates intimacy, pleasuring, and eroticism. It takes most couples 6 months to develop a comfortable, satisfying sexual style. It is destructive to expect romantic love/sexual passion to endure. Positive, realistic sexual expectations are the antidote. Sexuality is a good example of the healthy function of realistic expectations, protecting couples from disappointment, alienation, and inhibited sexual desire.

Exercise—Setting Realistic Couple Expectations

This is a writing and discussion exercise that involves comparing expectations before you married with present expectations. These involve major areas such as communication, money, children, sex, careers, where to live. Expectations also involve mundane areas: who cooks, cleans, makes coffee, decides whether to go dancing or to a movie, organizes friends for activities, decides where to go on vacation.

In what areas were your expectations met? What are the unmet expectations that result in disappointment or even despair? Where expectations were met or largely met, acknowledge the value of this achievement. For example, the couple who married with the expectation that within 3 years they would buy a house and be pregnant feel pride and satisfaction at achieving this goal. The couple both of whom enjoy extended families and find most relationships are good, but do not like two brothers-in-laws, still can acknowledge this as a strength. Expectations do not have to be met completely in order to feel satisfied.

Unmet or negated expectations cause stress. Be honest in discussing disappointed expectations. Share feelings and perceptions; do not blame your spouse. Own your feelings and take responsibility; do not use this exercise to put down or attack your spouse. It is your disappointments and frustrations that may or may not be shared by your partner.

In areas where expectations were not met, some were unrealistic, such as I will never get angry, I will never let you down, we will always feel loving when we go to sleep. Confront and change unrealistic expectations. When expectations were realistic, but not met, such as having a vital sexual life, both people working and saving money, or developing couple friends, this is a loss. In discussing failed expectations, explore how each feels and its impact on the marriage. Would it be best to let go of these expectations or replace them? If the latter, refocus on positive, realistic expectations and a plan to meet them. Translate expectations into healthy, reachable goals.

Discuss expectations that cause disagreement. One spouse is disappointed because she had not developed a positive relationship with her father-in-law, while the husband feels the situation is tolerable. Can this be improved, or are you wiser to accept it as is? Often the couple establish a mutual expectation; other times it is acceptable for expectations to be disparate.

Establish positive, realistic expectations for the future. Many are mutual, others personal. Include both major life issues and mundane areas. Develop positive, realistic expectations that enhance self-esteem and your marriage. What can you realistically expect from yourself, your spouse, the marriage? Share expectations about money and careers, where and how to live, balancing couple and group activities, travel versus saving money for a house down payment, how much time to spend with extended family as opposed to friends, how house chores are divided. Mutual expectations facilitate communication and satisfaction. Establish at least five shared expectations. With differences, be clear what they are. Even if you do not like it, be sure you can live with it.

Hopes, Dreams, and Expectations

In our marriage Barry is the dreamer; Emily prefers predictability and realism. Life changes have been fueled by Barry's dreams. Unfortunately, reality seldom turns out as well as he hoped. Emily is better dealing with the reality while Barry agonizes over why it did not work like his dream. This serves as an impetus for the next set of hopes and dreams. Hopes and dreams are different from realistic expectations. Barry is careful that his dreams do not subvert important realities in our lives. Be aware of the balance each person brings to the dreams versus realism continuum.

We urge you to express dreams and hopes, especially early in the marriage. This is the right time, rather than engage in "if only" thinking and feel burdened by resentments during later years. The early years involve choices and life directions which set a tone for your marriage. If plans do not work, they can be changed, but at a cost of time, effort, and money. If your dream is to live in a small city close to the mountains, acting on that dream now makes sense, not buying a house in the suburbs. If the hope is to have two children before 32, Norplant is a poor contraceptive choice. If your dream is to develop a small business into a franchise and make major money by age 40, signing up to work on a cruise ship for 3 years is a self-defeating diversion. Do not subvert your hopes and dreams. Allow room for dreams while maintaining realistic expectations. Do not set yourself up for failure by betting your career and marriage on a low probability plan. An example is both spouses quitting their jobs and becoming involved in a marketing scheme. A more realistic approach, used by a number of couples, is one spouse maintaining a salaried position while the other opens a small business or joins a commission-based sales organization. Dreams and realistic expectations can complement each other as long as you discuss pros and cons, evaluate alternatives, make plans, and work together.

What do you do when dreams and reality are disparate? What about the spouse who wants to play out his dream of spending a year on conditioning to compete in the Ironman Triathalon? The spouse who wants to have a baby rather than complete an MBA? The couple who works 70-hour weeks to establish a mail-order or Internet business, but it fails? The spouse who gives up his career to live in a rural area with a 3-month tourist economy? These are not right-wrong issues, but a matter of matching dreams, goals, and reality. Are personal and couple expectations congruent? No one other than you can decide what is right for you.

The spouse with the high risk or unconventional dream is asking the partner to give her a chance to try. It requires lobbying your partner. Couples break up over these issues, and sometimes that is the right decision. Other times, the spouse has the opportunity to play out the dream or a realistic modification.

The spouse needs assurance there is no secret or hidden agenda behind the dream. For example, the spouse who works overtime with the hidden agenda of meeting a mistress; the spouse who wants to get pregnant so she will have a socially acceptable reason to quit a job she hates; going to graduate school out of state to escape the marriage. Hidden agendas destroy trust.

The more unusual, high-risk, or variant the dream, the more you are urged to do a rigorous cost-benefit analysis (both practical and emotional), carefully research the issues, and have a backup plan if the dream is not viable. Seek consultation with respected, trusted friends and/or professionals. Develop life plans that fit your interests and values. High-risk dreams require special energy and commitment.

A Personal Note

We talked extensively about expectations and goals before marriage. We had a romantic and special premarital relationship in which we shared dreams as well as discussing hard issues. Shared expectations included leaving Illinois, being a middle-class couple, creating a respectful marriage, having at least two children, and a best friend marital style. Meeting these expectations strengthened our marital bond. Each had personal expectations that were met: Emily's goal of establishing her identity independent of the small town she grew up in and Barry's expectation to be a professional and explore the world. Sadly, there were expectations we did not meet, including having a cohesive family, financial independence, being socially sophisticated, changing our families of origin.

Our expectations continue to change and we reevaluate them on a yearly basis. Marriage cannot be taken for granted, even after 37 years. We find it worthwhile and enjoyable to discuss individual and couple dreams. Our expectation is we will continue to do this for the next 37 years.

Closing Thoughts

Developing positive, realistic expectations about personal and couple growth is a healthy resource for your new marriage. This facilitates understandings and agreements that enhance marital satisfaction. Rather than mourning the loss of idealized, romantic love, embrace positive, realistic expectations as a crucial resource for marital satisfaction and security.

CHAPTER 6

Sexuality: Creating an Intimate, Erotic Marriage

A folktale says that if a couple put a penny in the jar for every time they have sex during their first year of marriage and take a penny out each time they have sex afterward, there will be money left. This illustrates the myth that during the first year love and sex flow with no problems. The road to marital frustration and alienation is paved with myths and unrealistic expectations.

Emotional intimacy and sexual intimacy are different but well integrated in a healthy marriage. Traditionally, adolescent males and females learned very different lessons about sexuality. Women were supposed to value feelings, emotional connection, and an intimate relationship but devalue sex and eroticism. Men associated masculinity with sexuality and valued sexual frequency and performance. However, the man was not supposed to value emotional closeness, intimacy, or a committed relationship. Young men and women were socialized as if they belonged to different species.

In truth, there are many more similarities than differences between women and men. When assessing scientific (as opposed to ideological) data on intelligence, competence, and physical functioning, one is struck by gender similarities. This is equally true for emotional and sexual expression. Although there are differences—for example, women can conceive, breast-feed, have multiple orgasms—similarities greatly outnumber differences. Both women and men are capable of desire, arousal, orgasm, and satisfaction. Both experience and communicate empathy, closeness, sadness, and anger. The "war between the sexes" is not based on biological differences, nor is it predestined. Misunderstandings and conflicts are a matter of socialization and media hype rather than inherent biological or psychological differences.

Our premise, which has strong empirical support, is that intimate, satisfying marriages recognize shared values, capabilities, and interests. This promotes a respectful, trusting bond that provides a solid marital foundation. Emotional and sexual intimacy generate special feelings toward your spouse and marriage.

A favorite adage is that when marital sexuality is healthy, it is a small, but integral, component. Good sex contributes 15 to 20 percent to marital satisfaction and vitality. The main functions of marital sexuality are as a shared pleasure, to deepen and reinforce intimacy, and a tension reducer to alleviate the stresses inherent in life and marriage. Sexuality energizes and makes special your marital bond. When sexuality is dysfunctional, conflictual, or nonexistent, it serves as a major drain, robbing the marriage of intimacy and good feelings. Sexual problems (covered in Chapter 9) are the prime reason for separation and divorce in the first 2 years. The major sexual problems are a dysfunction, an affair, or fertility conflicts.

Emotional intimacy has a more subtle, but no less important, function in creating a viable marriage. Romantic love dissipates by the time of marriage or within the first year. If replaced by mature intimacy, the marriage has a powerful, solid source of reinforcement. Feeling cared for and caring for your spouse, sharing positive and negative feelings, engaging in empathic, supportive communication, feeling a sense of "we-ness," and establishing closeness are integral components of emotional intimacy.

Romantic Love and Passionate Sex

Our culture's glorification of romantic love and passionate sex subverts marriage. Couples can be loving and still have major sexual problems. Couples can be sexually desirous and functional, but for all the wrong psychological reasons. Love and sex are different dimensions. In a well-functioning marriage both the woman and the man are capable of emotional intimacy and sexual satisfaction. Integrating these dimensions requires communication and effort. It is anything but magical. That is the self-defeating promise of romantic love: If you love the spouse, everything will flow. This seductive cultural myth is reinforced by songs, movies, and novels. In truth, being swept away by romantic love and passionate sex predicts marital problems and sexual dysfunction.

Emotional intimacy encourages marital satisfaction. Romantic love leads to marital disappointment and alienation. Emotional intimacy is related to sexual satisfaction (especially for women). Women need to learn to value sexuality, and men need to learn to value intimacy. Ideally, both spouses can integrate emotional intimacy and erotic sex. Marriage functions best when each person is fully human, not governed by arbitrary (traditional) male-female roles. Each spouse valuing emotional intimacy and erotic sex facilitates a satisfying, stable marriage.

Unlearning Lessons from the Dating Game

A major barrier to marital communication is experiences while dating. Dating relationships are a terrible training ground for marriage. Once married, you have to unlearn negative attitudes and habits and learn healthy ways to communicate and experience intimate sexuality. The dating game has built-in insecurity, role-playing, adventure, and unpredictability. By their very nature, dating relationships end.

Traditionally, the man initiates and emphasizes sexual frequency and performance while the woman has the role of sexual gatekeeper. She emphasizes maintaining connection and intimacy. He views intimacy as being dependent, which interfered with autonomy. Same-sex friends agrees it was hard dealing with the opposite sex.

The most important barrier is distrust, which is endemic in dating relationships. Jealousy and instability are replaced by trust and confidence in your marital bond. This does not occur automatically (the first 2 years of marriage have the highest rate of affairs and separations), but from a conscious commitment to build a solid bond. Trust is much more than not having an affair.

Trust means confidence the spouse has your best interest in mind. You trust her with your strengths and weaknesses, hopes and fears. You trust the spouse would not intentionally hurt you or undercut the marriage. That does not mean you will not experience hurt, disappointment, conflict, and anger. However, you trust the spouse's intention is not to be destructive.

Another major barrier is fear of commitment, fears that are reinforced by premarital experiences of broken commitments. "Taking a break" from the relationship, playing hard to get to reignite interest, flirting and playing the field might spice up dating relationships but are poisonous in marriage. People leave dating relationships when they become difficult. Marriage involves valuing your bond through good and bad times. This does not mean putting up with anything; it does mean communicating and problem solving in the context of your intimate bond. The analogy Barry uses is that "dating skills are aimed toward sprinters, marriage skills toward marathon runners."

The Functions of Marital Sexuality

The major functions of marital sexuality are a shared pleasure, a means to deepen and strengthen intimacy, and a tension reducer to deal with the stresses of life and marriage. The traditional gender split was that females valued intimate sexuality and males valued erotic sexuality. There are myriad ways of being sexual. Sex meets healthy needs but also can serve unhealthy psychological motivations such as anger, anxiety, or placating the spouse. Traditional male-female arguments about sex interfere with pleasure and marital intimacy. Sometimes sex can be long, tender, warm, and involving (like a four-course gourmet dinner). Other times sex can be short and lusty (like a hamburger and fries). Marital sex is a mix and match depending on your feelings, needs, and practical and time constraints. If all sex were "quickies" or a 3-hour lovemaking experience, it would become boring. Sexuality can be intimate or playful, a late-night way to end the day or a middle-of-the-day main event, a way to reconnect after a conflict, or a pleasant reassurance. The essence of creative sexuality is awareness of your feelings and needs with freedom to communicate desires and share with your spouse.

The prescription for satisfying marital sex is integrating emotional intimacy, nondemand pleasuring, and erotic scenarios and techniques. These will not be present at each experience but are the foundation for healthy marital sexuality. Emotional intimacy is not just for the woman; it has great value for the man. Before age 30 males are easy, automatic, autonomous sexual responders—in other words, he needs nothing from his wife in order to function. To establish a solid sexual base and prevent problems, it is worthwhile to integrate intimacy and eroticism from the start. The core of intimacy is feeling comfortable and emotionally connected. You are an intimate team. The essence of sexual desire is anticipation of giving and receiving pleasure. Intimate sexuality is about sharing pleasure, not a sexual performance. The spouse is someone you feel open to and connected with, your sexual friend.

Nondemand pleasuring is key. Affectionate (holding hands, kissing, hugging) and sensual experiences (massages, bathing or showering together, cuddling on the couch, snuggling at night or in the morning) have value in themselves. Couples can enjoy nondemand pleasuring both inside and outside the bedroom. Not all touching can or should lead to intercourse. At times, touching can serve as a bridge to sexual desire, other times a way to stay connected. Sometimes you want an orgasm; sometimes you want a hug. Males have a hard time asking for a hug, so they initiate sex. Women have a hard time saying they feel lustful, so they initiate a hug. Optimally, both the woman and the man are comfortable initiating both nondemand pleasuring and intercourse.

Touching is a request, not a demand. "Intimate coercion" has no place in marriage. Intimate coercion is not the extreme of marital rape but the implicit threat of an affair if the spouse does not have sex, withholding love or money if a specific sex act does not occur, being distant or angry if there is no sex, or using sex as a bribe. Requests respect the individuality and autonomy of each spouse. Each person has a right to express feelings and wants. The spouse has a right to enthusiastically accept, say no, or offer an alternative. A demand says do this my way, now, or there will be negative consequences. A request says I want this, I am open to your feelings and needs, do not worry about a negative outcome. Requests facilitate intimate communication, demands set up an adversarial, performance situation. With demands, he wins the sexual battle but loses their intimate bond. With requests, both individuals and the relationship win.

Nondemand pleasuring facilitates emotional intimacy and sexual desire. It forms a bridge between affection, sensuality, and intercourse.

You do not have orgasms through intimacy and nondemand pleasuring. These increase openness and receptivity, but you need erotic stimulation for arousal and orgasm. Erotic stimulation includes intercourse but is not limited to intercourse. The essence of erotic stimulation is giving and receiving genital touching, which increases both subjective and objective arousal. One spouse's arousal plays off the other's. This is illustrated by the "give to get" pleasuring guideline. The major aphrodisiac is an involved, aroused partner. The more you turn your partner on, the more turned on you feel. Mutual arousal builds high levels of eroticism.

Erotic stimulation during the pleasuring/foreplay phase can include mutual manual stimulation; he does oral breast stimulation and manual vulva stimulation while she caresses his penis; she gives fellatio while he engages in breast stimulation and utilizes fantasy; they kneel, kiss, and give and receive genital stimulation; watch a sexy movie, undress each other and playfully touch; verbalize or play out a sexual fantasy; stand in front of a mirror so you have visual stimulation in addition to manual and oral stimulation. Multiple stimulation, giving and receiving a variety of erotic stimulation, enhances arousal. There are a wide variety of pleasuring positions, variations of stimulation, use of fantasy, lotions, music, movement, and erotic techniques.

Multiple stimulation can and should be integrated with intercourse. Why should erotic stimulation cease because his penis is in her vagina? Many couples find multiple stimulation is most important with intercourse, especially for women who want to be orgasmic during intercourse. Multiple stimulation during intercourse can include kissing or breast stimulation; switching intercourse positions two or three times; using his hand, her hand, or a vibrator for additional clitoral stimulation; she giving testicle stimulation; fantasizing; buttock stimulation; intercourse positions (like side-by-side) that provide additional genital contact; taking a break for manual or oral stimulation and then resuming intercourse.

Orgasm is a natural result of high arousal and allowing yourself to experience maximal pleasure. You are responsible for your orgasm; the spouse does not give you an orgasm. Part of that responsibility is to request the type, speed, and rhythm of stimulation that is most arousing. Orgasm is *not* the ultimate measure of satisfaction but is an integral part of sexuality for both the woman and the man.

We emphasize similarities between male and female sexual response, but there are differences. Male orgasmic response is stereotypic and predictable. He has one orgasm, accompanied by ejaculation, which occurs during intercourse. The most common male sexual dysfunction is premature ejaculation, experienced by half of males under 25 and 30 percent of older males. Female orgasmic response is more variable and complex (this does not mean better or worse). She might be nonorgasmic, singly orgasmic, or multiorgasmic, which could occur during pleasuring, intercourse, or afterplay. Less than 25 percent of women follow the male pattern of having a single orgasm during intercourse. Although the majority of women can be orgasmic with intercourse (utilizing multiple stimulation), most find it easier to be orgasmic with manual, oral, or rubbing stimulation. Approximately 15 to 20 percent of women develop a multiorgasmic response pattern. That does not mean the woman who has six orgasms has six times more pleasure. Orgasm as a performance goal—where you try to achieve the "perfect" orgasm, the "right" kind of orgasm, multiple orgasms, "G" spot orgasms, or whatever the new fad—is self-defeating. Sex is not about reaching an arbitrary performance criterion. Sexuality is about developing a couple style that facilitates desire, arousal, orgasm, and satisfaction for both the woman and the man. One objection marital therapists have about sex therapy is the overemphasis on orgasm and sexual function. The crucial factors in sexuality are desire, pleasure, and satisfaction. After a sexual experience, you feel energized and emotionally bonded.

Exercise—Nondemand Pleasuring

The focus of this exercise is to enhance communication and pleasure while reducing performance-orientation. There is a prohibition on orgasm and intercourse. This increases awareness and helps you focus on exploration, feelings, and touch.

Since it is traditionally the man who initiates sexual activity, let the woman take the lead. Ideally, both the man and the woman feel comfortable initiating and each is free to say no or suggest an alternative. To set a comfortable milieu, begin by taking a shower or bath together. Cleanliness (especially washing genitals) facilitates sensual and sexual feelings.

If showering, experiment with types of spray or temperature; if bathing, try a new bath oil or soap to increase awareness of sensual stimuli. Start by soaping your partner's back. Trace the muscles and contours; rub and massage gently. Ask the spouse to face you. Soap the front of his neck and chest. Move downward to the hips and wash the genitals as you would any body area. Let him soap and wash you. What feels particularly sensual?

Dry each other. Take your time and be tender. Stand still and take a good look at your spouse. Notice one or two things you find particularly attractive.

Proceed to the bedroom feeling natural being nude. If you do not feel comfortable walking through the house nude, put on a robe or towel, but take it off when you reach the bedroom. Pleasuring is best done in the nude. The room should be at a comfortable temperature with a moderate amount of light. If you prefer, darken the room, but be sure you can see your spouse's body. Put on your favorite music and/or burn a candle with a pleasant fragrance.

Let the woman start as pleasure-giver. Each spouse has an opportunity to be giver and recipient. A satisfying relationship requires comfort with receiving and giving pleasure. Interestingly, men find it harder to receive than to give.

The recipient has three tasks. The first is to be passive and receive pleasure. The second is to keep his eyes closed to allow concentration on feelings and sensations (also, this reduces the giver's self-consciousness). The third is to be aware of what parts of your body and what types of touch feel sensual.

She looks at his body in an open, exploratory manner and feels comfortable giving a variety of touch and body stimulation. Rather than try to second-guess him, touch for yourself—engage in stimulation you enjoy giving. The receiver is lying on his stomach, feeling as receptive, relaxed, and comfortable as possible. She can look at and touch him from the top of his head to the bottoms of his feet. The emphasis is on communication by touch rather than words. Talking distracts from the focus on sensations and feelings.

Begin by massaging his shoulders. Massage gently with your entire hand, moving slowly down his back and sides, avoid sudden movements. Be aware of what is appealing—freckles, tiny scars, muscle indentations. When you reach his waist, place your thumbs together, spread your fingers, and gently knead as you caress his sides and lower back. Move to his head, either give a scalp massage or run your fingers through his hair. You can give a vigorous back rub or run your fingers over his back in a playful manner. Explore and stroke his thighs and legs. Massage both buttocks simultaneously. The buttocks and anal area are among the most sensual parts of the body; they are erogenous zones with a multitude of nerve endings. Allow your touch to be sensual and enjoyable.

The task of the giver is to provide your spouse with a variety of experiences. The giver can enjoy various types of touch and experience your partner's body in a new way. These are guidelines, not hard-and-fast rules. Feel free to be creative.

Help your partner turn over on his back. He continues to keep his eyes shut. Gently explore his face. Notice signs of relaxation and comfort. Be aware of the difference between these expressions and the tension you have observed at other times. Gently massage his forehead. With your fingertips outline favorite facial features. Tenderly kiss his closed eyes. Kiss all parts of his face and neck.

Massage his nipples. Does touching them feel sensual? Males inhibit their natural response because they think men are not supposed to feel pleasure there. When exploring his chest, use smooth, tender strokes, covering the sides as well. How does it feel to touch his navel? Lightly touch his body hair. Run your hands sideways around the stomach. Do his stomach muscles react to your touch?

Look at the front of his body. Does he have an erection? Accept this as a natural response. Touch his penis when it is flaccid as opposed to when erect. Traditionally, the woman views the man's erection as a demand. Remember, there is a prohibition on orgasm. A common myth is that when the man has an erection, the woman must *do* something: have intercourse or at least bring him to orgasm. Interestingly, the man believes an erection *must* mean sexual arousal, and he rushes to intercourse even when he does not feel like sex. During this exercise, both can enjoy the erection without feeling any demand.

Explore his genitals—be aware of each part—penis, glans, shaft, frenulum, scrotum, testes. As you explore his testes, notice which is larger and what the shapes remind you of. Notice how his testes move inside the scrotum.

If the spouse is circumcised, trace the glans with your fingertips. If he is uncircumcised, gently move back the foreskin and explore the glans. Massage and caress his inner thighs and perineum. Notice how the scrotum changes as arousal and erection grow. Discontinue stimulation until the erection subsides. Erections naturally wax and wane (as does vaginal lubrication). Men become anxious when the erection wanes because they are used to going to intercourse and orgasm on the first erection. Waxing and waning of erections is a natural physiological response to prolonged, nondemand pleasuring.

Awareness that sexuality is more than genitals, intercourse, and orgasm is crucial for both the man and the woman. Touch the way you want. Vary playing, rubbing, caressing. If you feel anxious or uncomfortable, lay and talk and then continue. The giver proceeds at her pace and comfort level.

Continue body stimulation, enjoying slow, tender, rhythmic, flowing touching. Enjoy his whole body, including the penis as a natural, healthy part of him. When she feels comfortable with his body and sensual touch, switch roles.

The woman lies on her stomach and allows herself to relax. He finds a comfortable position whether sitting, kneeling, or lying. He does touching and pleasuring for himself, not trying to repeat her patterns, second-guess what she wants, nor turn her on. This exercise is for exploring and sharing pleasure. Focus on pleasuring the entire back of her body. Do not rush the process. When she turns over, do not focus on her breasts or vulva. Men touch with the goal of arousal; instead focus on comfort and pleasure.

The man can integrate nongenital and genital pleasuring. Both the giver and the recipient can experience her breasts in a sensual manner. He can explore a variety of touches; she is aware and open to sensations and feelings. With the palm of his hand, start at her waist and move to the neck with one long motion. Be careful not to press hard; breasts can be sensitive. Sometimes the difference between pleasurable and irritating touch is less than an inch or a minor difference in pressure. Trace her nipple with your fingertips. Does it become erect?

Massage her stomach, then explore her genitals. Run your fingers gently through her pubic hair and caress her mons. Spread her labia with your fingers. Be comfortable with the sight and feel of her genitals. Identify her clitoris and clitoral shaft. Look carefully at her labia, noticing how the labia surround the vaginal opening. Spread the vaginal opening with two fingers and notice the color and texture of the interior. Gently insert one finger into her vagina and notice the sensation of containment. Feel the warmth and dampness. Touch the mons, perineum, and around the urethra. Move slowly and gently. Invite touching and exploration.

Intermix nongenital touching—do not concentrate on her genitals. Focus on openness and pleasure, not arousal or orgasm. Do a sensual whole body massage.

End the exercise by holding your spouse, experiencing feelings of warmth and tenderness. Lie in bed and share feelings. What have you learned of sensuality and pleasure? How can you generalize this to lovemaking and intercourse?

Emotional Intimacy

Sexual intimacy energizes your marital bond. Emotional intimacy nurtures and reinforces your bond. Emotional and sexual intimacy are strongly linked for women, less so for men. Both emotional intimacy and sexual satisfaction are integral to a vital marriage.

Intimacy is an example of gender-based premarital learnings interfering with a healthy marriage. Men need to nurture and value emotional intimacy. Learning this early in the marriage, before a marital crisis, is preferable. Barry has counseled countless couples where the man saw the marriage slipping away and said if only he had known how important it was to keep emotional connection and for her to feel cared about. In a satisfying, stable marriage both the husband and the wife value emotional intimacy.

The core of intimacy is feeling understood, supported, and loved. Therapists emphasize empathy and validating feelings. Validation does *not* mean agreement. It means you are listening in a respectful, caring manner and you accept the spouse and her feelings. Difficulties and conflicts do not center on objective measures of right-wrong but on desires, feelings, and perceptions. A validating, emotionally accepting milieu alleviates a significant percentage of marital difficulties. For problems that require examining alternatives and conflict resolution, emotional intimacy establishes a solid base for working together as a respectful, trusting team.

Mature intimacy replaces the intense, romantic love feelings that propelled you into marriage. Emotional intimacy is less intense and idealistic but supports a genuine, mature, stable relationship. Emotional intimacy keeps alive loving feelings.

Intensity is a core element for the emotionally expressive couple style, but intimacy is important for all marital styles. Loving, intimate feelings cannot be taken for granted. In words and actions, emotional intimacy needs to be nurtured, expressed, and reinforced.

Exercise—Building Emotional Intimacy

Spontaneity and naturalness are emphasized when discussing emotions. We applaud spontaneous feelings, but it is naive to believe spontaneous expression alone will sustain your marriage. This exercise emphasizes intentionality and the value of planned intimacy. Think of this as an "intimacy date."

Traditionally males have undervalued intimacy, so let him be the initiator. Be sure you are alert and focused, have enough time (at least half an hour—an hour is preferable), and will not be interrupted (put the answering machine on and do not answer the door). He can enhance the milieu by making tea or having a glass of wine, burning a pleasant-smelling candle, or playing music in the background. Make this a personal invitation, not "we have to do our exercise."

Talk about an experience where you felt emotionally intimate. It could be a premarital or marital experience. It need not be a major occasion. Examples include walking on the beach and feeling close, revealing life hopes, talking together the day after you first made love, saying you were sorry after a fight, showing your spouse the neighborhood you grew up in, deciding you want a baby, going on a picnic and talking for two hours, feeling romantic after a friend's wedding, taking a walk in the rain, sharing excitement about a promotion, staying up all night to wallpaper your first apartment. Focus on feelings, not just events. How open were you? How close did you feel? How trusting were you?

Discuss the state of emotional intimacy in your marriage. Be specific and honest. What do you say and do that facilitates intimacy? How frequently does it occur? How intense are the feelings?

The next topic is difficult. What inhibits intimacy? Focus on what you do, not on what your spouse does or does not do. It is easier to blame your spouse than assume responsibility for your behavior. Specifically, what do you do or not do that blocks emotional intimacy? Is it intentional or unintended? What are the advantages of maintaining barriers to intimacy? Are you willing to give up these protections?

Make three requests of your spouse that would enhance feelings of intimacy. Remember, these are requests, not demands. What could your spouse say or do that would increase feelings of intimacy? Examples include the spouse calling home daily or every other day, nondemand touching before going to sleep or on wakening, walking at night at least once a week and talking about feelings, saying "I love you" in a genuine manner, once a week going to dinner or for a drink and discussing hopes and dreams, after the baby is asleep putting on music softly and dancing, making birthdays and your anniversary special, romantic gestures like bringing flowers or an inexpensive personal gift, not calling names or engaging in dirty fighting, greeting each other with a hug. Each spouse makes three specific, personal requests to deepen emotional intimacy.

TOBEY AND WALT

Tobey and Walt had been married 14 months. Both were disappointed in the marriage, although for different reasons. Tobey wondered if she had married the wrong man: Walt was distant and secretive, totally different from the 16 months they were a dating couple. Tobey was 30 and wanted to begin a family, but she did not want a child unless she was sure the marriage was viable and stable. Tobey blamed the problems on Walt's emotional withdrawal.

Walt's disappointment focused on dramatically reduced sexual frequency. They had been a sexually active premarital couple. Sex had decreased 2 months before marriage, which Walt attributed to hassles planning the wedding and conflicts with relatives. However, it had not resumed after the ceremony and there were bitter arguments about initiation. They had sex less than twice a month, and Tobey complained about the sex. Attempts to discuss problems quickly broke down into name-calling and tears. The downward cascade included put-downs, attack-counterattack, defensiveness, denial, and character assassination. The marriage Tobey and Walt had entered into with love and hope was in big trouble.

Tobey and Walt realized they could not reverse the trend on their own. At Tobey's urging, they consulted a marriage therapist with a subspeciality in sex therapy (this made therapy more acceptable for Walt). Rather than a symptom of craziness or panic, seeking professional help demonstrated good judgment and a sign of how much they valued their marital bond.

In the initial couple session, the therapist focused on miscommunication, especially each spouse's intentions. Tobey wanted increased emotional intimacy, but Walt saw her as his worst critic. Walt felt this was a betrayal, a perception that shocked Tobey because it was the opposite of her intention. This is a common pattern. The wife pursues closeness and becomes critical when she does not receive it. The husband is hoping for a harmonious relationship and good sex, but is put off by criticism and reacts by avoiding. The more he avoids, the more she pursues, using escalating aversive communication to get his attention. He feels defensive, avoids, and stonewalls. Each attacks the other's behavior as mean and unreasonable. Recognizing the self-defeating pattern is an important step, but it is not enough. Each spouse must take responsibility for changing his or her behavior.

Tobey needed to state her desire to be emotionally close, focus on specific negatives and requests, and refrain from putting down Walt as a person or husband. Walt needed to share thoughts, feelings, activities, and interests. When he felt criticized or nagged, he would express this, respond nondefensively, listen, and validate her concerns. Both needed to trust the other's intentions and stay on the same intimate team. Sexuality had become a battleground of traditional male-female roles. Both wanted sexuality to energize their intimate bond, but that was not the present reality.

The therapist met individually with each of them to explore psychological and sexual issues. In the individual session, Walt discussed expectations about marriage. Walt was desperately afraid of a nonsexual marriage similar to that of his family of origin and his best friend's failed marriage. Walt had never shared these fears with Tobey. He worried about Tobey's disapproval and not measuring up. He felt vulnerable to criticism, and inadvertently Tobey had stepped into the role of his worst critic.

Tobey did not understand the changes in Walt. His caring had disappeared, and he reverted to the male role of being demanding, especially sexually. The therapist discovered Tobey was an ardent reader of "pop psychology" books and a regular viewer of TV talk shows. These reinforced her worst fears about men and marriage.

She was creating a self-fulfilling prophecy. Tobey agreed to "go cold turkey" on the books and talk shows and focus on Walt as a person and their marriage as a process. Knowledge is power, but many pop psychology books and media presentations are "crazy making."

The therapy sessions were conducted as a couple. The therapist provided feedback and suggestions. He advised that instead of threats of divorce, they focus energy on building a vital marital bond. Communication and sexual exercises were assigned between sessions. Good intentions are not enough. Couples have to actively build, practice, and reinforce intimacy and sexuality experiences. Walt made personal sexual initiations and requests. He realized sexual quality was more important than frequency. Although Tobey was okay with "quickies," she much preferred quality sexual scenarios involving pleasuring and oral sex. Walt was surprised by her request to wash genitals before oral sex but realized this facilitated responsiveness.

The therapist made a suggestion to improve communication. When Tobey said "I want to talk," Walt had a knee-jerk reaction that something was wrong and he was going to be blamed. The therapist suggested they talk while doing an activity—taking a walk, raking leaves, doing dishes, over a cup of coffee. They agreed to focus on a specific topic. This reduced Walt's defensiveness and allowed communication free of criticism and blaming. Tobey stated whether she wanted to just share feelings or to focus on problem solving. Most of the time Tobey wanted to share and talk, not for Walt to solve a problem. As emotional intimacy grew, they were able to recognize and accept differences in communication styles, how much individual as opposed to couple time they wanted, differences in attitudes toward money, and different ways of relating to extended family.

Tobey and Walt discussed career decisions and Tobey's desire to have a baby. Walt agreed to wait a year before making a career change and to begin a family now. Luckily, Tobey and Walt were in the three quarters of couples who found it easy to get pregnant. Sex with the hope of becoming pregnant was an aphrodisiac. They were comfortable with their complementary couple style, and the baby was an affirmation of their confidence in each other and their marriage.

Tobey and Walt agreed to 6-month therapy follow-ups for the next 2 years. This was to prevent a relapse into bad habits and encourage generalizing personal and couple gains. Tobey and Walt were motivated by knowing they would be accountable, the therapist's urging to value intimacy and sexuality, and their desire for a satisfying, stable marriage and family. Emotional and sexual intimacy provided special feelings that reinforced their marital bond.

Closing Thoughts

"Love is not enough." You need to develop and maintain an emotionally intimate relationship that nurtures your marriage and a sexually satisfying relationship that energizes your marital bond. The core of marriage is a respectful, trusting friendship. Emotional and sexual intimacy make it special. Nurture and value your intimacy.

CHAPTER 7

Becoming a Family

One of the most important and life-changing decisions is whether or not to have children. Traditionally, children and family were the prime function of marriage. Children were a mandate, not a choice. The only marriages that remained childless were those struggling with infertility. Those couples were treated with silence and sympathy.

Marriage has validity in itself; you do not need children to justify your marriage. Nor are children necessary to justify sex. The main functions of marital sex are a shared pleasure, a means to deepen and reinforce intimacy, and a tension reducer to deal with the stresses of life and marriage. Conceiving a child is a potential function of sex, not a necessary function.

Traditionally, becoming pregnant was a major impetus to marriage. In the supposedly conservative 1950s, one in four brides was pregnant at the time of marriage. Now, approximately one in four women either has a child or is pregnant when she marries.

We are strong advocates of planned, wanted children. We are in favor of contraception, planned pregnancies, childbirth classes, prepared childbirth, sterilization when the couple are sure they do not want more children, adoption for infertile couples, and choice in terms of therapeutic abortion. What underlies these seemingly disparate concepts is the value of planned, wanted children.

Children and family is a high value for most couples, a value we share. We raised one adopted child and two biological children. One of the highlights of our lives was Barry's being present at the birth of our two sons. Our personal value is prochild and profamily. However, this is not a "should"; it is not the right choice for all couples. More than 85 percent of couples have children, whether biological, adopted, or stepchildren. We believe if couples carefully considered their lives, values, and situation, that would decrease to 70 percent or less.

A Choice, Not a Mandate

If both spouses were willing to discuss feelings, wants, and reality factors concerning children, it would raise anxiety but be in your long-term best interest. Of all life's decisions, the choice to have a child is one of the hardest to reverse. You can change jobs and houses, move to another community, even change marital partners easier than stop being a parent. Parenting is at least an 18-year commitment that is time- and energy-consuming. One of Barry's favorite sayings is "the age of your child is more important than your age in determining your life organization."

In considering whether to have a child, discuss emotional, financial, practical, and situational factors. Be aware of external factors—the urging of parents, friends, siblings, religious teachings. Cultural pressure is strongly prochild. Parents especially are in favor of your having a child so they can be grandparents. They had children, so you should too. Religious groups are prochild and profamily. There is nothing wrong with this as a cultural norm, but each individual and couple need to choose what is right for them—not be controlled by cultural ideals or myths.

Having a child is basically an emotional choice. Ideally, the child is planned and wanted, an affirmation of marital viability and desire for a family. There are few decisions in life that are as emotionally complex as whether to have children, when to have them, and how many to have. If couples decided only on the basis of financial, practical, and logical factors, few would have children and the human race would decrease. Just the opposite is happening: We are facing a population explosion, especially in developing countries, that threatens the earth's resources and quality of life.

The primary emotional reasons a couple choose to have a child is to experience the process of pregnancy, participate in parenting, and watch the child develop into an independent person. Pregnancy, childbirth, and parenting are among life's unique and special experiences. Couples have children to fulfill emotional needs with the hope their lives will be enriched by the parenting experience.

Couples who decide not to have children deserve to have this choice respected. The traditional view was that the "right" choice was to have children. Couples who chose to remain childless were stigmatized as immature, selfish, or hostile to traditional values. This is unfair and does not honor people's individuality and choices.

Myths about Children

Popular myths include:

1. The more the merrier.
2. An only child will be maladjusted.
3. You must have a child by age 30.
4. You should not have a child after 40.
5. A child bonds the marriage.
6. It is crucial to have both boys and girls.
7. Planning children robs sex of fun and spontaneity.
8. Children stabilize a tenuous marriage.

Each individual and couple need to honestly and carefully explore attitudes, values, feelings, goals, and life circumstances. There is not an all-purpose, right decision. We suggest the following guidelines:

1. Having children is a choice agreed to by both people.
2. The marriage is on solid footing emotionally, financially, and sexually before having a child.
3. You are married at least 2 years before beginning a family.
4. Children are planned and wanted.
5. Children are at least an 18-year commitment. You have the financial, practical, and psychological resources to make this commitment.

Infertility Issues

For 85 percent of couples under 30 and 75 percent of couples over 30 getting pregnant is too easy: The fear is an unplanned pregnancy. Couples who want to become pregnant and have difficulty find this frustrating, then frightening and psychologically painful. Even more than a sexual dysfunction or affair, infertility strains the marital bond. The infertility workup is physically and emotionally difficult, but you are optimistic it will result in a pregnancy. As time goes on, the tests and interventions become increasingly invasive and expensive. The month is an emotional roller coaster of sex on demand during the high probability week, feeling depressed and even rageful when your period comes. Psychologically and relationally this is a terrible drain. If the couple are not empathic and supportive, it will tear apart their marital bond. More than half of couples do become pregnant, a source of relief and joy. Other couples choose to adopt a baby, a hard-to-place child, an older child, or utilize overseas adoption. Adoption is a stressful, but worthwhile, endeavor. We suggest joining an adoption information and/or support group.

Some couples decide to remain childless. They embrace the advantages of being a couple: time and freedom, financial resources, ability to pursue careers, flexibility in lifestyle, more energy to devote to the marital bond.

Infertility is a major challenge to the marriage, but there are alternatives. The couple can survive the stress and be resilient.

Use of Contraception

A core guideline is to use the first 2 years of marriage to develop your couple style and build a strong bond of respect, trust, and intimacy. Ideally, this means waiting at least 2 years to have a child. A planned, wanted child is an affirmation of the vitality and security of your marital bond.

This means using effective contraception. A perfect contraceptive would have the following characteristics: totally effective, no side effects, separate from sexual activity, easily reversible, requires little effort to use, could be used by the man or woman, and inexpensive.

Unfortunately, there is no perfect contraceptive, although there are good alternatives. Each couple decides which contraceptive is best for them. The most commonly used contraceptive is the birth control pill. Other popular options are condoms, diaphragms, injections, patches, Norplant, intrauterine devices, cervical caps. Some couples use a female contraceptive plus a condom (condoms alone are not a highly effective contraceptive). The more you view contraception, family planning, and the decision to have a baby as a joint endeavor, the better for your marriage.

The Choice to Have a Baby

If you are in the majority of couples who decide they want a child, what is the next step? People say stop using contraception and enjoy lots of sex. That is only partially correct. Acknowledge this is the right time in your lives and marriage to become pregnant. The decision to conceive is a couple commitment. One of the most depressing statistics is the most common time a couple break up is 3 months before or 3 months after the birth of a first child. Rather than an affirmation of the marital bond, the stress of having a child severs the bond.

It is a major transition from being a couple to being a family. The process is facilitated by talking and planning. Being aware of the high probability week before she ovulates is crucial. The best strategy for getting pregnant is to have intercourse 2–3 times 4 days before you ovulate until the day of ovulation. Having sex with the hope of getting pregnant is fun and can be an aphrodisiac.

For most couples, getting pregnant is the easiest part of having a baby. The 9 months of pregnancy help you prepare for this life change. The first 3 months of pregnancy are the time for the woman to be as healthy as possible. This means no smoking, drinking, or drug use; eating regularly; moderate and regular exercise; and reduced stress.

It is crucial to have prenatal care with an obstetrician you feel comfortable with and who will address your questions about health and the development of the fetus. Throughout pregnancy share what is happening physically and emotionally. Stay connected psychologically and sexually. Sexuality requires communication and openness to experimenting with various intercourse positions (especially side rear-entry and man kneeling–woman sitting) and nonintercourse erotic expression, especially in the 3rd-trimester.

A significant number of couples attend prepared childbirth classes, which we highly recommend. This encourages approaching childbirth as an intimate team. It took two to conceive this child; be together in bringing her into the world. Prepared childbirth facilitates the transition to parenting. The class allows you to share knowledge, practice breathing exercises, prepare for difficulties (including a caesarean section), and learn techniques to cope with discomfort and pain. Rather than the pregnancy and child being solely the woman's domain, the man has an integral role of being the coach and supporter.

JILL AND BART

Jill hoped to marry in her early 20s, following the model of her older sisters. She had been engaged at 24, but had the wisdom to realize this would be a fatally flawed marriage. A good dating couple, they were unlikely to create a viable marriage.

Three years later Jill met Bart, marrying when she was 29. Jill wanted to have a baby before 30, but was wise to realize the importance of building a solid marital bond before becoming a family. Jill and Bart learned to deal with differences and conflicts, especially being a two-career couple.

Bart, who very much enjoyed the intimacy and stability of a shared life with Jill, was reluctant to have children at this time. Bart had seen two friends' marriages break up. The men, financially responsible for the child, had limited parental time and contact. Bart wanted to be sure this would be a viable, secure marriage before making the commitment to becoming a family. Intellectually Jill understood this but felt Bart was emotionally withholding. Both wanted their marriage to work; they felt stuck in a struggle over differences in life plans. Sex had been an easy, flowing part of the relationship, and Jill was a conscientious birth control pill user. One of their biggest fights was when she threatened to stop using contraception.

Choices are not made in a vacuum. Their best couple friends became pregnant in July which served as an impetus for Jill to talk seriously about their plans. Jill and Bart agreed to discuss career and life plans and what it would mean to have a baby. Bart was genuinely interested in Jill's feelings and desires about where to live and how to coordinate careers. A successful career was important to Jill, but she did not need to live in a large metropolitan area for that to occur. Jill had a strong preference for a medium-sized New England city. They agreed to focus their job search on three New England cities. The first person who received a good job offer would accept and the spouse would focus all his or her search efforts there. Jill and Bart trusted they could deal with the hard decisions necessary to promote two careers. This was not a feel-good statement but a commitment to deal realistically with a complex life planning.

Career plans, conflict resolution skills, and where to live were progressing better than baby talks. The more Jill lobbied for getting pregnant, the more defensive and avoidant Bart became. Jill's emotionality increased as the friend's pregnancy proceeded. Discussio s broke down with her crying and accusing and Bart stonewall.ng. Bart suggested they see a counselor to break the impasse. Jill readily agreed but insisted they stay focused on the issue of whether to have children. In college, she had seen a social worker for an elevator phobia that turned into 2 years of general psychotherapy. Jill did not want to repeat that. They found a marriage therapist who specialized in short-term, focused therapy.

The therapist saw them together and then set up one individual appointment. In her individual session, Jill said she loved Bart and trusted this would be a stable marriage, but she talked primarily about her strong desire to have children and her frustration with Bart. She agreed to continue birth control until they reached a decision. Jill was bewildered and then worried when Bart's meeting evolved into five individual sessions. Bart was not willing to disclose specifics of the sessions but assured Jill it was about his issues, not her.

At the conjoint feedback session, the therapist encouraged Bart to share what he had learned. Bart's parents were divorced when he was 5. He lived with his mother who remarried when he was 8, and his stepfather died of a heart attack when Bart was 16. Bart had regular, but emotionally distant, contact with his biological father. Bart saw him every other weekend and spent two weeks with the father's extended family at a lodge in the mountains during the summer. Bart was initially close to his stepfather, but as that marriage deteriorated so did their relationship. Bart was disappointed in fathers and not at all sure he could be a good parent. He was grappling with the ambivalence of whether he wanted to—this was a secret he had kept from Jill and was now frightened by her reaction. Rather than being judgmental and punishing, she was empathic and encouraged him to discuss this ambivalence with her. She felt Bart would be a good father, but she was not going to force him. Jill wanted to be the supportive, caring spouse, not the demanding, punishing spouse. This was immensely helpful to Bart. He did not want to be controlled by his fears. As he explored past fears and present realities, Bart saw his life, marriage, and parenting in a more positive, optimistic light.

Jill made a suggestion that made a dramatic difference. They would baby-sit friends' children for a few weekends and see how they functioned as a couple around children. Bart had not baby-sat as an adolescent and had few caretaking experiences, none with children under the age of 2. Not surprisingly, two couple friends were enthusiastic participants in the experiment. Bart found Jill's suggestions and feedback about children very helpful. He felt panicky when left alone with more than one child, so the first two times they did everything in tandem. By the third time, Bart was enjoying himself and sure he could be a responsible, competent parent.

The decision to stop using birth control was a joint one. Jill was eating better, exercising more, and in consultation with her physician, stopped taking medication and, drastically reduced over-the-counter drugs. She took vitamins and ate well 3 months before becoming pregnant and throughout the pregnancy. Jill ensured a healthy pregnancy with regular prenatal care. Jill and Bart signed up for a prepared childbirth class and read a book on parenting from birth to the baby's first birthday. They also enrolled in a six-session "Becoming Parents" class that emphasized both couple and parenting challenges. (Appendix B contains suggestions for finding marital enhancement classes and Appendix C about resource books for new parents.)

Bart's father and men of that generation had been bystanders at the birth of their children and helpers to their wives in taking care of babies. Bart wanted to be an integral part of the whole experience, a "first-class father," involved, competent, and not dependent on the mother. Bart talked to new fathers and pressed them to move beyond the joking stories of missed sleep and sex for specific suggestions. Jill and Bart talked at length with two couple friends who had recently had children.

Jill and Bart stayed an intimate team throughout the pregnancy. Talking, planning, attending classes, doing childbirth exercises brought them closer. Labor was 16 hours and more difficult than they had anticipated, but Bart was there as a coach and helper. They chose an obstetrician and birthing center of a hospital with care. The nurse-midwife was especially helpful and caring. The birth was an emotional highlight of their lives. Being a participant in his son's birth promoted bonding for Bart. He watched the baby as Jill got much needed rest.

A baby dramatically changes your lives and marriage. Jill and Bart experienced loss of sleep, the stress of caretaking, less couple time, few prolonged lovemaking sessions, and change in routines. Yet they felt like an intimate couple who were developing a cohesive family unit. This was a source of pride for Bart and great satisfaction for Jill.

Making the Right Choice for You

In our lives, the decision to have children was easy and one we never regretted. We enjoyed parenting younger children much more than adolescents, although we realize parenting is an 18-year commitment. There is not one right choice that fits all couples. You have to weigh values, feelings, goals, life experiences, and what would be healthy for you as individuals and your marriage.

The cultural myth is that unplanned pregnancies only occur to unmarried women. In truth, more than one third of marital pregnancies are unplanned. A significant minority decide they cannot adapt to the pregnancy at this time and choose a therapeutic abortion. More commonly couples decide even if unplanned, the child is wanted. The fact that the most common time a couple separate is 3 months before or 3 months after the birth of a first child reflects how important and impactful the decision is. Ideally, becoming pregnant is a mature, joint decision, a validation of marital viability and confidence.

The decision to have a child should come from healthy motivations. Examples of unhealthy motivations include to shore up a shaky marriage, rescue self-esteem, respond to pressure from family or friends, acquiesce to spouse's ultimatum, do the socially acceptable thing, or prove something to yourself or family. Healthy motivations include a planned choice, an affirmation of the marriage's viability, a desire to parent, the experience of seeing a child develop, or the desire to be a family. The same decision—to conceive—will have dramatically different consequences if it is positively motivated than if it is negatively motivated. The following exercise is oriented toward couples who are confused, ambivalent, or stuck about whether or not to have children.

Exercise—Discussion and Decision Making

Deciding whether to have a child is a major life commitment that deserves time and attention. Psychologically, this can be a difficult exercise. The exercise is divided into four components:

1. Each individual writes positive and negative factors for having a child.
2. Share the written material and discuss pros and cons.
3. As a couple, write out important issues to deal with and discuss.
4. Proceed with mutual decision making.

The structure for the writing exercise is for each spouse to list feelings under four columns:

1. Positive feelings about having a baby.
2. Negative feelings about having a baby.
3. Positive emotional affects on marriage.
4. Negative emotional effects on marriage.

On a second piece of paper, focus on practical, financial, and situational factors:

1. Positives for having a baby.
2. Negatives for having a baby.
3. Positive effects on marriage.
4. Negative effects on marriage.

Honestly disclose emotional and practical factors. Do this for yourself, not to win over your spouse. Be as specific and realistic as possible. For example, positive feelings include holding an infant, sensations of breast-feeding or rocking a baby, being affectionate and cuddling a toddler, teaching the child to play soccer, watching the child develop, taking pride in introducing the child to her grandparents. Negative emotional effects on the marriage include feeling stressed and overwhelmed by caretaking, losing couple time and connection, feeling tired and sleep-deprived, lessening sexual frequency and vitality, feeling burdened by responsibilities. Examples of positive practical factors could include baby serving as an impetus to move to a larger house, receiving practical and financial support from extended family, developing friendships with parents of young children, planning long-term financial goals for the child. Examples of negative practical factors include financial stress, less personal and couple time, problems with backup and emergency child care, not being able to take couple trips, medical bills, not getting work promotions because you cannot readily travel.

Share these lists a day before your discussion. The purpose is to disclose thoughts and feelings, hopes and fears, and have them understood by your spouse. At this point, do not begin weighing alternatives, trying to persuade the spouse or rushing to a decision. Clarify feelings, worries, concerns, hopes, and values. Ask open-ended questions and empathically reflect your spouse's feelings, concerns, hopes, and desires. Clarify both positive and negative factors and feelings so you share the same information base. Some couples find this mechanistic and tedious, but many are surprised at what they hear and discover. Your spouse's feelings and concerns are more complex and ambivalent than expected. Sometimes, the spouse is shocked to discover that she misunderstood his hopes, values, and concerns.

The third phase is to jointly write positive and negative feelings and positive and negative practical factors. Writing makes this concrete and facilitates discussions and clarifications. At this point, you can weigh alternatives and make points to your spouse. You have clarified feelings and perceptions and are moving toward a decision. Seldom is it easy; if it were, you would not have gone this far in the exercise. There is usually ambivalence and uncertainty on one or both spouses' part. You commit to the decision to become pregnant now, postpone the decision for a given time, or decide you will remain childless. If the latter, will one spouse volunteer for a sterilization procedure? If you cannot decide, then proceed to phase 4.

Obviously, the decision-making process is complex and difficult. Otherwise, it would not have gotten to this phase. We advise against coercion, ultimatums, or forcing a decision. A baby affects both individuals and their marriage: The decision needs to be mutual. Express feelings and wants: This is the time to be clear and strongly express desires, but do so fairly—without threats or hidden agendas.

Discuss the child issue at least once a week and preferably twice a week for at least 5 weeks (and up to 15 weeks). This is not to wear the spouse down but to seriously examine individual and couple desires and fears with the goal of reaching a mutually acceptable decision. Utilize the subjective 1–10 scale to state how strong your desires and concerns are. For example, ability to tolerate childlessness is a 5. The spouse's fear that having a child would destroy her career and sense of well-being is a 9. Although the desire to have a child and please her parents was a 4, she volunteered to have a tubal ligation. The husband's desire for children was a 5 and his fear of financial responsibilities was a 4, so he agreed with this decision.

The decision to have a child asks you to weigh emotional and practical factors. It is based on present feelings and your best prediction of what will happen in the future. There is complexity and ambivalence because of the importance of this life-altering decision. No wonder so many people leave it to chance or one spouse makes a unilateral decision (to stop using birth control or be sterilized).

What if these discussions do not result in a resolution? You can postpone for 6 months and revisit it then. We recommend seeking outside consultation with a psychologist, marriage therapist, minister, physician, or trusted friend to help you get "unstuck."

The Dangers of Not Deciding

We emphasize planned, wanted children and viewing parenthood as a choice. This sounds enlightened and psychologically healthy, but what about people who prefer to do it the old-fashioned way: see what God (or chance) ordains? Is that so bad? Obviously it has worked for couples over the ages, but it does have risks. The likelihood is you will become pregnant and need to be willing to accept this.

The most dangerous situation is where one spouse acts in a secretive or manipulative manner. For example, the man does not disclose he had a vasectomy or the woman says she is using a diaphragm but is not. Being tricked or lied to disrupts trust and invites the spouse to act out in revenge.

The "folk wisdom" that once a baby arrives, he will be accepted by the reluctant parents is often not true. This is one reason why a couple separate. Contrary to popular mythology, there is neither a maternal nor a paternal instinct. Parenting is a choice, not a biological given. In our lives, we very much enjoyed parenting, especially the baby and childhood phases. It required enormous energy, time, and commitment. It is hard to imagine parenting without that commitment. One who forces a child on a reluctant spouse runs the risk of being a single parent.

Parenting is one of life's most difficult commitments to abandon. If the child is 6 years old and you decide parenting is not what you want, what do you say or do with the child? If a parent "burns out" when the adolescent is 14, who will assume responsibility? Acting emotionally or impulsively is risky when it involves an 18-year commitment.

The Adoption Option

One of the most frustrating and stressful times for a couple is when they decide they want a baby and discard birth control but do not become pregnant. There is optimism when beginning fertility treatment, but over time it is replaced by frustration and desperation. It is not until this time that adoption is discussed. That is unfortunate because adoption is a viable alternative. Most couples want to adopt a healthy American infant. Unfortunately, adoption agencies have a long waiting list for infants. There are other options, including older children, hard-to-place children, and overseas adoption. There are classes and self-help groups that provide information, practical advice, and emotional support. We adopted a hard-to-place child. Couples who seriously examine their motivation and are willing to deal with the special challenges of adoption are encouraged to pursue this.

Making a Wise Decision for You and Your Marriage

Whatever decision you make should be accepted by friends and family. Whether you decide to remain childless, have 1 child,

2 children, or 5 children, the decision is yours and only yours to make. Even if you decide against the guideline of waiting at least 2 years before starting a family, it is your choice. Once you have made the choice, commit yourself to successful implementation.

If you decide not to have children, you do not need to defend or justify that. Take advantage of the increased freedom to build an individual and couple life that is satisfying and you are proud of. If you choose the traditional path of having a family, be involved parents while balancing personal and marital roles. Parenting is one of life's most challenging and unique experiences. Enjoy it for all it is worth. If you are going to be a parent, do it right.

Having people who share your life organization and values is helpful. Develop couple friendships in which you have similar-age children so you can share experiences and support. As children develop, they require different parenting skills. The attitudes and skills required for parenting a 2 year old are very different from those required of parents of a 14 year old. The trap is focusing so much on parenting you forget about being a couple. Remember, the most important relationship in a family is the husband-wife bond. Your marital bond needs time, attention and nurturing. You are not shortchanging the children: The best gift to a child is parents who have a healthy, stable marriage.

Closing Thoughts

Deciding whether to have children, when to have them, and how many to have is one of life's most important decisions. We advocate talking and planning, making the decision that is right for you. Do not be controlled by cultural "shoulds," pressure from parents and friends, or fears. A strong guideline is to wait 2 years before having a child.

A planned, wanted child acknowledges and affirms the viability of your marriage. It is a major transition from being a couple to being a family. Being good parents and maintaining a vital marriage is complementary, not in conflict. Make a commitment to personal, couple, and family growth. You feel pride and satisfaction in your life when you maintain a healthy balance of personal, couple, and family time. The most important relationship in a family is the husband-wife bond. The basis of a healthy family is a healthy marriage.

CHAPTER 8

We Can Work It Out:
Resolving Conflicts

The romantic love myth promises that as long as you love each other everything will be fine. "Love is the essence of life" and "Love conquers all." If there is love, how can there be conflict? Romantic love and conflict are incompatible. The problem lies with the concept of romantic love. One of the most important skills for a newly married couple is to recognize, address, and problem-solve differences and conflicts.

Conflict is inherent in sharing your lives. Skills for dealing with conflict are integral to a healthy marriage. What is poisonous is fighting dirty by putting the spouse down, threats or ultimatums, being manipulative, fighting the same battles over and over again, acting out anger, being revengeful or spiteful. Dirty fighting tears at the marital fabric. Rather than viewing your spouse as an intimate friend, you see her as the angry critic intent on blaming you and putting you down.

We advocate the positive influence model of dealing with differences and conflicts. This entails valuing your marital bond of respect and trust while dealing with problems and conflicts. Focus on resolving issues, not winning at your spouse's expense nor putting the spouse down. Deal with the conflict in a respectful, not attacking, manner. State feelings and concerns; be sure they are understood and validated before making a request for change.

This is a request, not a demand. Do not threaten your spouse or seek retribution. Consider a range of alternatives to resolve the conflict rather than "my way or no way."

Using the positive influence model, the couple try to resolve the conflict in a "win-win" manner or at least so that each spouse can live with the agreement. Willingness to deal with differences and problems by learning conflict resolution skills is a crucial resource for newly married couples.

Conflict Avoidance

The naive hope, especially for couples with a conflict-minimizing style, is that marital conflicts can be avoided. The desire is to ignore the conflict and hope it will go away. A man who grew up in a home where his parents were always bickering and once a week exploded into a major confrontation was determined to avoid conflict in his marriage. He ignored and avoided issues so there were no fights. He was the good guy who did all the dishes and responded anytime she had a complaint. When there was a disagreement over spending, he told her to do whatever she thought best. When neighbors were loud and rude, he ignored it. When she was irritated, he went jogging so he did not have to talk. He was shocked when he learned she was having an affair. Her rationale was she needed to escape from an emotionally empty marriage. Even then, he did not express feelings of hurt or anger.

The problem with avoiding or ignoring problems is that when you share a married life, there are real issues, differences, and conflicts that have to be dealt with. Making a big deal over each issue is counterproductive. Some problems seem less serious the next day, and minor differences disappear with time. However, there are real-life conflicts over mundane and serious issues that, if not faced, fester and become virulent. It is better to address problems preventively or in the early stages before negative attitudes, habits, and resentments become entrenched.

In another conflict avoidance strategy the spouse denies there is a problem, saying the partner is a worrier or is bored and looking for problems. This is common with alcohol or drug abuse, anxiety problems like obsessive-compulsive disorder, or introversion and social isolation. The person is afraid to step up to the problem, so stonewalls and blames the spouse. They have a pseudo argument about denial and nagging. Avoiding problems makes them worse. The spouse feels she is being played with, eroding her trust in him and their marital bond.

Some couples say,"Don't sweat the small stuff." It might appear that who does the cooking, who picks up who at the train, rakes the lawn, cleans bathrooms, calls in-laws, are nickel-and-dime issues. In reality, daily hassles set the emotional tone for your marriage. Do you see each other as involved and giving or as isolated and defensive? Is there a genuine sharing, or are tasks done grudgingly? Does he let it go or keep obsessive count? Complementary couples have separate domains and chores but maintain a sense of appreciation. They share the nitty-gritty tasks of life and marriage. Alienation is caused if one spouse feels under-valued or taken advantage of.

The "trendy" model is fifty-fifty equality in all tasks, that is, each spouse does half of the cooking, cleaning bathrooms, mowing the lawn. It sounds good but does not work. People have different skills and interests. A shared, equitable division of tasks is more functional. Be especially aware of how the onerous chores are divided. Small stuff matters.

The most destructive conflict avoidance strategy is to counter-attack and intimidate the spouse into silence. This is used primarily by men. It is a strategy that works in the short term, but it sets the ground for anger and alienation, subverting your marriage. Aversive control kills trust and intimacy.

The Difference between Angry Feelings and Anger Expression

"Pop psychology" advice about anger is confusing and often harmful. The catharsis theory postulates that people internalize angry feelings that build and then explode. The way to deal with this is to express anger: "Let it all out." This simplistic advice is usually wrong, often harmful to the individual, and destructive for your marriage. Anger and anger expression are multicausal and multidimensional. Any self-help advice (including ours) must be considered in the context of each person's situation, feelings, values, and marriage.

Anger is a secondary emotion; the primary emotion is hurt or disappointment. Being aware of and responsive to the primary emotion is optimal. People have a right to their feelings, including hurt and angry feelings. Being aware of and in touch with your feelings is healthy. The ability to express hurt or angry feelings in a manner that enhances personal well-being and facilitates the relationship is a crucial skill. Express feelings in a clear, direct, and assertive manner. This means moderate emotional expression, not "letting it all hang out." Interpersonal violence and intimate coercion are poisonous. Do not express anger through violence or threats.

Take responsibility for your feelings. Do not blame your spouse. State your feelings and perceptions. Make requests for change. Be open to your spouse's feelings, perceptions, and alternatives for resolving a conflict. Assertive expression of feelings is goal-directed: The focus is on problem resolution, not catharsis or hostility.

Conflict often involves anger, but conflict is not about anger. Conflict is about differences, desires, and ways to reach goals. Healthy conflict resolution involves low-to-moderate anger expression. Many conflicts do not even involve anger. The essence of healthy problem resolution is to accept conflict as a natural occurrence, a challenge, and an impetus for change.

Marital Styles and Ways of Dealing with Conflict

Emotionally expressive couples welcome conflict and meet it head-on. This style involves forcefully presenting feelings, arguing, and lobbying the spouse to do it your way. Conflict is carried out with high intensity; each spouse is made aware of the other's feelings. The one with the strongest feelings usually wins. Change occurs; they do not let the problem fester. The relationship remains vital. The dangers with this style are that the resolution is impulsive and not a good solution, the couple "go to the mat" too often, and risks to the marital bond are ignored. The fights become vicious, undermining respect and trust.

The conflict-minimizing couple presents the other extreme. Their strategy is to avoid conflict, especially emotional conflict. They accommodate, minimize, deny, and alter situations so they do not have to confront each other and the issue. The advantage is that life is peaceful and predictable, the focus is on productive and pleasant agendas. It is easy to enjoy positive aspects of the marriage. The dangers are that the couple denies a conflict until it becomes a chronic problem; they stagnate and do not make healthy changes. In avoiding conflict, they lose a sense of genuine connection. When a serious problem occurs, they have neither the skills nor the confidence to deal with it.

The complementary couple style is the most efficient for conflict resolution. The strategy is to decide whose domain is affected; it is that person's responsibility to resolve it. This allows the relationship to flow smoothly, the partner is supportive, and the spouse whose domain it is deals with the conflict in the most effective way she can. The conflict is not ignored but resolved in favor of the person in whose domain the conflict occurs. The dangers with this system are that the couple does not fully engage the issue, the resolution is not optimal, roles become rigid, and negative feelings turn into resentment.

The best friend couple style finds conflict both unsettling and frightening. Conflict disrupts the relationship, especially when there are strong feelings and a need for change. They try to engage the conflict and utilize the positive influence process. Resolving the conflict can promote individual and couple growth. The danger is that frustration builds when the problem is not resolved and continued conflict tears at the marital bond—especially emotional intimacy. The spouse says if you are my best friend why do you not give me this. They avoid the issue and each other. Not all conflicts can be resolved, a harsh truth for the best friend couple style.

Exercise—Conflict Resolution Skills

This exercise focuses on trying to resolve two real-life conflicts. One involves a nitty-gritty hassle (who does the cooking, how social events are planned, who calls who during the day, preferences for country music or jazz). The second conflict involves a major life decision (whether to move to a larger apartment or save for a house, stop using contraception and start a family, enter therapy to deal with a phobia, go back to school and/or switch careers). We suggest addressing the nitty-gritty hassle first. You can develop the skills and confidence to resolve differences and conflicts.

Remember, conflict is a natural part of marriage and conflict resolution skills are crucial to ensure marital satisfaction and stability.

In discussing a nitty-gritty hassle, use the speaker-listener communication format. Each spouse states his or her feelings and perceptions. Take responsibility for your feelings; do not blame your spouse. Most important, clearly state your intention to reach an agreement rather than manipulate the spouse, put him down, or make a power play.

In the typical gender conflict the woman wants to be listened to and the man wants to resolve the problem. This can serve a complementary function, not be a source of anger. Problem solving is a four-step process:

1. Listen in a respectful, caring manner to each spouse's feelings and perceptions.
2. Generate a range of alternatives to resolve the problem.
3. Reach an agreement that is likely to work.
4. Monitor, revise, and successfully implement the agreement.

In the first phase, be sure each spouse has his or her say: feelings are shared and validated. People, especially males, have a tendency to argue rather than accept and validate a spouse's feelings. Validating feelings is not the same as agreeing with the complaint and proposed resolution. For example, in a conflict about who takes care of the cat and makes sure the house is locked at night you might disagree on what is the best system while still affirming how important it is to get the cat in so she does not run away. In creating alternatives, be sure you take the time to explore a range of ways to resolve this rather than going with the easiest answer. Agreeing to a plan that is not workable or does not resolve the problem risks the spouse's becoming irritated and resentful (a common trap for conflict-minimizing couples). Seldom is there only one way to do something, and seldom is there a perfect solution. Some couples decide to take turns on an every-other-day basis. Another alternative has one doing the chore for a month and the spouse taking it next month. Others decide to do it in tandem or divide the task—one takes care of the cat, the other closes up the house. Be sure you have a clear agreement. You could write it down and have it readily available to consult if there is a difficulty or confusion. Couples settle for vague feel-good agreements that sound fine but do not work. Women want to feel okay about the process; and men want to be sure it will resolve the conflict. This gender difference can be a strength. These are complementary approaches and compatible goals.

Nothing succeeds like success. Reach at least one nitty-gritty agreement before tackling a large issue conflict. Be sure you understand and can utilize the positive influence process of conflict resolution.

Examples of major areas of conflict are she wants to move to another state, he wants to quit his job and return to school, she wants a child and he wants to save for a house, one wants to join a church but the other is not interested. When addressing a major issue, it is unlikely there is a simple, perfect resolution. Begin by carefully listening to your spouse's feelings, perceptions, desires, and concerns. Acknowledge and validate her viewpoint before expressing your feelings and perceptions. Clearly state feelings and desires. Keep your emotion moderate (high-intensity anger, helplessness, or neediness diverts from problem solving). Your intention is to reach understandings and agreements, not put something over on your spouse or get your way. After discussing alternatives, state your preferences and lobby for what you believe is a good agreement. Be clear about your feelings and preferred resolution, but do not threaten, intimidate, or coerce your partner. Be sure the agreement is not harmful to either spouse. Optimally, the resolution is helpful to both people and your marriage. Minimally, both can live with the agreement. Life issues can be resolved if you make a good faith effort and stay with the positive influence process.

Some agreements are made for the benefit of one spouse (e.g., the person returns to school and works part-time for a temporary agency). Acknowledge that this resolution is in one spouse's best interest. Do not keep count; the next conflict is not settled for the other spouse. Each conflict is considered on its merits. Be aware of negative patterns such as one spouse always gives in, idealistic solutions that are not practical, the spouse who lobbies hardest gets his way, you settle for a lukewarm compromise. Monitor these traps: They indicate poor conflict resolution skills. Learn to respect and deal with differences; do not ignore them nor constantly struggle over them. Healthy marriage involves a balance of self-acceptance and acceptance of your spouse combined with the positive influence process of change and agreements. A common male complaint is that once married the woman wants to change him. A common female complaint is that the male wants to quickly solve the problem so he can feel expert rather than deal with her feelings and needs.

Work through each step in the conflict resolution process. To recap:

1. Listen to each person's feelings and perceptions in a respectful, caring manner. Validate feelings; do not be critical or indulge in put-downs.

2. Create alternatives that are likely to resolve the conflict while meeting the needs of each spouse and your marital bond.
3. Discuss and lobby so you reach an agreement that resolves the conflict and both people can live with. Be sure you do not coerce or intimidate your spouse.
4. Monitor the agreement to ensure successful implementation. Be open to revising and modifying it (success does not mean being perfect).

Conflicts, disagreements, and anger are not fun but can promote individual and couple growth. The conflict resolution process increases respect and trust for your spouse and marital bond.

Conflict and Anger

Conflict and anger are thought of as negative emotions that are disruptive for the marriage. Most of the time, that is what happens. Conflicts are not dealt with well nor resolved. Anger escalates into defensiveness, criticalness, hostility, and contempt. Anger expressed is anger reinforced. The anger cycle becomes powerful and destructive. Angry conflicts that fester poison your marital bond, reducing respect and trust. When anger increases and results in defensiveness, attack-counterattack, or getting even, then anger controls your relationship and tears at your marital bond.

Conflict and anger can serve healthy functions in your marriage. How the anger is expressed and dealt with is what makes it helpful or problematic. The positive functions of conflict are raising issues, confronting self-defeating behavior, and promoting change. Anger is a way to express feelings of hurt and disappointment so that tough issues are faced and dealt with, not denied or minimized. Anger itself is not a poisonous emotion. It becomes poisonous if anger turns into criticism, contempt, defensiveness, and put-downs. Healthy conflict resolution promotes a vital, secure marriage.

Couples wish they could avoid conflict. We are fans of prevention; many conflicts are preventable. Prevention and early intervention are good strategies. The optimal strategy is to honestly discuss differences and causes of conflict. Do not argue as if it were "right-wrong." Be empathic, understand feelings and issues from your spouse's perspective. Acknowledge common ground and shared values. Accept differences in approach and style. For example, one spouse's style is to work on a task in a focused manner until completion while the other's style is to work on three tasks and when she becomes bored switch to another. Being aware of and accepting this style difference reduces stress. Accepting differences can prevent angry conflict.

It is crucial to be aware of your spouse's motivations and intentions. Usually, the motivation is to be helpful, seldom is it to put down the spouse or be harmful. If the motivation is negative, we strongly suggest therapy because this is a major threat to marital viability.

Assume your spouse's behavior is well-intentioned and caring. A spouse who nags about returning to school, stopping smoking, losing weight, seeing a therapist, keeping contact with an estranged sibling, is not trying to coerce or put you down. Instead of counterattacking, listen in a nondefensive manner. Accept this as a well-intentioned request, not an ill-intentioned demand. One problem is that the advice is unsolicited. With the positive influence model, we suggest asking if your spouse is open to hearing feedback and requests. Be clear about your intention before making suggestions. Awareness that your spouse's intentions are positive makes it easier to deal with the feedback and problem.

Some conflicts cannot be prevented or avoided. Conflict is a natural part of marriage and the human condition. Prevent the conflicts you can, quickly deal with conflicts over unimportant issues, be willing to address conflicts that disrupt or block individual or couple satisfaction. View these as a challenge that, when successfully resolved, will increase respect and trust. For those conflicts which are not resolvable, you need to maintain a dialogue so that the problem does not cause resentment or subvert your marital bond.

JEFF AND STACIE

Jeff is 28, Stacie, 27; they married 18 months ago. They have developed a healthy conflict resolution pattern, although there is room for improvement.

Premarital experiences with conflict reflected poor learnings. Like many couples there was a powerful romantic love attraction with idealization of the partner and relationship. Conflict was viewed as a test of love. For Jeff and Stacie, it was either perfect romantic love, in which case they would marry, or the conflict would end the relationship. They had three breakups and reunited, but they did not resolve the issues. This dichotomous view of conflict (a typical trap) is antithetical to the positive influence model of conflict resolution.

Two conflicts continued to plague their marriage. First, Stacie wanted more time with Jeff and wanted to know where he was when they were apart. Second, Stacie wanted a commitment to have at least two children. Rather than addressing these conflicts, they hoped love would be enough. The third conflict, not having enough money to afford a decent apartment, was resolved by Stacie's getting a promotion and Jeff's business growing.

Marriage is a confrontation with reality, not the magic of romantic love. For Jeff, marriage was more satisfying than he expected given the complaints he heard from male friends and relatives. His major concern was Stacie's neediness and nagging. On the other hand, Stacie was disappointed and upset with Jeff and the marriage. She naively hoped that once married, Jeff would be open to her influence and requests. The nitty-gritty conflict about couple time and the major issue of children were not resolved. She could not understand Jeff's defensiveness; it made her suspicious. Jeff and Stacie had fallen into a classic pursuer-distancer dance with neither spouse having empathy for or understanding the partner's position.

Traditionally, it is the woman who feels responsible for the emotional tone of the marriage. In this couple, Jeff worried about the downward cycle. He did not like feeling defensive and avoiding Stacie. Jeff's parents had a best friend marital style. That is what Jeff had expected and Stacie said she wanted.

Jeff was willing to listen to Stacie's feelings and concerns for as long as she needed to talk. They had four long conversations in which Jeff respectfully and carefully listened and validated her feelings. For the first time in a year, Stacie felt heard and her concerns taken seriously. Jeff asked her to switch roles and listen to his feelings and concerns. He made it clear his intention was to build a respectful, trusting marriage but felt put off by Stacie's nagging and suspicions. Jeff wanted to maintain individuality and autonomy and for Stacie to realize this was not a rejection of her. Specifically, he wanted to continue playing on a baseball team, be a volunteer fireman, and maintain a friendship with Joe, someone

Stacie disliked. Jeff committed to discussing any potential high-risk situation (Stacie was specifically worried about a woman from the team or fire department coming on to him and his ability to say no). Jeff wanted her to trust that he was a responsible person and husband. They agreed to set aside quality couple time, at least 2 hours during the week and a 3-hour block on the weekend.

The child issue was dealt with surprisingly easily. Jeff assured Stacie he wanted children, but his preference was to wait until they were married 3 years before becoming pregnant. Jeff wanted to be sure each was established in his or her career and they had saved enough money so Stacie could take at least 6 months off work after the baby was born. Jeff disclosed his fear: Stacie would be like his mother and not pursue a career after she had children. Jeff was a small business owner; for them to live the life they wanted Stacie's income was crucial. Stacie assured Jeff that one reason for entering the physical therapy field was it allowed her to work part-time. She wanted to combine a career and parenting. Stacie's older sister was a positive model. She did desktop publishing at home so she could be with her children. Sharing intentions, fears, and concerns allowed them to develop a 5-year career and family plan. This conflict turned into an area of relationship strength.

As important as these agreements were, the most important outcome was that Stacie and Jeff were now confident they could deal with differences and conflicts. Jeff was pleased to have a complementary marital style and confident in their ability to resolve future problems. Stacie felt secure, trusting Jeff and their marital bond. Her friends and mother emphasized being hypervigilant in marriage or Jeff would have an affair or cheat her of what she wanted. The necessity to fight for intimacy and security was a core part of Stacie's socialization. She now realized this was not healthy. Stacie and Jeff were committed to maintaining a complementary marital style. This included being able to address and deal with conflicts without needing to question their trust bond.

Conflicts That Are Not Resolvable

The majority of nitty-gritty conflicts and major life issues can be dealt with. This does not mean a perfect resolution but reasonable understandings and agreements. Sometimes you agree to something you do not like but can live with. Much of the time conflicts involve ongoing dialogue in which you discuss and revise understandings and agreements.

Some conflicts are not resolvable. Examples include the spouse who cannot stop smoking no matter what he tries, the spouse who is unable to lose 30 pounds, the couple whose best efforts to move to a nicer home are thwarted by practical, financial, or job factors, the spouse who is not able to overcome her fear of flying, the couple who are unable to maintain a decent relationship with in-laws.

One of the great dangers of the human potential movement is overpromising that everything is changeable and making people feel badly about weaknesses and vulnerabilities. The Alcoholics Anonymous Serenity prayer asks for the courage to change what is changeable and to accept what cannot be changed and the wisdom to know the difference. This is a healthy guideline. An irresolvable conflict does not mean the marriage is dysfunctional or fatally flawed. It means you as individuals with your character-istics and vulnerabilities are unable to resolve a specific problem.

We suggest two guidelines for dealing with unresolvable conflicts since research findings indicate that as many as two thirds of con-flicts require ongoing dialogue or acceptance because they are not resolvable. The first guideline is to accept reality and stop trying to change the spouse or situation. The healthy strategy is acceptance: Do not make this issue a major relationship stress. This strategy is easier to adopt for complementary and conflict-minimizing couples. Emotionally expressive couples keep hammering at the issue hoping the spouse will change. Best friend couples find it hard to accept that they cannot resolve an issue. The second guideline is to respect your spouse's right to his personal style and to ensure that the conflict has minimal impact on you and your marriage. Do not make his prob-lems your problems. For example, the spouse's unresolvable smok-ing, eating, or job problem need not become your problem or dominate the marriage.

Unresolvable conflicts involving major life issues are particu-larly difficult. Examples include one spouse wants to change to a lower paying career that will require a major change in standard of living, one spouse plans to take a job that demands a great deal of business travel, a religious conflict that affects a child, one spouse decides to run for public office over the other's objections.

These present major challenges to your marital bond. As long as there is no hidden agenda and the intention toward the marriage is positive, these conflicts can be dealt with. For example, Barry sees political couples for whom conflict over time and the sacrifices necessary to be in the public spotlight are intense. Nonresolvable does not mean irreconcilable. The spouse agrees to do what is necessary to be publicly appropriate, and the political spouse agrees to devote the time and energy to maintain marital vitality. Neither is totally happy, but this understanding allows the marriage to proceed in a healthy manner.

Dealing with Conflicts versus Going to the Mat

Respecting your ability to address conflicts and trusting your spouse's intentions when dealing with difficult issues promotes a healthy marriage. Do not act like you are walking on eggshells—express feelings and deal with hard issues. The positive influence model asks each spouse to share attitudes, feelings, and desires in an open and problem-solving manner. Work as a respectful team to reach the best agreement or resolution possible.

This is very different from "going to the mat," which is popular in American culture whether involving business conflicts, financial conflicts, or relationship conflicts. Increasingly we are a litigious society. Lawyers threaten to sue and destroy the person. It is a war, except the weapons are words, accusations, and money. Going to the mat is the conflict resolution process run amuck. This is a special trap for emotionally expressive couples. The struggle to express feelings and win your point overcomes your sense of coupleness. Threats and ultimatums are the negotiating tools. You risk marital respect and trust—a very dangerous gamble. We suggest resorting only to this once or twice in a marriage. Some couples go to the mat on a weekly or monthly basis—that is poisonous for your marital bond.

Closing Thoughts

The traditional view was that newly married couples should avoid conflict. Romantic love and time would overcome differences and problems. What an unrealistic marital model.

Differences and conflicts are integral to marriage. A core marital skill is the ability to address and resolve conflicts. Ideally, conflict resolution skills using positive influence promote individual and couple growth.

More than stress involving content issues, the couple becomes angry, alienated, and distrustful as the emotional process worsens. Breaking the downward cycle is crucial in order to maintain marital viability. You can develop a functional style of conflict resolution. Listening in a respectful, caring manner and validating feelings and perceptions are the first step. Exploring alternatives that meet individual and couple needs and successfully resolving the problem is the goal. You can lobby and advocate for your position without making threats or issuing ultimatums. Reach an agreement or resolution that optimally meets individual and couple needs but at the least both can live with. Conflict resolution skills are a crucial marital resource.

CHAPTER 9

Sexual Problems:
Dysfunction, Affairs, Infertility

Sexual problems are the major cause of separation and divorce in the first 2 years of marriage. This is a surprise to those who believe the claim that people are having the most exquisitely satisfying sex in the history of the world. Although there is more information and discussion of sexual issues than at any time in human history, this has not translated into healthier sexual functioning or greater sexual satisfaction. Couples are not functioning better sexually than their parents' generation. What has changed are the types of problems. Sexual dysfunction in the 21st century is less likely to be caused by lack of information or repressive sexual attitudes. Problems of inhibited sexual desire, premature ejaculation, female nonorgasmic response, erectile dysfunction, and painful intercourse are frequent. There is a troubling increase in secondary dysfunction (i.e., the person or couple had been functional, but sex is now problematic), especially inhibited sexual desire. Rates of sexual problems (fifty percent of married couples complain of sexual dysfunction or dissatisfaction) have not changed in 20 years but have shifted to those caused by unrealistic expectations, performance anxiety, and disappointment and alienation.

When sexuality goes well, it plays a positive, integral role in your marriage. The positive functions of marital sexuality are a shared pleasure, a means to reinforce and deepen intimacy, and a tension reducer to deal with the stresses of life and marriage. Sexuality energizes your marital bond and makes it special. Sexuality contributes 15 to 20 percent to marital vitality and satisfaction. When the couple have sexual problems, especially early in the marriage, it is a major drain. Sexuality plays an inordinately powerful role, robbing the marriage of intimacy and vitality. Sexual issues must be addressed and resolved, or the marriage is in danger.

Sexual Dysfunction

A male with an erection problem mislabels himself "impotent." This becomes his self-definition not just sexually but in terms of general self-esteem. The nonorgasmic woman mislabels herself "frigid." She feels deficient as a woman and a wife. Sexual dysfunction dominates self-esteem and drains couple satisfaction.

Is sexual dysfunction an individual or couple problem? Understanding it as a couple problem increases the probability of successful resolution. This is true even when the problem predates the relationship. The man who has always been a premature ejaculator or the woman who has never been orgasmic are more likely to change if the problem is treated as a couple issue. It is a couple task to develop a sexual style that is comfortable and functional for both people. This challenges the "guilt-blame" trap and allows the couple to address sexuality as an intimate team. A newly married couple who successfully confront a sexual dysfunction learn about themselves, each other, and their sexuality. This serves you well and inoculates you against sexual problems as you and your marriage age.

Extramarital Affairs

People are shocked to learn the most common time for an extramarital affair is the first 2 years of marriage. Extramarital affairs weaken the trust bond and throw the marriage into crisis. The spouse questions the worth of the marriage.

The marital commitment is challenged when one or both spouses have an affair. The myth is that affairs are a result of boredom and occur after years of marriage. In reality, affairs are most common early in the marriage. What does an affair mean in a new marriage? Does it indicate the marriage was a mistake? The spouse no longer feels love? Is it due to lack of attraction? Reactions are guilt, blame, anger, threats, and counterthreats.

The most common cause of an extramarital affair is high opportunity. People (especially males) fall into an affair rather than plan to have an affair. Male sexual socialization emphasizes that "a real man is ready to have sex with any woman, anytime, in any situation." Saying no is not easy, even after marriage. This is a self-defeating way of thinking about sexuality, especially its impact on marital intimacy and trust. This is not to excuse the man's affair but to make the point how easy it is to fall into an affair.

The more an affair substitutes for the marriage as a source of emotional and sexual fulfillment, the greater the threat to the marital bond. "Comparison affairs" are the most disruptive and threatening. The spouse is compared with the person she is having an affair with and found wanting. Comparison affairs are the most common type of female affair. People leave marriages because of a comparison affair. Even when the affair ends, its legacy is still in each spouse's mind. The comparison affair occupied a great deal of time and emotional energy. If the other person ended the affair, there is "if only" thinking. There are strong ambivalent feelings, including a sense of loss. Even if the spouse does not learn about the affair, there is uneasiness that something is wrong. Often, the spouse discovers the affair in a traumatic manner. He might receive an anonymous phone call, hear about it from a neighbor or work colleague, or see them together. Humiliation and betrayal turns to anger. Even when the affair has ended, angry thoughts, including the desire for revenge, remain. Feeling judged and criticized by the spouse and ex-lover is a poisonous aftereffect. Dealing with an extramarital affair is a major challenge for the marital bond.

Infertility

Couples do not expect to have a fertility problem. Throughout adolescence and young adult years the constant theme is do not get pregnant, use contraception. The assumption is that getting pregnant is easy. It feels immensely unfair to be married, want a baby, and not be able to conceive. A fertility problem is a greater stress on the marriage than a sexual dysfunction or affair. Approximately 15 percent of couples under 30 and 25 percent of couples over 30 have difficulty conceiving.

The majority of couples eventually do become pregnant. The guideline is that if you do not become pregnant within a year, consult with your gynecologist who will refer you to an infertility specialist. If the infertility problem is not resolved, assessments and interventions become increasingly intrusive and expensive, causing major stress on the individuals and marriage. Whether infertility lies with one spouse or is a combination of factors, it is best to address infertility as a couple issue.

Coping with Sexual Problems

Ideally, sexuality is a positive, integral component of your marriage. A dysfunction, affair, or a fertility problem (unwanted pregnancy or infertility) robs sexuality of its positive function and plays an inordinately powerful negative role. Our coping model involves the following guidelines:

1. Be honest with yourself and your spouse in assessing the type and severity of the sexual problem.
2. View sexuality as a couple issue. This does not mean the spouse caused the problem, but you need to be intimate partners in confronting the sexual problem.
3. Address the problem, but do not allow it to define self-esteem or dominate your marriage. The sexual problem is real and needs to be resolved; neither minimize it nor give it controlling power.
4. Use all your resources to understand and resolve the problem. These include marital or sex therapy, medical specialists, reading, a marriage enrichment program, a self-help group, consulting a minister, family members and/or friends.
5. Affirm what you value about your spouse and marriage. Maintain motivation until the sexual problem is successfully resolved.

Frequency and Types of Sexual Dysfunction

Many newly married couples experience a sexual dysfunction or dissatisfaction. Almost every marriage will have at least one experience where sex is unsatisfactory or disappointing, if not a "bomb." Human beings are not perfectly functioning machines. Couple sexuality has built-in complexity and variability. Sex is not always easy, flowing, or satisfying. Sex is portrayed in movies as intense, erotic, and always successful—an unrealistic model. In fact, movies almost never portray marital sex; it is either a pre-marital or extra-marital affair. Develop positive, realistic expectations for marital sexuality. The goal is not to be the best sexual couple in town. It is to develop a couple sexual style that is comfortable and satisfying for both spouses and that energizes and makes special your marital bond.

Every couple has at least one experience where sex is a "failure." A sexual difficulty is not considered a dysfunction unless it has existed for at least 3 months. Occasional or intermittent sexual problems are normal. Unfortunately, most couples do not address the sexual dysfunction until it has existed for years. The therapist has to deal not only with the dysfunction but layers of confusion, frustration, blaming, and anger. Sexual problems do not remain stable but over time become burdensome, severe, and chronic. The healthy strategy is to address sexual problems early in the marriage while they are in the acute stage and motivation to revitalize sexuality is high.

Female Sexual Dysfunction

The most common sexual complaints are:

1. Nonorgasmic response during intercourse.
2. Inhibited sexual desire.
3. Nonorgasmic response during partner sex.
4. Painful intercourse or discomfort.
5. Arousal dysfunction.
6. Primary nonorgasmic response (preorgasmic).
7. Vaginismus.

The most common sexual complaint, not being orgasmic during intercourse, is *not* a dysfunction; it is a normal variant of female sexuality. The husband insists she function just like him: "have one orgasm that *must* occur during intercourse." This performance goal assumes the male sexual pattern is the only normal, natural one. Scientifically this is incorrect and harmful. The traditional sexual problems were caused by lack of information, inhibitions, and guilt; the new problems are caused by unrealistic expectations and performance demands.

Miscommunication, frustration, and blaming are caused by lack of understanding regarding male-female sexual response. There are many more similarities than differences. Accepting commonalities facilitates marital sexuality. There are differences, one of the most important being female orgasmic response is more variable and complex than male orgasm—this means different, not better or worse. The woman could be nonorgasmic, singly orgasmic, or multiorgasmic, which might occur during pleasuring/foreplay, intercourse, or afterplay. There is not one "right" orgasmic pattern, nor are multiple orgasms superior to a single orgasm. Orgasms during intercourse are neither healthier nor more mature than orgasms through manual, oral, or rubbing stimulation. The mythical distinction between "vaginal" and "clitoral" orgasm is not scientifically valid.

Each couple develops their unique sexual style. The essence of sexuality is giving and receiving pleasure-oriented touching, not a competition for the "right" orgasm. One third of sexually functional women never have orgasm during intercourse. This is normal, not a dysfunction. The majority of women can be orgasmic with both nonintercourse stimulation and during intercourse, but find it easier to reach orgasm during nonintercourse sex. A significant proportion use simultaneous clitoral stimulation (with her hands, his hands, or vibrator) during intercourse. Some women prefer orgasm during intercourse, others prefer orgasm during oral sex, others with manual stimulation. The key to female sexuality is developing a comfortable desire, arousal, orgasm, and satisfaction pattern, not achieving a rigid performance criterion.

Inhibited sexual desire is the most common female sexual dysfunction, involving one third of women. For half, this is a lifelong (primary) problem. The other half experienced desire, often at the beginning of the relationship, but it has dissipated.

The key elements for sexual desire are anticipation, deserving, and receptivity. Does she think about, fantasize, dream, look forward to sex? Does she feel she deserves sexual pleasure? Is she receptive and responsive to her partner's initiation? Whether a movie, athletic event, or vacation, half the fun is anticipation. In planning and anticipating, she "psychs herself up" and is open to the sexual experience. Openness and receptivity enhance sexual desire. Often desire increases as a response to touching rather than preceding touching—"responsive desire" is normal and healthy. Contrary to popular myth, sexual desire is not a biological need governed by hormones. Nor is desire a static state. Sexual desire is influenced by psychological, physical, relational, and situational attitudes, experiences, and feelings.

Desire is facilitated by feeling close and connected, open to engage in pleasurable and erotic touching, using thoughts and fantasies as turn-ons, looking forward to sexual play, seeing sex as a tension reducer to deal with the hassles of life, sharing arousal and orgasm. Sex is a symbol of intimacy; affection and sensual touching can serve as a bridge to sexual desire. Desire is subverted by sexual and emotional poisons and turnoffs. These include performance anxiety, anger, guilt, depression, anticipatory anxiety, distraction, sexual aversion, disappointment, alienation, feeling pressured or coerced, obsessions and compulsions, shame, fear of pregnancy. You can confront these poisons and turnoffs; build anticipation and sense of deserving; think, talk, and feel like an intimate team; increase comfort, pleasure, and eroticism. Sexual desire cannot be treated with benign neglect nor taken for granted. Individual and couple bridges to desire need to be built, nurtured, and reinforced.

Female dysfunctions, including nonorgasmic response, lack of arousal, painful intercourse, and vaginismus, need careful assessment and treatment. There are a myriad of possible causes of secondary nonorgasmic response, the most common being anger or disappointment at the spouse or marriage. Others include not putting energy or attention into your relationship, anticipatory or performance anxiety, depression, sex being quick and mechanical, spouse too intercourse-oriented, lack of sexual communication, his sexual dysfunction. Prior orgasmic experience is a good prognostic sign. You will be orgasmic again if inhibitions are identified and resolved. Rather than the wife's blaming herself or feeling blamed by the husband, the couple need to rebuild sexual comfort and confidence.

Painful intercourse is best understood as a combination of physical, psychological, and relational factors. Women often feel worse after consulting a gynecologist who does a cursory exam and says "you're fine, the problem is in your head." The husband who reacts to her pain by blaming makes the problem worse. Put-downs and accusations do no one any good. Choose a sensitive, competent gynecologist to conduct a thorough assessment of hormonal factors, infections, muscle tears, blockage, or tissue irritation. Often, there is not a specific medical cause. Nonetheless, the pain is real. It is in your vulva, not your head. The most common causes of painful intercourse are lack of vaginal lubrication, awkward or irritating penile intromission, and lack of flexibility in the vaginal walls. Interventions include increased couple awareness and communication, focus on pleasuring, use of a nonallergenic vaginal lubricant, she guiding intromission, and use of pubococcygeal (pc) muscle exercises to improve strength and flexibility of the vaginal walls.

Masturbation has traditionally been blamed for sexual problems, with women discouraged from masturbating. In truth, women who masturbate report greater body and sexual awareness, learn their arousal and orgasm pattern, and are more likely to be orgasmic during partner sex. Self-exploration/masturbation (which can include vibrator stimulation) is the easiest way of learning to be orgasmic. She explores her body, is aware of what feels good, identifies special turn-ons and techniques to increase arousal, and gives herself permission to let go. Rates of masturbation increase among newly married women.

Being orgasmic with a partner requires communication and working together. The woman's feeling responsible for herself, her sexuality, and her orgasm is crucial. It is not the man's responsibility to "give her an orgasm." She develops her "sexual voice." He needs to be respectful and attentive to her requests and guidance, and share her pleasure. She needs to respect and accept herself as a sexual woman, sharing her awareness and turn-ons.

Vaginismus is rare but very disruptive to self-esteem and couple sexuality and can prevent conception. Finding a competent, supportive gynecologist for diagnosis is important. Vaginismus involves an involuntary spasming of the vaginal opening that prohibits or makes intercourse very painful. The good news is vaginismus can be successfully treated. She increases comfort and feelings of control, learns genital relaxation techniques, and gradually increases receptivity to objects in her vagina. He is actively supportive while honoring her veto of anything sexually aversive. Intercourse is at her initiation, and she guides his penis into her vagina.

Male Sexual Dysfunction

Sexual dysfunction is more common among women than men, but more traumatic and threatening for men, especially at the beginning of the marriage. Too much of the man's self-esteem is tied to his penis. Males have unrealistic performance expectations. An example is three quarters of males believe their penis is smaller than average, a statistical impossibility. The essence of sexuality is giving and receiving pleasure-oriented touching, not a performance dominated by competition and fear of failure. Sexuality is intimate and interactive. She is his intimate friend, not a demanding critic.

The most common sexual dysfunctions are:

1. Premature ejaculation.
2. Erectile dysfunction.
3. Inhibited sexual desire.
4. Ejaculatory inhibition.

Premature ejaculation is by far the most common problem, approximately 3 in 10 men have poor ejaculatory control. This varies in severity from ejaculation right before or during intromission to ejaculating within a minute of rapid thrusting. He does not experience voluntary control. Premature ejaculation causes sexual dissatisfaction for the man and woman. A common cause is the association of high sexual excitement with anxiety about rapid ejaculation. Premature ejaculation is a strongly overlearned pattern. Do-it-yourself techniques to reduce excitement include wearing two condoms, using a desensitizing cream on the penis, biting his lip, thinking nonerotic thoughts such as how much money he owes. These serve as a sexual distraction. He reduces arousal but does not increase ejaculatory control.

Learning ejaculatory control is a couple task. Increase awareness and comfort; do not reduce arousal. The treatment strategy is counterintuitive: increase stimulation and learn to accept greater pleasure. Identify the point of ejaculatory inevitability (after which ejaculation is no longer voluntary—he will ejaculate no matter what). The next step involves practicing the stop-start technique with manual and/or oral stimulation so he maintains arousal without ejaculating. As he approaches the point of inevitability, he tells her or nonverbally signals so she stops stimulation until the urge to ejaculate decreases (usually 10 to 30 seconds). She resumes stimulation 30 to 60 seconds later. With practice, comfort and confidence increase. Transfer this to intercourse using the "quiet vagina" technique of the woman guiding intromission with little or no movement. He increases awareness and comfort with the sensations of vaginal containment. In subsequent sessions, she utilizes slow thrusting. When he approaches the point of inevitability, he signals her to stop. The process includes gradually increasing movement, the male controlling thrusting, and different intercourse positions. It is harder to maintain ejaculatory control in the man-on-top position with short, rapid stroking.

Erectile dysfunction is relatively rare for males under 35, but it dramatically impacts the marriage. The majority of erectile problems in younger males are caused by anxiety, specifically anticipatory and performance anxiety. The man who does not get erections by any means should consult a urologist. Common medical problems interfering with erection include medication side effects, alcoholism or drug abuse, vascular or neurological disease, and poorly controlled diabetes.

Males learn about arousal as an easy, automatic, autonomous process, proceeding to intercourse on his first erection. When this is disrupted, he becomes caught in the cycle of anticipatory anxiety, tense or failed intercourse, and sexual avoidance. The couple works as an intimate team to regain comfort and confidence with erection. Sexuality is an active process of giving and receiving pleasure. Sex is not a spectator sport (passively observing the state of his penis). Sex is about sharing pleasure and eroticism, not a pass-fail performance.

Put a temporary prohibition on intercourse so you can experiment with the process of waxing and waning of erections. Your partner uses manual or oral stimulation to an initial erection and then ceases stimulation; this naturally results in your erection waning. You cannot will or force an erection but can remain open and receptive to her stimulation. Males are used to predictable, automatic erections and proceeding to intercourse on his first erection. There is nothing wrong with this scenario, except he panics if he loses his erection. You can learn to experience the natural physiological process of waning and the erection becoming firm again. Make requests for erotic stimulation and special turn-ons. If you do not regain an erection, this need not result in feelings of embarrassment or failure. Enjoy pleasuring you can give to her, or have erotic, nonintercourse sex to orgasm for one or both. Sensual and erotic scenarios enhance couple intimacy. Intercourse is a natural extension of the pleasuring process, not a pass-fail test.

Inhibited sexual desire is rare for newly married males. First, identify inhibitions and turnoffs. Common causes are anxiety about erection or ejaculation, a variant arousal pattern kept secret from your spouse, concern over sexual orientation, fears of pregnancy, intimacy, or commitment. This requires couple sex therapy since the man is defensive about inhibited desire and views the spouse as his critic or enemy rather than intimate friend. Desire is the essence of sexuality. Sexual inhibitions, avoidance, and secrets subvert desire and intimacy.

Ejaculatory inhibition is rare and usually does not come to the attention of a professional until the couple are ready to become pregnant. Men with ejaculatory inhibition are viewed as "studs" who can continue intercourse indefinitely. In truth, ejaculatory inhibition interferes with intimacy and pleasure. The man learns to request multiple stimulation and utilize "orgasm triggers." He learns to trust her and let go and allow arousal to flow to orgasm. You cannot force orgasm but can increase involvement and erotic stimulation. Orgasm is a natural result of increased arousal. Orgasm triggers include rhythmic thrusting, tightening leg muscles and letting go, focusing on erotic fantasies and images, verbalizing how turned on you feel, testicle stimulation, tuning into her arousal.

MOLLY AND BRENT

Molly and Brent were married 19 months and entered sex therapy feeling great embarrassment. They were referred by a gynecologist who they consulted about fertility problems. They felt doubly stigmatized by the sexual dysfunction and infertility. Brent had severe premature ejaculation; he ejaculated before his penis was in Molly's vagina. Brent felt defeated and avoided couple sex, using masturbation instead. Molly had a history of child sexual abuse and inhibited sexual desire. At first, Molly was not concerned by Brent's sexual avoidance because it coincided with her low desire. However, both wanted children and sexual dysfunction sabotaged this goal.

Molly and Brent were a demoralized couple. The therapist assured them there was no reason to believe they would not conceive. The question was whether they deserved a satisfying sexual relationship. Did they want to improve sexual intimacy and pleasure or just have procreative sex? Molly surprised herself (and Brent) by saying she was interested in sexual pleasure as well as conception.

Molly accepted the concept of sex as a couple issue and being an intimate team easier than Brent. Brent clung to the view that he was responsible for all the problems: If he could only *perform* better, everything would be okay. Goal orientation and performance pressure maintained the premature ejaculation problem.

Molly and Brent started with nondemand pleasuring to increase comfort and sensuality. Molly enjoyed the touching and intimacy. Touching was voluntary (as opposed to coercive and abusive), a mutual give-and-take (as opposed to doing what the man demanded), involved and intimate (not mechanical and alienated). Brent was her intimate spouse (not a man who wanted to "get off"). Brent had great empathy and respect for Molly dealing with sexual trauma. This broke his obsessive preoccupation with performance and allowed him to be a caring spouse. The temporary prohibition on intercourse facilitated Molly and Brent's developing a comfortable, pleasure-oriented sexual style.

Intercourse was gradually reintroduced, with Molly in control of initiation and guiding his penis into her. Developing ejaculatory control during intercourse was slow but steady. They conceived after 4 months. Having intercourse with the intention of getting pregnant was a sexual aphrodisiac. Sexuality is an intimate, nurturing part of their marriage, no longer a source of embarrassment or trauma. Molly and Brent resolved to remain an intimate sexual couple throughout the pregnancy.

Dealing with an Extramarital Affair

The best strategy for extramarital affairs is prevention. The joke in the mental health field is affairs are good for the psychotherapy business. Affairs put individuals and the marriage into crisis. Why are affairs more likely to occur during the early years of marriage? What are the most common types of affairs? What does the affair mean? Contrary to simplistic advice, affairs are multicausal and multidimensional with a range of meanings, individual differences, and outcomes.

The three most common types of affairs are:

1. High opportunity/low involvement affair.
2. Ongoing, compartmentalized affair.
3. Comparison affair.

Although husbands are twice as likely to have an affair as wives, it is the woman's affair that poses the greater threat to the marital bond. This is not intended as a sexist statement but reflects the reality that because it is a reversal of the traditional double standard and the wife's affair is likely to be a comparison affair, it destabilizes the individuals and marriage.

The high opportunity/low involvement affair is the most common male pattern, reflecting traditional sex role socialization of separating sex from intimacy. This is likely to be a "one-night stand," someone he meets on a trip or in a bar, a paid experience with a prostitute, or going to a massage parlor. It reflects the male norm that a "real man never says no to sex." Men do not consider this an affair, much less a threat to the marriage. They are wrong.

An ongoing, compartmentalized affair is sexually motivated and plays a continuous, although limited, role in the person's life. This is the type of affair where they hook up at a monthly sales meeting, meet once a week at a motel, get together at a bar two or three times a month, when traveling to a city meet for sex, or sneak away once a quarter for a weekend. This is viewed as a harmless, yet exciting, way to spice up life. He maintains an erotic outlet, separate from the marriage. The splitting of eroticism from intimacy and the emotional betrayal devitalize the marital bond.

The comparison affair meets emotional and sexual needs not met by the marriage. This is the type of affair people leave their marriage for. You compare the lover with the spouse. It is a major challenge to your marital bond. Even if the marriage survives, the spouse questions attractiveness, desirability, personal and sexual worth.

Why would a person have an affair in the first 2 years of marriage? The most common cause is a high opportunity situation. Other causes are not feeling sexually sure of himself, to see if others find her desirable, want to return to the intrigue of dating sex, a way to maintain emotional distance, hostile acting out against the spouse, an energizer to deal with career disappointment, a way to maintain a premarital affair, or a secret arousal pattern he acts out. For some, the affair is a means to gather courage to leave a fatally flawed marriage. For others, it is a cry for help that says attend to this marriage. An affair sends a message. You need to identify the issues behind the affair. Sometimes the affair is a symbol of a nonviable marriage. More often it is a symbol of a problem that needs to be resolved if this is to be a vital marriage. What is the impact of the affair on each spouse and the marital bond?

We suggest marital therapy to help understand and deal with the affair. Do not pretend it did not happen or minimize its impact. Do not impulsively end the marriage because of an affair. With the help of a professional, carefully examine what you can learn about yourself, your spouse, and your relationship to understand the causes, meanings, and impact of the affair.

Couples who choose to maintain their marriage make an explicit agreement to prevent future affairs. They do this by honestly sharing what kind of people and what kind of situation are high risk for each spouse. Sharing vulnerability increases awareness. The couple makes an explicit agreement to monitor and avoid high-risk situations. An additional agreement is that if the spouse finds himself in a high-risk situation, he commits to discussing it before acting out. This agreement and commitment help rebuild their trust bond.

Dealing with Infertility

Couples never imagine they will have to confront a fertility problem. If they do not become pregnant after 12 months, the first question is "Whose fault is it?" This is a self-defeating way to approach an infertility problem.

Fertility problems are a couple issue. Being stuck in guilt and blame subverts your marriage. Medically, it is common for there to be a female, male, and couple component. Even when it is strictly a male factor (lack of sperm) or a female factor (blocked fallopian tubes), it is healthier to treat this as a couple issue. Avoid the guilt-blame trap, focus on resolving the problem. Explore alternatives (surgery or other medical interventions, artificial insemination, adoption, enjoying a couple life without children, being involved godparents, adopting overseas).

More than any other sexual problem, infertility puts stress on a married couple, especially those committed to parenting. It does no one (nor the marriage) any good to deny or minimize the disappointment and fear of never having a child. Couple therapy with a clinician who has a subspecialty in fertility issues is strongly suggested. Share fears, perceptions, and concerns with the therapist and each other.

Seek medical assessment and intervention with a fertility specialist (gynecologist, endocrinologist, and/or urologist). Choose a competent physician with whom you have rapport. Fertility is not just a medical problem but involves your sense of personhood and the meaning of the marriage. You need to discuss costs, benefits, and potential risks, especially of high-technology interventions. Many fertility specialists have a mental health professional on the staff, a sign of how complex and stressful the process is. A self-help group, Resolve, is a resource to help couples accept infertility and explore alternatives.

Some people say divorce this spouse so you can have children with a different spouse. Although many couples divorce over the stress of infertility, most who approach this issue as a team agree on a mutual course of action. This can range from using special interventions to become pregnant, adopting an older child, choosing to remain childless. There is not an easy, perfect resolution, but there are viable alternatives that preserve and can strengthen your marital bond.

Closing Thoughts

Sexual problems need not overwhelm your marriage nor cause you to view divorce as the only alternative. Most sexual problems can be addressed and resolved. Others need to be accepted and coped with. Couples who successfully resolve sexual problems early in the marriage inoculate themselves against sexual difficulties later. It is not easy to address a sexual problem, but if you approach this as an intimate team and maintain motivation, sexuality will nurture your marital bond rather than subvert it. Resolving sexual issues early in the marriage is worth the effort, resulting in a resilient, vital marriage. Sexuality energizes your marital bond and makes it special.

CHAPTER 10

The Most Common Stress:
Dealing with Money

The issues that cause most marital conflict are money, sex, and children. Financial problems are underestimated as a source of distress among newly married couples. Interestingly, couples are more willing to talk about sexual problems than money problems.

Couples are surprised to find how complex and serious money problems can be. Whether a young couple just starting out or a second marriage in which one spouse gives or receives child support, the naive hope is that they can avoid difficult discussions about financial matters. More people keep money secrets than sexual secrets.

In the traditional marital model, the husband is the primary (or sole) breadwinner. It is his role to generate income, make financial decisions, and be responsible for the financial viability of the family. He gives his wife an "allowance" to manage the house and children. In the financial game they play, the husband complains that his wife neither understands money nor appreciates how hard he works or the pressure he is under. She complains that he does not understand how much food, clothing, and the children's needs cost—there is never enough money. They approach money issues as if men and women belong to an entirely different financial species.

Although the husband complains about the wife's financial stupidity, he prefers it that way: He wants to maintain financial control. The woman prefers to work around or manipulate the husband so she gets what is needed for the children and household. It is a disrespectful, nontrusting financial dance.

In these roles, adults knew more about their parents' sex life than their financial life. Children are aware of financial stress and conflict but unsure what the issues are. Seldom did they know how much the parents made or how money was budgeted. This is true whether they grew up in privileged circumstances or in poverty. Few newly married couples have a positive model for money management and financial decision making.

Recognizing Differences

Each spouse brings to the marriage attitudes, experiences, and feelings about money. For example, a man enters his second marriage with fearful attitudes. His parents were forced to sell their home when his father lost his job. In his first marriage, both worked; they saved money, bought a nice house, and took expensive vacations. The divorce was draining emotionally and financially. Legal fees were astronomical. In bitter divorces, only the lawyers profit. He felt burdened by child support payments and believed the ex-spouse misused money, causing further agitation. Although he earned a good income, he was very cautious about spending. His attitude about sharing money with the new spouse bordered on paranoia. This was her first marriage. She felt she was paying for the problems of his family of origin and first marriage.

Couples argue about money as if it were a political debate: One side wins, the other loses. She lobbies to get her way, acting as if it is a right-wrong factual issue. In truth, money issues are multidimensional. People's perceptions and feelings are as important as precise calculations. Values, confidence, and trust are as important as W-2 statements. Money has as much to do with feelings and perceptions as facts and figures.

People recall grandparents talking about the economic depression of the 1930s and how those experiences influenced attitudes and emotional reactions to money. Their parents talked about steady economic growth in the 1950s where the goal was to buy a home in the suburbs. Economic realities change, whether the job market, inflation, interest rates, salaries, stock market, job security. The get-rich, consumer-oriented "yuppies" of the 1980s had a major influence. Start-up companies, the stock market frenzy, and the winner-take-all economy of the 1990s had its positive and negative impacts.

People fear theirs could be the first generation with a lower standard of living than their parents. Newly married couples expect both spouses to work in order to maintain a reasonable standard of living. Yet the financial understandings of two-career couples are confusing and contradictory. How do you feel if the wife is earning more than the husband? Will they move for the husband's job if it negatively impacts her career? How does this affect spending decisions? How does this affect respect and trust in your marriage?

You need to consider your financial backgrounds, how money was dealt with in the family of origin, how you earned and spent money during your single life. This increases awareness and facilitates sharing preferences and desires as well as identifying fears and worries.

The most important factor is an agreement that there will not be financial secrets. Examples of secrets include one spouse having credit card debt, a family inheritance of $20,000 that will be disbursed at age 30, a bad credit rating you hide from the spouse, likelihood of inheriting a large sum of money when a grandparent dies, stock you did not tell the spouse you have, delinquent child support or alimony payments, responsibility for debts from a failed business, overdue college loans.

We strongly advocate discussing financial issues, preferably before getting married. Financial secrets impact your trust bond. You are better revealing these up front than hearing it through someone else, the spouse receiving a late-notice phone call or discovering a bill. Your intention was to avoid embarrassment or confrontation. However, the discovered secret turns a difficult situation into a marital crisis.

In discussing experiences and attitudes about money, do not turn it into a right-wrong argument. Listen in a respectful, caring manner to your spouse's personal and family experiences. How important is money in life? Growing up, did she earn her own money? What did she spend it on? What are his financial dreams and goals? His fears and concerns? What are her present income and future plans? What are the assets and what are the debts? Share your wants, concerns, hopes, and fears. Once you have a shared information base, it is easier to make financial decisions and plans.

Problems with Income

Almost all couples complain they do not have enough money. Even couples whose joint yearly income is $450,000 worry they do not have enough and read with envy of people who make a million dollars a year or whose investments double in value.

It is easier to be honest about income than expenditures, but people keep secrets about income too. For example, those in sales exaggerate commissions with the rationale that you have to project a successful image. Whether this is good business policy is questionable, but it is definitely not a good marital policy. Another example is the woman who said she earned half as much as she did so as not to embarrass her husband and make him feel inadequate. He was enraged when he learned the truth. Or the man who assured the spouse they could live on his salary of $40,000 but had to carefully budget and save for a house. When applying for the home mortgage, she was shocked to learn he earned $70,000.

We recommend disclosing all sources of income—weekly paycheck, sales commissions, bonuses, money from stocks or inheritance, child support payments, even money paid under the table or not reported to the IRS. Make a differentiation between reliable and variable income. Be honest with yourself and your spouse. How secure is your job? What is your projection of income next year? In 5 years? Is this reasonable and satisfactory, or do you need alternative means to generate income?

Problems with Spending

Spending is the more common problem and harder to be honest about. People dislike budgets because it is difficult to remain accountable. We strongly recommend making and keeping a budget. Couples who have a budget do not get into serious financial problems.

The reason it is so hard to keep spending under control is that as income goes up so do expectations: There is never enough money for everything you want. If income decreases, it is hard to return to restricted spending habits. For many couples the best strategy is to make money less important in their lives and learn to live within their means and be prudent spenders and savers.

Another pattern is to rationalize spending by saying it is not for yourself but for the children, spouse, or house. How can you feel bad or blamed if the money was for a good cause? An understandable, yet self-defeating, rationalization is that people work hard, so they deserve the luxury of an expensive weekend escape or a new suit.

In dealing with spending problems, the first step is to collect data on how much you actually spend. Be honest with yourself and each other. We suggest keeping data for 2 months, writing down all expenses over $2. Establish categories for stable expenses such as mortgage or rent, car payment, health insurance, college loans, child care. Categories for variable expenses include gas, food, clothing, credit cards, entertainment, personal expenses, hobbies, eating out, and donations. Do not try to hide or finesse the real costs. If it is viewed as a joint project, not guilt/blaming, it is likely to result in an honest assessment.

Once you have the data, what should you do with it? It is easy to identify two or three areas where you can cut overspending: $200 a month for drinking, dancing, and movies can be cut to $125; eliminate high-interest credit cards; buy fewer books or tapes, instead borrow from the library (our publisher did not like that suggestion). In a common pattern one spouse feels the other is overspending and demands she stop picking up tabs for friends, not buy more shoes, stop calling her best friend long-distance, not send flowers to relatives. These demands are often "I'll stop buying books if you stop buying scarves!" Tit-for-tat agreements do not work; they break down into blaming fights. Each person needs to take responsibility for reducing his or her spending. Couple agreements about joint expenses are necessary, but coercing or cajoling the spouse to stop spending does not work. You can change your behavior easier than changing your spouse's behavior. That is a very important guideline that generalizes to all kinds of couple differences and conflicts. First be responsible for your behavior.

What to do when one spouse's spending is out of control and damaging to the couple's finances? This needs to be addressed as a couple issue. Make an agreement with a negative contingency applicable to both people. For example, the agreement is if the balance on the joint credit card is more than $2,000, then both spouse's credit cards are cut up.

Systems to Deal with Money

There is not "one right way" to handle money; it differs depending on circumstances, values, and goals. It is important to recognize financial problems, realistically assess them, and reach clear agreements about money. Money problems breed disrespect and distrust that can subvert the most hopeful, loving marriage.

The money management system we advocate is the husband and wife as serious, equitable financial partners. Both need to be aware of income and expenditures.

The most important decision is whether money is shared equally. In our marriage, all income and major spending decisions are shared. However, this does not fit all couples or situations. There are a number of viable financial arrangements. The most common are:

1. All income and expenses shared.
2. Expenses shared proportionately to income.
3. Hers-his-ours, each person keeps financial autonomy, except for joint expenses, which are shared equally or proportionately.
4. Income shared equally: any expense above a certain figure ($100–$300) decided jointly, other expenditures decided individually.
5. All income and expenses joint, but each spouse has monthly stipend (between $100 and $500) that does not have to be accounted for.

One important variation, especially for couples one or both of whom have been previously married, is to keep separate money and debts incurred before marriage. For example, child support from the first marriage is not included in the couple financial system. Some couples do not include family inheritance in their financial arrangement.

It is critical to develop a clear, mutually acceptable financial system. Just as important is having a backup system to deal with a crisis; for example, if one spouse were to lose his job or incur major medical bills. A money system need not be set in concrete. There is room for adjustment and negotiation as your financial situation changes. However, this cannot be unilateral. There must be discussion and agreement.

Some financial systems do not work but instead breed resentment and distrust. Examples are money used as a threat or club to punish the spouse; money as leverage to control the spouse's behavior or feelings; money given with strings attached; a hidden financial agenda; a spouse being made to feel guilty because of lack of income or money spent on children. Guilt, conflict, and resentment poison a relationship. Money as a bribe for sexual behavior (the spouse who "rewards" the partner for oral sex) can destroy both the sexual and the financial relationship. Money as a relationship reward or punishment is destructive.

LEANNE AND ALEX

The negative effects from financial problems were evident for Leanne and Alex, who had been married 14 months. Leanne was 28; it was her first marriage. Alex was 30, this was his second marriage. Alex had a 5-year-old son for whom he made monthly child support payments. Leanne and Alex met through mutual friends and quickly developed an intimate relationship. The principal concern was how Leanne would relate to Alex's son. Since that went well, they felt there would be no impediments to a successful marriage. Leanne was anxious to have a child of her own, and she assumed Alex would be excited to have a baby. Neither Leanne nor Alex raised issues about income or budgeting in premarital discussions.

Leanne worked full-time in a hospital as a medical technologist, a well-paying job with full health insurance benefits. Alex began a small business 8 months before they married. His three-employee business involved landscaping and tree trimming. Alex needed to remain competitive with franchise companies. Although he would have liked to, Alex did not offer health insurance. He was pleased with the family insurance (including coverage for his son) through Leanne's policy.

Alex insisted Leanne maintain full-time employment with the health insurance benefit. He attacked her as selfish and short-sighted about their financial future. Leanne angrily counterattacked that he was the selfish one. She contemptuously said if he were a "real man" he should be able to support both of them and not leech off her health insurance, especially for *his* son. Money fights often degenerate into an attack-counterattack mode. The couple abandons a problem-solving focus. The argument degenerates into personal put-downs and character assassination. Instead of dealing with the problem and resolving issues, it becomes a blaming, disrespectful, dirty fighting fiasco.

Arguments about money, work, and health insurance continued on an intermittent basis. Alex and Leanne could enjoy themselves, do things as a couple and with friends, and problem-solve other issues. However, when it came to money, the discussion always degenerated. Increasingly, a sense of helplessness and hopelessness pervaded these conversations. Leanne shared concerns with family and friends. After months of hearing the same frustrating stories, they took an increasingly anti-Alex stance and told Leanne to do what was best for her. Leanne threatened to quit her job. She was becoming increasingly dissatisfied with both the hospital and the marriage. Alex talked to his friends and accountant who reinforced his position that Leanne was being unrealistic and unreasonable. Their positions became polarized, and alienation increased.

Leanne and Alex signed up for an adult education class at the community college on money management. It was an excellent program taught by an instructor with a banking and credit counseling background. The most helpful exercise involved keeping detailed records of income and expenditures. It was easy to track Leanne's income because she received the same paycheck every 2 weeks. She was surprised at the dramatic differences in Alex's income. In one month he earned three times as much as she, but the next month took home less than Leanne. This increased her empathy for Alex's feelings of financial insecurity.

Keeping track of expenses was an eye-opener and strong impetus for sticking to a budget. They were shocked at how much money was taken from the ATM machine and wound up in the "miscellaneous" category. With two incomes they were able to save money, but they were amazed and chagrined by how much money passed through their household. They agreed to a substantial contribution to their savings account as the second payment after the mortgage.

If the course had been graded, both Leanne and Alex would have received an A for knowledge. However, they still felt stuck about making career, money, and family decisions. The instructor observed that there is a strong emotional component to money problems and suggested a referral to a marriage therapist who had expertise in family financial issues.

Alex was anxious about the initial therapy session. In his first marriage, they saw a couple therapist before separating. Alex connoted seeing a therapist with fear the marriage was tenuous. Leanne was enthusiastic because the class had given them good financial tools so they were in a better position to confront emotional blocks. In the initial session, the therapist affirmed the vitality and viability of their marital bond while pointing out the emotional drain money arguments were having. They were functioning as an intimate team and had learned to function as a parental team, but financially they were untrusting strangers preparing for war. This metaphor had a strong effect. Alex assured Leanne that was not his intention.

The first assignment was to nonjudgmentally review learnings about money before they became a couple. Each discussed how the family of origin handled money, what was talked about and what was not, how money was earned and spent as an adolescent and young adult, and hopes and expectations about money. After initial anxiety, they were able to share information, feelings, and perceptions. The spouse being a respectful listener and not inter-jecting ideas or trying to make a point facilitates communication.

At the next session, Leanne and Alex shared insights. The therapist acknowledged these and asked what fears had stopped them from sharing financial hopes and worries before they married. Leanne tearfully said her worst fears had been confirmed. She could not deal straightforwardly with Alex. In her family, the man's needs came first: He was the ultimate financial decision maker. The woman's hopes and needs were relegated to a distant second. Leanne felt she would have to work around Alex if she were to switch to a part-time job and have a baby. She feared Alex was engaged in a power play and resented him trying to control her.

Alex had always felt financially insecure. His father had been a self-employed builder who made a great deal of money and the family lived very well, but had been bankrupt three times—the last time for good. Alex wanted the sense of freedom and autonomy that comes from working for yourself but was fiscally conservative and would never risk bankruptcy. He saw the financial arrangement with Leanne as ideal: They had the security of her steady income and health insurance, which allowed him to take risks and develop a successful business. He felt tricked and betrayed by Leanne's desire to work part-time. Alex felt she was selfish and irresponsible, which was how he viewed his first wife.

Both were surprised and hurt by the spouse's misreading of the situation and the other's hopes and intentions. They realized why lessons from the class had been so hard to implement.

The therapist observed that each feared being manipulated, although that was not the intention of either. Rather than their reverting to a defensive or, even worse, counterattacking, mode, the therapist encouraged acknowledging each other's feelings and concerns. Validating your spouse's feelings and perceptions does not signify you agree with them, but it does mean they deserve respectful attention. A solid base of emotional understanding allows you to examine alternatives and problem-solve. Leanne understood Alex's fear of financial insecurity, and Alex understood Leanne's desire for a job in which she could combine career and family. For Leanne, having a child was more important than money. She had to trust she could deal directly with Alex about her feelings and needs. Alex respected and trusted Leanne as long as he was not afraid she had a hidden agenda or was being manipulative.

The health insurance dilemma was resolved rather easily. Leanne's professional organization offered a health maintenance plan they were eligible to join. Alex preferred insurance whereby he could choose his own doctor, but at this point the health maintenance plan was an acceptable alternative. Leanne made it clear she was a serious financial partner who could plan and monitor both income and expenditures. Leanne agreed to keep the family financial books. This took an incredible emotional pressure from Alex. Alex blamed women for financial problems: He blamed his mother, his first wife, and had been blaming Leanne. Emotional trust combined with the money management skills from the class made Alex confident they would succeed. Alex and Leanne could stay on the same financial team.

Leanne and Alex realized there would be hard issues but felt they had the practical and emotional resources to effectively resolve problems. They agreed to maintain a budget and schedule monthly meetings to discuss financial plans. After saving $4,000 as a reserve, Leanne would resign from the hospital. She would work part-time for an HMO. Alex applied for a business line of credit as a backup. They understood each other's hopes and fears, and were confident they would continue to function as a financial team.

The Importance of Addressing Financial Problems

It is better to prevent a problem or resolve it at the acute stage before it becomes severe and chronic. When the financial problem is acute, the couple are motivated to address it, are hopeful, and will work to find a resolution. When the problem is chronic, layers of frustration, resentment, and blaming interfere. Chronicity and feelings of helplessness and hopelessness are as problematic as the financial issue. You have to break through the defensiveness and blaming before beginning to deal with money problems. Benign neglect is not the way to resolve financial issues.

Money problems seldom remain at an equilibrium. They become worse over time. Expenses and bills get out of control, partly because you are paying interest and late charges. The cycle of guilt and blame becomes entrenched. Bitterness increases even if one or both spouses take second jobs. Each resents the other for not doing enough.

The time to address money issues is early in your marriage before self-defeating attitudes and habits dominate. The naive hope that money problems will cure themselves is replaced by resentment and bitterness as the problems become chronic. You might not reach a perfect resolution, but you can significantly improve your financial management skills. A favorite adage is "There are always positive alternatives."

Exercise—Financial Planning and Problem Solving

Each spouse needs to be honest in assessing individual and couple income and expenditures. It is easier to start with the income part of the ledger. Each person lists all sources of income: regular pay, monthly commissions, child support, money from parents, year-end bonus, inheritance, income from investments. Be truthful and comprehensive, differentiate between guaranteed and variable income. Be sure you are not over- or underestimating. Even if this money is in cash or occurs once a year (even if you do not report it to the IRS), be sure it is in your couple calculation.

The expense component is more difficult but even more important. Divide these into joint expenses, his expenses, her expenses. Joint expenses include child-oriented expenses, whether for biological or stepchildren. Gather the data from your checkbook, log book, professional expenses, or monthly budget. The subtle prompt is to encourage making and maintaining a budget.

Being honest about expenses is more difficult than being honest about income. Fixed monthly expenses—rent or mortgage, car payments, taxes, health insurance, child support, children's music and other lessons—are easy to track. It is harder to be honest and realistic about variable expenses like food, clothing, entertainment, medical, gifts, hobbies, eating out, utility bills, or phone bills. It is even harder to plan for big-ticket purchases like cars, furniture, or painting the house. Too often, an emergency fund, vacation fund, and savings fund are ignored.

Once you have gathered these data, realistically assess financial problems. Almost every couple finds at least one (and usually more) issues that vex them. Do not fall into the attack-counterattack mode. Focus on problem solving and regaining control of your finances. There might not be a perfect resolution, but there are positive alternatives.

There is never enough money—whether you make $55,000 or $550,000. You have to learn to budget and make wise financial decisions. Few people enjoy money management. It is not like sex where positive feelings and experiences are the reward for dealing with issues.

There is always a new financial problem or new item to budget for. Money agreements, staying on a budget, even saving do not make you feel good and add pleasure to your life. What they do is remove a source of stress, worry, and conflict.

Once you have assessed the money situation and made a budget, make specific agreements to deal with specific problems. Carefully assess alternatives and develop agreements that are clear, honest, and realistic. They are unlikely to be perfect (few agreements are), but be sure you can live with them. At a minimum, the agreements resolve an acute crisis.

Dealing with a financial crisis is easier than an overall agreement on how to organize finances and prevent future crises. For example, couples cut up credit cards, take a second job, borrow from parents, move to a cheaper apartment, sell one car. That is like a crash diet to lose 20 pounds. Unless you change eating habits, you will regain it in a matter of months. You need to change the way you communicate about and manage money.

Long-term financial planning and agreements can involve going back to school or obtaining technical training, a 2-year plan to develop your own business, a rigorous budgeting system that is carefully monitored, setting up a contingency plan with a financial reserve, saving to buy a house. Good intentions are not enough. Write out your agreement. A crucially important step, often ignored, is a system to implement and monitor agreements. Long-term agreements should be monitored every 3 months or at least in 6 months. Expect problems and lapses. Learn from mistakes, and get the system back on track. The worse mistake is to give up—this only makes your financial situation worse.

We suggest couples review their financial status every 3 months to be sure agreements stay on track. Redo this exercise each year to reach new agreements and set financial goals.

When One Spouse Is Very Dissatisfied

The marital bond is under major pressure when one spouse is extremely dissatisfied with the couple's financial status. Examples include not having the lifestyle you expected based on your family of origin, one spouse wants to save for a house down payment but the other would rather spend money on travel, one spouse does not care about earning a lot of money but the other spouse does, credit card debt is out of control, one spouse's income is based on sales commissions (which are unpredictable) and that upsets the spouse on salary, they cannot agree on a budget, she feels he is underfunctioning in his career, child support payments are late or lacking, spouse without children resents money spent on stepchildren, one spouse wants to plan while the other resists financial planning.

We suggest marital therapy. Explore feelings and perceptions about money, review positive and negative learnings from the family of origin, improve communication, understand emotional blocks. Awareness of how your marital system affects and is affected by financial issues is very helpful. Guidelines for choosing a marital therapist are available in Appendix A.

An alternative way to address financial problems is to seek specific financial counseling provided by accountants, credit counseling agencies, financial planners, and financial counselors, or you can ask a friend or relative who is skilled at financial management to serve as an informal consultant or mediator. Address problems so resentments do not build and subvert your marriage.

Our Self-Disclosure about Financial Problems

All marriages have areas of weakness, including ours. Although we are better than at the beginning of our marriage, we have a chronic problem of poor financial management. We are better at income production than controlling expenses and staying on a budget. Sometimes this turns into an acute financial crisis. We always survive, but "robbing Peter to pay Paul" is stressful. Barry is the one who frets and worries about money, although he is no better at sticking to a budget than Emily. We utilize the services of an accountant to ensure our finances do not get us into major problems.

Although we have read books and adopted money management techniques (keeping a monthly budget, obtaining a home equity loan, having health and retirement payments taken directly from the paycheck), we reluctantly accept that money management is our Achilles' heel. Our goal is to ensure money problems do not stress our marital bond or become unmanageable.

We joke that if one of our books becomes a best-seller, this will be our salvation, but we would find ways to overspend. In this and other areas we are a good example of the adage "there are no perfect people and no perfect marriages."

We hope our self-disclosure does not negate the guidelines and exercises we have proposed. Barry has successfully used them with newly married couples. It is an example of things being easy in the book but hard to implement. A guideline we follow is not to blame the spouse, and we try to avoid power struggles. We accept joint responsibility for financial problems and cope as best we can.

Not Comparing Yourselves with Others

Unfortunately, people compare in a number of areas, money being a prime example. Whether comparisons are with parents, siblings, friends, or media personalities, they are more than inappropriate, they are harmful. The only reasonable comparison is with yourselves and your goals. You will always find someone who makes more money, has a more expensive house, a fancier car, better investments. You and your spouse have to establish personally relevant goals for income, spending, and savings.

The most negative effect of comparisons is that they interfere with realistic expectations. Being realistic is the key to avoiding financial problems. Our culture emphasizes hitting the jackpot, making a fortune in the stock market, and conspicuous consumption. People brag about how much money they will make in a new business, investment, or a get-rich-quick scheme. There is tremendous publicity about winning lotteries or athletes, music stars, and corporate executives making obscene sums of money. This feeds the comparison mania that sweeps our culture.

The ability to borrow money and spend more on houses, cars, vacations, and luxury items discourages careful budgeting and saving. The couple feel if people who married at the same time can buy a $280,000 house, why not us? We are not advising you to put on a blindfold or reduce awareness of the real world, but we suggest not allowing yourselves to be controlled by what others do or say. Be realistic about yourselves, your life plans, and your financial goals.

Closing Thoughts

Money is a major source of conflict in marriage. Finances are not just a matter of numbers and accounting. Money is a complex, emotionally charged phenomenon. You need to honestly communicate and deal constructively with the financial issues facing your marriage. Develop a financial management system that you respect and trust.

CHAPTER 11

Tag Team Parenting

Children are a choice, not a mandate. A destructive cultural "should" is that a married couple *must* have children. Empirically, couples who decide to remain childless report greater marital and sexual satisfaction. We chose to have children and have a prochild bias, but it is not the right choice for everyone. This chapter is for couples who have or are planning children and want to successfully integrate parenting into their lives and marital style.

The Transition to Parenting

The majority of couples decide to have a baby (many are pregnant or have a child from a previous marriage or relationship). Since you want to have a child, how can you approach parenting in a healthy manner?

The transition is easier if the baby is wanted and planned. A biological reality of pregnancy is you have 9 months to prepare. We strongly urge couples to attend prepared childbirth classes as well as classes in parenting an infant. Childbirth and parenting are a team project. Emphasize the challenges and rewards, but be aware of the stresses and traps.

Traditionally, males and females had very different roles. The woman's body dramatically changes. Childbirth, breast-feeding, and taking care of the baby dominated her life, with the man having a minimal role. This was the most frequent time for males to begin an extramarital affair. The danger of separation is highest 3 months before or after the birth of a first child, in part because traditionally there was no common ground for the couple.

As with other marital issues, prevention is the best strategy. Ideally, from the decision to have a child, meeting with the obstetrician, attending classes, being present at the birth, rooming in at the hospital, taking care of the baby, you are a parental team.

Adopt positive, realistic expectations about parenting. Be open to the changes and challenges of a three-person family. The birth of a child increases interaction with family of origin and extended family. Remember, your family of creation takes precedence over the family of origin. Ideally, you would enjoy the help and support of grandparents, but be clear you are the parents and primary caregivers. There is a danger of getting into right-wrong power struggles with in-laws on how to take care of the baby or raise children. A preventative strategy is to solicit advice, but let them know you are not open to unsolicited advice. They can enjoy being active, involved grandparents, but the responsibility and authority lies with you, the parents.

Sharing Tasks and Sleep Deprivation

Even if you developed satisfactory agreements and a couple style before the baby, you will need to renegotiate these. Every aspect of your life changes with a baby. The biggest changes are lack of privacy, reduced couple time, less energy to be sexual, and sleep deprivation.

Couples without babies have much more freedom. A baby's needs are immediate and concrete: to be held, fed, changed. You can put off adults for hours, days, or weeks. It is hard to put off a baby for more than 5 minutes, whether in the middle of the day or 2:00 in the morning. When the baby is hungry she wants to be fed immediately, when dirty she needs to be changed quickly, and when crying she wants to be held and comforted right then. You cannot leave the baby alone; people complain they no longer have the time or privacy to go to the bathroom. A 10-minute shower is a luxury.

Perhaps the biggest change involves sleep habits and sleep deprivation. Some babies settle into a sleep pattern. More often, sleep is irregular, especially during the first year. Babies sleep a great deal, but wake often—from 2–6 times during the night. Breast-feeding provides significant advantages for mother and baby. However, it puts a major burden on the woman to wake and breast-feed. The man learns to comfort the baby and change diapers, but he cannot breast-feed. Some couples use a middle-of-the-night bottle with formula or expressed breast milk, but it does not always work. Sleep deprivation is a normal part of the transition to parenting, not a sign of personal deficit. Usually it is the mother who experiences greater stress. The problem is exacerbated when the couple fall into the trap of blaming/ defensiveness.

Being a parental team is just as important as being an intimate team. That does not mean tasks are divided fifty-fifty. Complementary couples divide tasks based on skill and interest. It is clear who has prime responsibility and who does backup and support. Often, these are based on traditional gender roles, but need not be.

The most common pattern is the woman takes a leave of absence or cuts back on work commitments, men seldom do. Best friend and emotionally expressive couples share tasks and are flexible about who does what. Ideally, both the father and the mother are capable of doing all the tasks involved in parenting. Men find this a challenge. The traditional male role does not promote nurturing, even with babies. Babies require consistent caretaking, holding, and nurturing—this can be done by father or mother.

Other household tasks must be attended to; life does not stop because you are parents. Whether paying bills, cooking, or cleaning there are changes now that you are a three-person family. It is hard to maintain reasonable schedules. Disruptions are caused by a sick child, a bad night's sleep, visits from relatives or friends. Flexibility and support are important. With a baby, tasks cannot be done with the efficiency and timeliness you expect in an office.

Your Husband–Wife Bond

The husband–wife bond is the most important relationship in the family. This bond is weakened after the birth of a baby, which does not mean it was the wrong decision nor that your marriage is in trouble. It means there is less time and energy for your relationship. This is normal; there is no reason to blame each other or feel guilty.

When you have a baby under 6 months old, it is hard to go out as a couple (unless you have grandparents, siblings, or good friends to baby-sit). Sex is rushed, squeezed in when the baby is sleeping, keeping one ear open in case he cries. Gynecologists recommend not having intercourse until after a postpregnancy exam (6 weeks after childbirth). Some couples feel comfortable with erotic, nonintercourse sex during this time. Others stop being sexual for 2 to 4 months during the late stage pregnancy and 6 weeks to 4 months afterward.

Pregnancy and childbirth cause a major change in the woman's body and self-image. Regaining sexual desire is gradual, and functioning is variable. The danger is falling into a blame-guilt struggle about sexuality that increases self-consciousness and resentment. Being intimate friends promotes a gradual increase in sexual desire, comfort, arousal, intercourse, and satisfaction. Do not compare sexuality with before the baby: It is comparing apples and oranges.

The essence of the husband–wife bond is a respectful, trusting friendship that is strong enough to endure the stress of becoming parents. Your bond is challenged by the tasks and hassles of parenting. This is a major reason why we suggest waiting 2 years before having a child.

Maintaining a respectful bond and working as a parental team are a higher priority than sex. Both emotional and sexual intimacy can suffer, especially the year after the baby is born. Couples who understand that intimacy is more than intercourse are in a good position to navigate this transition. We urge couples to make time for each other and talk about adult topics in addition to parenting. Plan intimate time (which may or may not include intercourse) when the baby is napping. If you have in-laws or good friends to baby-sit, go out for a couple date and talk about yourselves and adult topics, not babies. A great resource is couple friends with a baby who will switch baby-sitting. Two of you taking care of two babies is not much harder than one baby.

LAURIE AND BILL

Laurie was 29 when she became pregnant. She and Bill had been married for 2 years and 8 months. They read articles, took self-assessment tests on the Internet, talked to friends who recently had a baby, and for 2 weekends baby-sat Bill's 18-month-old nephew. During the pregnancy they enrolled in a prenatal course and a prepared childbirth class, and after the birth they joined a church-sponsored discussion group for new parents. They felt as prepared as possible. Both were confident in their desire and ability to parent.

Bill was surprised that no matter how well prepared he was, the actual experience was more taxing than he had imagined. Bill's biggest adjustment involved disrupted sleep and reaction to the baby's crying. It did not help that their daughter was colicky between 4 and 9 months. Bill was an action-oriented problem solver who found it frustrating not to be able to get her to stop crying. After 2 or 3 minutes he handed her back to Laurie. Laurie would breast-feed, but she was worried the baby was not getting enough milk. An experienced mother from the Le Leche group assured Laurie breast-feeding was going fine; it was not her fault the baby was in a colicky phase. The consultant suggested they check the baby's diapers, ensure nothing was scratching or irritating, and she was not thirsty. Otherwise, put the baby in a holding cuddly and carry her around. Bill used the cuddly and learned to tolerate her crying without panicking.

Bill and Laurie both did the tasks associated with parenting, from midnight waking to singing to her. Bill surprised himself by being more adept at changing diapers than any of his male friends. He particularly enjoyed giving baths. Laurie enjoyed putting their daughter in the cuddly and going for walks, careful her neck and head were adequately supported. Laurie found breast-feeding very satisfying. Bill was better at dressing their daughter, although Laurie chose the outfits.

Bill and Laurie prided themselves on having orderly, well-thought-out careers and finances. Bill managed a computer store, and Laurie was a compensation specialist in a corporate office. They hired a daytime nanny who started two months after the baby was born. Life with a baby requires flexibility; babies are not orderly. This is especially true of child care arrangements, for example, when the baby or one of the adults becomes ill. Bill had to adjust to disrupted sleep, which interfered with his orderly life. The bigger burden rested on Laurie, who had to be available for breast-feeding.

When the first nanny turned out to be unreliable, Laurie stayed home with the baby. She resented this, but it was hard to discuss her feelings with Bill. They thought of themselves as excellent problem solvers, but lack of sleep, baby crying, and complex emotions blocked communication. Both wished there was a grandparent to watch the baby. Bill wished they had a traditional marriage in which Laurie was a full-time homemaker. Laurie preferred to work and her salary was crucial to their standard of living.

Couple friends agreed to take the baby overnight. Bill and Laurie went to a hotel that had a full range of workout and spa facilities. Laurie felt like an adult for the first time since their daughter was born. Bill got 10 hours of uninterrupted sleep, and they made love twice. Over breakfast the next morning, Laurie and Bill discussed feelings and perceptions about child care and how each was coping. They tried not to blame or be defensive, each stating feelings and concerns in a productive, nonattacking manner. They agreed there were problems to be dealt with, blaming the spouse was a cop-out. They felt reenergized and better able to address parenting and couple issues.

The system they devised was Bill gave the bath and put the baby to bed. Laurie did night awakenings and feedings. When the baby woke in the morning, Bill would get up, change her diaper, bring her to Laurie to breast-feed in bed, and then took the baby while Laurie got another hour of sleep. If Bill's sleeping was difficult during the night, he went to the guest room. They interviewed child care people together. Both needed to agree before hiring the person. They divided house chores in a new manner and planned to assess how it was working in 3 months. Rather than frustration building and keeping grudges (a particular trap for Bill), they set aside half an hour when the baby was asleep to air concerns and conflicts.

Bill and Laurie were surprised how complex the transition to parenting was. Since this was a planned, wanted baby and they were well prepared, they thought it would be easier. The reality of a child and parenting is complex. Laurie and Bill enjoyed being parents and wanted a second child in 2 or 3 years. They realized two children would be a major transition.

Laurie shared with Bill what she learned in a college marriage and family course: "The husband–wife bond is the most important relationship in a family." Bill agreed, saying it had to be more than a slogan; they had to put it in practice on a daily basis. In balancing the balls of parenting, working, paying bills, household chores, family and friends, it is easy to take the marriage for granted and treat it with benign neglect. Easy, but costly. Your marital bond needs consistent energy, time, and reinforcement. Time for yourself and the marriage is not cheating the child. The child benefits from a healthy family anchored by a vital marriage.

After the First Year

When couples think of parenting, they think of babies. Yet there are many phases in parenting. The skills involved in parenting an infant are very different from parenting a toddler, which in turn are different from parenting a preschooler. Parenting again changes as the child enters school and throughout the school years. Parents speak of ages 7 to 11 as the "golden years of childhood" where the child's intellectual and personal growth is extraordinary and the family is still the center of the child's life. One of the biggest transitions occurs at puberty and entering junior high. The peer group and being your own person become more important than family bonds. Parenting adolescents can be stressful, but adolescents need involved, responsible parents. Parenting does not end at 18 or even 21. The role of the parent changes from being responsible to being a consultant. The hope is that by 25 you have an equitable relationship with your adult child.

A favorite metaphor is the emotional bank account theory of parenting. Babies, toddlers, and children provide consistent reinforcement. There are regular, small deposits into the parental emotional account and few withdrawals. You want to build a strong account because with adolescence emotional deposits are irregular and sometimes there are major withdrawals. You want to be sure you have reserves and a solid parent–child relationship so it can weather adolescent turmoil.

The concept of being a parental team continues to serve you well throughout these years. Being a team does not mean you cannot enjoy one-on-one parenting. One-on-one time with a child is vital and particularly satisfying. This is especially true when you have more than one child. Family time is important, but so is individual time with each child. Rather than viewing them as "the kids," focused time and attention reinforce that each child is a unique person with unique strengths and needs.

Exercise—Parenting Time and Satisfaction

In the course of family life, things are so hectic and rushed you feel overwhelmed. So much energy is spent on the nitty-gritty daily routine and dealing with crises that couples find it hard to make time to look at the big picture and assess parenting, what is and is not working, and develop a change plan. This exercise asks you to take the time and assess parenting, carefully examining areas of satisfaction and dissatisfaction.

We ask each spouse to independently engage in this assessment, then share and discuss. Divide parenting time into two categories. The first is mundane tasks such as changing diapers, feeding, picking up toys, making the baby's bed, dressing the child, getting her in and out of the stroller or car seat. The second category is interactive experiences: holding and rocking the baby, reading to the baby, going for a stroll, introducing her to family members and neighbors, playing games, singing to the baby. One parent might like a particular activity—learning to identify body parts—considerably more than the other parent. Sometimes, giving her a bath feels like a mundane task, other times it is a very pleasant experience.

Each person separately records the activities he or she has with the child, recording both frequency and time. List tasks and interactions each day, how frequently they occur, and how much time is spent. Rate experiences on a scale from -5 (highly aversive) to 0 (neutral) to +5 (highly satisfying). Aversive versus satisfaction ratings are tricky. For example, a task like changing diapers is a -2 or -3, so does not need to be assessed each time; a summary rating is sufficient. Other tasks such as feeding the child might vary from a -4 to a +3. What makes it aversive one time and pleasant the next? This is even more important for interactive experiences: Why does reading to the child vary from +4 to -2? Why does one spouse find reading to the baby consistently +5 or +4, while the other parent rates it +1 to -3?

In reviewing time and satisfaction ratings, people are often surprised. Many men are distressed to find how little satisfying time they spend in parenting. Women find they spend so much time attending to nitty-gritty tasks they do not have the time to teach or enjoy the child.

Share ratings with your spouse. Be open to the spouse's feedback and perceptions. Are you ignoring positive interactions? Do you overplay the time or aversiveness of a task? What does it mean if each spouse views parenting differently?

In looking at ratings and perceptions, what does it say about your parenting style? How functional is your parenting? How enjoyable? We are not advocates of trying to be "perfect parents," but do encourage you to be involved, competent, and satisfied parents.

Each parent can pick one task and try a different way to approach it so feelings of competence and satisfaction increase. For example, if baths are a difficult task, you could try working together where one does the bathing and the other talks to and entertains the baby and then wraps him in a towel. This allows you to work in tandem, although each has a specific role (which you could maintain or change weekly). Do not try to develop a "perfect" system but a functional, satisfying one. This can involve changes for one parent or changes in how you interact as a parental team.

Be aware of deposits in your parental emotional account. These can come from special experiences or spontaneous interactions with your child. Others are planned and built in. For example, Barry particularly enjoyed taking babies and young children for strolls, wrestling on the floor, reading stories, learning the alphabet and counting. Emily enjoyed breast-feeding, giving baths, telling stories, singing to the baby, identifying and tickling body parts. Find at least one experience that provides special feelings for deposit into your parental emotional account.

Parenting changes as the child develops. Once you have mastered one stage, you are challenged to learn another set of parenting skills as your child's needs change. You definitely cannot rest on parenting laurels. Be open to the changes and challenges of parenting.

Individual Autonomy, Being a Couple, and Parenting

Life is a balancing act. It is crucial to maintain a positive balance among individual autonomy, being a couple, and parenting. All three are vital; do not let the ball drop in any of these areas. If you are not doing well individually or as a couple, it is significantly harder (although not impossible) to function well parentally. It is true that some couples feel the best thing they do is parenting.

What most influences family satisfaction is a healthy husband–wife bond. When that is weak or nonexistent, family functioning and stability are threatened. You are not being selfish or short-sighted attending to individual and couple needs. It is a wise emotional investment for you and your children.

The key family concepts are emotional cohesion and functional, flexible roles. This is easier to reach when each parent is a well-functioning individual. This gives you energy to focus on the important, but time- and energy-consuming, tasks of parenting. Being good people and a healthy couple help you to be better parents.

There is no such thing as a "perfect parent," "perfect child," or "perfect family." Be involved, responsible parents who care about the needs and feelings of their children. The extreme of the 1950s was the child-centered family with rigid parental roles. The extreme of the 90s was the chaotic, stressed family in which children's feelings and needs were ignored or minimally met. Since you chose to have children, you owe it to yourselves and the child to be involved parents. Individuals and families face more structural stress and time constraints than in the "good old days." Do not fall into the trap of berating yourself because you do not have the time and energy your mother had. You want to be the best parent you can be, not a mythical "perfect mother."

In many ways, fathers have it easier. The traditional father role was the distant, emotionally unavailable disciplinarian. Men want to be better fathers than their fathers were. The male trap is to be uninvolved with the baby because he feels incompetent or awkward. Men believe women have a maternal instinct and, especially if she is breast-feeding, the father has a limited role. We urge the man to be involved from the first, joining in prepared childbirth and prenatal classes, being present at the birth, holding the baby, changing diapers, giving baths, putting the baby to sleep, playing with and talking to the infant. You cheat yourself and the child if you start fathering at 4 when he is ready to play ball. The earlier and more frequently you parent, the stronger the father-child bond. You want to be a fully functioning father, not settle for just the athletic and disciplinarian roles.

How Parenting Can Strengthen Your Marital Bond

Being a parental team and a marital team is reciprocally reinforcing. Tag team parenting and supporting each other's parenting increase respect and trust. Some couples do well in their adult relationship but have difficulty parenting. They are the exception, not the rule. There is a positive correlation between being a good couple and being good parents. Maintaining a balance between coupleness and parenting enhances both roles and each person's psychological well-being.

The major complaint of mothers is feeling isolated and burdened by responsibilities, especially with babies and preschoolers. The husband's being an involved father, sharing tasks and worries, relieves her and increases trust and respect.

The male's major parenting complaint is lack of time and skill, as well as absence of peer and family support for the father role. A wife who encourages and reinforces how integral the father's role is builds a sense of being a team. Comfort and confidence with fathering comes with practice and feedback. Rather than her being competitive and putting him down for not doing it right, her active encouragement and reinforcement for what he is doing well and constructive suggestions for change make all the difference. Being with families in which the father plays an active role can be an invaluable resource. Couple friends who try to be an equitable parenting team is another resource.

As an example of tag team parenting, the spouse who is feeling tired or overwhelmed can tag off to the partner. He is willing to step in without blaming or berating. He assumes prime parenting responsibility, whether for 10 minutes or the day. They have confidence in and support each other's parenting skills. This does not mean you are clones: Each has a distinctive parenting style. Work together or take turns depending on who is the prime parent for that task.

Couples who adopt a complementary marital style find it is easily transferable to their parental style. Each parent takes primary responsibility for tasks and acknowledges and reinforces the other's contributions and domains. These couples often follow traditional parenting roles (as do conflict-minimizing couples). Usually the mother is the prime parent. The father has specific tasks such as putting the children to sleep or being the responsible parent on Saturday and Sunday afternoon while she works out, meets friends, or does career tasks. In the complementary model, marital and parental roles are congruent. Roles and tasks are clearly defined, and each respects and supports the other's contributions.

Couples with a best friend or emotionally expressive marital style emphasize flexible parental roles. Tasks are distributed on an equitable basis. This is a more idealistic model, vulnerable to practical problems and miscommunication. It demands more interaction and negotiation. Parenting is not divided into component parts; each parent knows all aspects of the child. A man in his second marriage said that with the daughter from his first marriage he never even knew the name of her pediatrician. With the daughter from this marriage he knows not only the pediatrician but the children she plays with and their parents as well as the child care person. He feels involved in all aspects of her life, a fully functioning parent.

Closing Thoughts

Being parents dramatically changes your lives and marriage. We strongly suggest establishing a solid marital bond, waiting at least 2 years, discussing the implications of having a child, and the baby being planned and wanted. Develop positive, realistic expectations about parenting. Be aware that during the first year you will experience sleep deprivation, have less couple time, and probably less sex.

In the same way you establish a marital style, you need to establish a parental style. Ideally, the parental and marital styles complement each other. Remember, the most important relationship in a family is the husband–wife bond, which requires attention and reinforcement. It is in the child's best interest for you to maintain a healthy marriage. Parenting is a time and energy-consuming challenge that can enhance your life and family satisfaction.

CHAPTER 12

Organizing Your Lives:
Career Conflicts and Decisions

In one of his most famous adages, Freud said the two most important tasks of adulthood are to love and to work. Feeling competent and satisfied with work promotes psychological well-being and enhances your marital bond. Competence and achievement are core elements of psychological well-being.

Career success is much more than money or status. Some people earn a great deal of money but feel very dissatisfied. More typical is the person who underfunctions at work and is dissatisfied with both the job and the money. Career frustration and dissatisfaction have a major impact. Is that an individual or a couple problem?

Each person needs to take responsibility for his/her work life. Career is a domain where personal autonomy and individual differences are respected and honored. Yet it has a major impact on your marriage. In healthy marriages, career decisions are open to discussion and a positive influence process.

The ideal prescription is to choose a career where the work is interesting and challenging, you develop skills and competencies, and there are opportunities for advancement and reasonable income. There is not a "right" career: It is a process of matching interests, skills, and satisfaction with the type of work, people, environment, and money. The worst situation is work that is aversive or boring, you are incompetent, and you feel resentful. The match of interests, skills, and career opportunities is critical. Often, people fall into a job without asking whether it fits their needs and personality. It can be a high-prestige job like a lawyer or a low-prestige job like a dishwasher, but job dissatisfaction lowers self-esteem and stresses your marital bond.

Traditional Male/Female Work Roles

Traditionally, the male was the only or primary worker. The couple and family organized around his work and schedule. If he was offered a promotion, they moved for his job. His income determined the family's standard of living.

Now the norm is two-career families. However, the woman's work is still considered secondary, especially in couples with a complementary or conflict-minimizing marital style. She has a job, not a career. Her income is supplementary, not integral. Her major role and satisfaction come from parenting and the home, not paid employment.

An advantage of traditional gender roles is that they are accepted and supported by the culture. The disadvantages are that they inhibit people's choices, are unfair to working women (who are paid less and whose needs are treated as secondary), and limit family income; the man uses his job to define himself: He is a "success object." The traditional system reinforces arbitrary gender roles instead of honoring individual differences, preferences, and male-female equity.

Even in the 1950s traditional gender roles were not followed as rigidly as cultural mythology. These roles are less relevant in the present and will become irrelevant in the technological, global economy of the 21st century. What will replace traditional work roles, and how will that affect marriages? Choice, diversity, and change will be career guidelines, presenting new challenges and pitfalls for both individuals and the couple.

Gender Roles and Careers

Traditionally, the man's career defined his self-esteem and their lives. The woman's career was to be wife and mother. If she worked outside the home, it was a job, not a career. Life choices and organization are very different now. Both the woman and the man can have careers, and hers can be as important as his. Obviously, this is not true of all couples or marital styles (especially not for traditional couples).

Three economic trends impact careers:

1. With the global economy, company restructuring, decreased unionization, and multiple career changes, there is less security.
2. With increased living expenses and decreased benefits, the majority of couples need two incomes to maintain their desired standard of living.
3. Educational and career opportunities have increased for women, especially college-educated women.

The two-career couple is the norm, not the exception. With women delaying age of marriage and establishing career expertise, it is expected she will work after the children are born. She is aware of (or has experienced) the importance of an income if separated or divorced. She is an autonomous person who values individuality and choices, including career choices. Career opportunities (especially those for well-educated or highly trained women) have significantly increased.

There are a number of advantages of both people earning income. A common pattern is for one spouse to have a dependable source of income that allows the other freedom to take career risks. Traditionally, this involved the wife's having a secure job while the husband sought a graduate degree, began his own business, or was paid on commission. Gender roles govern these choices less in the 21st century—often it is the man who maintains the stable income, allowing the woman career freedom. This works particularly well with children; she has greater flexibility in combining parenthood and career.

Shared responsibility for income production transfers to shared responsibility for financial decision making and life planning. Each spouse being capable and interested in work and money issues enhances individual and couple functioning. However, this is not without potential problems and pitfalls. When your marriage is different from what you grew up with and/or the cultural norm, you have to devote special time and energy to successfully implement a new system. This means talking and planning to insure it will be successful and not create unanticipated problems.

The best example is when the wife is more professionally and financially successful than the husband; this pattern is occurring with greater frequency. Barry practices marital therapy in Washington, DC where 40 percent of wives earn more money than their husbands, the largest proportion in the nation. This raises a number of issues and challenges that, if not addressed, can disrupt the marriage. Money issues are the most common source of stress among couples. Men feel threatened when the spouse has a higher income, and women feel he is underfunctioning. This is not rational but is powerful and reinforced by male colleagues and relatives. American society is overly competitive. Career and money are overused as measures of self-worth. That is not psychologically healthy, but it is the reality.

Barry worked with a couple in which the man was a competent, well-respected state government manager earning $65,000 a year, which was more than his father, siblings, or friends. His wife was in computer marketing/sales. Her commissions and bonuses resulted in an income of $145,000. On an objective level the couple should have been pleased with their joint earnings. Unfortunately, the income disparity caused major relationship stress. He felt emasculated because she earned twice as much. He felt she did not value his career or competence. She resented not being able to celebrate bonuses or enjoy perks because he was overly sensitive. She wanted him to be ambitious and earn more money. Although this was a major issue, it could not be openly discussed, each felt defensive and not understood.

Two-career marriages raise complexities and challenges. These can be dealt with as long as both spouses are willing to discuss difficult practical and emotional issues. The hope is that you can maximize the advantages while minimizing the pitfalls. Being equitable financial partners involves assessing money and income potential, not just spending decisions. It means discussing each person's career plans, hopes, and fears. Income is an important factor but certainly not the only or even most important one. Although it is nicer to be paid $80,000 than $45,000, this is lost if you hate the job or feel forced to do something you are not competent to do. If given the choice of earning $12 an hour doing an important job working with people you like or earning $20 an hour as a bill collector working for a mean-spirited, hostile boss, what would you do? What would you want your spouse to do? When the man was the only income producer, he chose the higher paying job but resented it. Two incomes gives him more degrees of freedom. Traditionally, the woman chose the pleasant job because income and career advancement were not vital. She still might, but both the woman and the man can carefully assess options. How does job choice, income, competence, and satisfaction affect your marriage?

If she receives an excellent job offer in another city, will they relocate? If he is accepted into graduate school out of state, will she give up her job and move with him? What is the right mix of autonomy and coupleness when planning careers? Couples struggling with these issues comment how much simpler life choices were for their parents.

Opportunities and choices are a plus but require thought, exploration of feelings, discussion of values, planning, and decision making. This is a multifaceted decision not just about career and money but the career paths of two individuals, their values, quality of life, and maintaining a healthy marital bond. For couples who want to combine career, marriage, and parenting, there is a crucial additional level of complexity.

An important guideline, especially for conflict-minimizing couples, is not to agree to something that sounds good but does not work. The prime example is taking jobs in different cities. It could make good career sense but puts great stress on the individuals and their marital bond. Reaching an agreement about careers and quality of life takes thought, examining alternatives, and discussion. At a minimum be sure each person can live with the agreement. Ideally the agreement would promote the careers of both people and facilitate marital growth.

Careers versus Jobs

A career involves commitment. You prepare through education and training, are eager to refine skills and increase competence, seek opportunities to advance, accept new challenges, and devote more than 40 hours a week to your career. You take pride in achievements, competencies, and successes. A job has different practical and psychological implications. A job is a 9-to-5 obligation, a means to earn income. When less self-esteem is invested in a job, you devote little time or energy to planning. You leave after 40 hours. You don't take the job home with you as you do with a career. There is less emotional investment, so switching jobs is less stressful.

Traditionally, a career was for men and a job for women. Her career was being a wife, mother, and homemaker. The man's career defined his self-esteem and the fiscal viability of the family. The rules were simple and easily understood, but limited individual choices, flexibility, and opportunities. What if he wants to change careers? What about the ambitious woman who plans for a thriving career? The man involved in sports, charities, or community activities who wants only a 40- (or 30-) hour-a-week job? The woman who does not want a low-pay job, but wants to pursue a career on a 25-hour-a-week basis? One of the advantages of being a therapist is it allows women to combine parenting and a career.

Careers are not just the traditional ones of banker, lawyer, teacher, dentist. They include small business owner, sales and marketing, master plumber, computer consultant, artist. Careers involve time, education, training, status, income, and, most important, commitment. The danger is that too much of the person's energy and self-esteem is controlled by the career, often at the expense of psychological balance, marital intimacy, and parenting. The advantage is that a career promotes pride and achievement, is a positive organizing force in life, and facilitates the well-being of your marriage and family.

Approaching one's occupation as a job can be a good thing. Many men and women prefer to invest time and energy in children, hobbies, sports, community action, cultural events. This facilitates balance in life, including the quality of your marriage. At midlife many formerly career-driven men switch gears and approach their livelihood as a 40-hour-a-week job rather than an organizing life force. For others, reality factors intervene: The job is boring, they like the people more than the work, there is no room for advancement, they would rather switch jobs every 2 years than worry about a career.

You are responsible for your career or job choices, not your spouse. This includes communicating honestly what is happening and what your plans are. Loss of respect can be a fatal blow for the marriage. A major precursor for loss of respect is that the spouse lies or covers up work problems and failures. The spouse who over-promises, says she is making more money than she actually is, the spouse who claims skills and competencies he does not possess or brags about commissions or bonuses that never come through, is setting the ground for marital distrust and conflict. Marketing people say it is crucial to present an optimistic, can-do image. That may or may not be good business advice, but it is definitely not good for a marriage. Self-respect and respect for your spouse is based on realistic expectations, not overpromising, pretending, or covering up.

People complain career issues are more confusing and anxiety-provoking than when they were students. At least in school, goals and measures of success were clear. Progression is from freshman to senior, and there is an objective marker of success, grade point average. When the person pursues a training program, apprenticeship, associate degree, or college degree, there is a structure and endpoint. Although people complain about rules and bureaucracy, there is a clear goal and time frame. In the "real world," career paths and goals are nebulous. There are more choices, yet change is difficult and riskier. People make poor decisions, are not honest about subjective or objective evaluations, do not develop competencies, or are unrealistic about pay and alternative jobs.

The guideline in making career choices is to be aware of interests and aptitudes, commit to appropriate levels of training, master skills and competencies, and take satisfaction from work and achievements. A common mistake people make is to wander from job to job, never making a commitment. A common trap is to make choices based on money and/or prestige but wind up hating the work. The healthy guideline is to commit to personally relevant goals where you are interested, can succeed, and enjoy your work. This can be a nontraditional career such as owning a craft design business, providing public service by managing a quality child care center, or having a day job and pursuing a writing career at night. With a traditional career, the crucial ingredient is being sure it genuinely matches your interests and skills. With a nontraditional career, be sure it is a feasible plan and you put the time and energy into successful implementation. The trap is that the person has a dream but not the motivation or commitment to follow through. Dreams are easy. The more your dream differs from the career mainstream, the more time, energy, and discipline are necessary to make it a successful reality.

What if a career plan is not working? This is where gender differences are most pronounced. Females are likely to blame career failures on themselves, seek help or advice, and give up too easily. Males are likely to deny the problem, keep failures secret, blame outside forces, and not act until it is a disaster. As in other areas of life, admitting problems and learning from mistakes is crucial. Women are embarrassed about failures, put themselves down, and retreat. Men deny failures, blame others or events, and hide rather than learning from problems.

Be honest with yourself and your spouse about career difficulties. A major disaster for the two-career marriage is the couple who are competitive and one-up each other. Honesty is a prime casualty. Competition is the motivation, not sharing, cooperating, or supporting. You do not admit doubts, setbacks, or defeats. You are in trouble when you think of the spouse as your worst critic or the enemy.

IRENE AND SAM

Irene was a 27-year-old accounts manager at a furniture store when she met 28-year-old Sam, who had graduated college 4 years earlier and was trying to develop a career as a musician. Irene had dropped out of college after a year and a half to work in retail sales for a large department store, a job she hated. A friend heard about an opening at the furniture store. Irene had 3 months' on-the-job training in accounting and in 2 years was promoted to accounts manager. She enjoyed the salary, bonuses, and responsibility but could not see doing this for the next 40 years. Irene wished she had finished college and gave those with a degree inordinate respect. Although she had dated other college-educated men, Irene felt Sam was the brightest and most creative man she had been involved with. Sam was thrilled with this adulation because he was at odds with his parents over career issues. Sam's mother was an assistant dean at a community college, and his father was a partner in an international accounting firm. Having begun college as a finance major, Sam switched to an English major with a journalism minor. Sam's pursuing a music career while working low-wage jobs infuriated his father and disappointed his mother. Irene's admiration and support were a tonic for Sam.

After 3 months of dating, they moved in together and married 10 months later. Irene's parents were divorced; her mother managed an apartment building and her father owned a small business. Both sets of parents were concerned about the life course of their adult children and were hopeful this marriage would provide a stabilizing element.

Irene and Sam talked a great deal about their families, what they did not want to replicate. Irene saw her parents as unhappy with their careers. She did not want to manage real estate or own a small business. Sam insisted education, money, and prestige were not what he wanted. He was not going to be a clone of either parent. He wanted to be a creative musician.

Sam and Irene had not discussed personal career goals, fears, or concerns. It was easier to say what they did not want and critique the careers of others than talk about their hopes and anxieties. This is a very common trap. We strongly suggest couples discuss hard practical and emotional issues before marriage, which includes a 2- or 5-year career plan involving money and training needs. Unfortunately, Irene and Sam ignored these crucial conversations. She assumed with his degree Sam would eventually have a well-paying career and reach ambitious goals. Irene expected him to support her returning to school full-time. Sam assumed Irene shared his view of personal and artistic freedom. He also assumed her steady income would stabilize their lives and allow him to concentrate on his music. Sam viewed Irene as an ally against his parents.

Irene did not want to stir up conflict; she wanted to support Sam's growth and music career. She thought he was a talented musician and enjoyed listening to performances and talking with other musicians. However, she did not like the smoky bars and worried about rampant abuse of alcohol and drugs. They tried to accommodate each other's schedules: Irene had a rigid 9-to-5 workweek, while Sam's schedule was irregular, performing on weekends with occasional gigs out of town. They enjoyed weekends exploring a new town during the day and playing music at night.

During the first months of marriage, Sam became erratic with day jobs. With Irene's income he was less concerned about expenses. He bought additional equipment and took lessons to expand his musical repertoire.

Irene's employer would fund college courses only if the subject was accounting or a closely related business area. However, Irene was interested in public health policy. Sam did not offer to help pay for her academic program. He would unleash antieducation diatribes that irritated and confused Irene. She felt Sam did not understand or value her goals. The crunch came when Irene had to pay tuition for a night course on health policy—and was $300 short. Irene asked her in-laws for a loan and they offered to pay for the whole course. This enraged Sam. He accused Irene of being a traitor, which Irene felt was unfair and hurtful. Career plans and goals were becoming a major source of marital conflict.

Irene signed up for the course and told her in-laws the loan would be repaid by the end of the semester. Irene was a more aware and conscientious student than she had been at 19, and really enjoyed the health policy field. She discovered financial aid resources and career opportunities, especially with a master's degree. Irene was very enthusiastic about pursuing this career path, although as a part-time student it would entail a 5-year commitment. She wished she could take two courses a semester and two courses during the summer, but this did not meet Sam's approval. His music was improving, although he groused about not getting "breaks." His earnings from music were increasing although overall income was decreasing because he seldom did day work even when employers called. Irene was the prime income producer and the ambitious spouse. She was becoming increasingly discouraged with the role reversal, but she was afraid to discuss this with a recalcitrant Sam.

When couples do not openly communicate and rationally discuss career and financial issues, it leaves them vulnerable to emotional explosions. One night after a gig, Sam and Irene were discussing music over beer with friends. Sam was pontificating about the musical calling and the "jerks who worked dull, stupid jobs." Irene asked whether that included her, and Sam shot back, "What good does your job do for anybody?" Late nights and alcohol are a dangerous combination for a marital explosion. Irene's frustrations burst forth and Sam's resentment about the establishment and money were played out. It was their worst fight, filled with name-calling that degenerated into attack-counterattack. Sam did not come home that night.

Neither wanted to feel alienated. Sam hoped his apologies would satisfy Irene and the matter would drop. Irene apologized for her attacks and put-downs but was assertive in insisting they discuss careers and money, generate alternatives, and reach an agreement about personal and couple goals. She suggested they use the career counseling services at the community college. Irene found a counselor who was sensitized to issues of two-career couples and nontraditional careers. Some of the meetings were individual, others conjoint. The counselor emphasized that career decisions were an individual responsibility: You make choices for yourself, not the spouse. Comparisons and competition distort your decision-making process.

Irene made her academic and career choices. She talked to Sam in detail about how he could support her plans. Irene was afraid Sam would undermine her goals, but once Sam was aware of how committed she was, he took a helpful role. This was easier than expected, but they had to talk about practical matters. Irene wanted to work part-time so she could take two courses per semester. That meant either getting a loan from Sam's parents or his returning to day jobs.

Sam was used to taking an adversarial stance with authority figures. The counselor made it clear he was neither an establishment figure nor a father substitute. He urged Sam to make choices that were in his best interest with a commitment to successfully implement his plan. Sam was not meant to be an accountant or an academic. What would fit him?

Sam wanted to succeed at music, but if that was not viable, he was filled with anxiety and despair. He had no backup plan. Sam would not make a good music teacher, nor did he have an interest in music stores. For the great majority of people, music is a better avocation than vocation. The counselor suggested that for the next year Sam continue to give his best effort to succeed in music but consider alternative, nonestablishment careers. Sam could not let fears control his career choice nor allow his resentments to subvert Irene's career goals. These were sobering thoughts. Sam agreed to read books and articles about nontraditional careers and do information interviews with musicians about how they decided to pursue musical careers and how satisfied they were.

A year later Irene and Sam met with the counselor for a follow-up session. Much had changed. Irene was rapidly progressing in school and planned to pursue graduate school for a masters in public health policy. Sam decided he would continue music part-time, and entered a 3-year apprenticeship program to become an electrician. They had an understanding they would move to wherever Irene could get into the best graduate program. Sam admired Irene's professional ambition, and Irene admired Sam's technical proficiency. Since Sam was busy and productive, he was a happier person and a better spouse. They felt satisfied with the process of career planning. Sam did not have the typical male hang-up of having a better educated, higher income spouse. As long as both felt productive and satisfied, money and career differences could be integrated into their marriage.

My Career, Your Career, and Our Life

Career decisions are more complicated than for your parents' generation. You need to think and talk through alternatives. Even couples who prefer the traditional model of the male being primary or sole income producer need to realize the economy or situation could change and eliminate that option (temporarily or permanently). Both people need to be able to function in the work world. For the majority of married couples, both people work throughout their marriage. Less than 20 percent of married women never work.

Women have greater flexibility and career alternatives. For example, she can have 2 or 3 years where there is no job on her résumé. If this happened to the male, he would be on the defensive justifying the empty space. Women can work in jobs or careers, part-time or full-time. If she needs to reduce or stop work for children or to care for an aging relative, she might have that option. She has freedom to quit a job she hates. The downside of this flexibility is impediments in salary and advancement. Although it is less true of professional careers, women are often treated as second-class citizens. They are paid less for the same work, not given opportunities, and have arbitrary limits placed on advancement. In addition, women have jobs (especially part-time) in which health insurance and benefits are absent or woefully inadequate.

The male has a different potential set of advantages and disadvantages. No longer is all the pressure on him to be a "success object." The spouse shares in career and financial concerns. The man is more than his job: Men are urged to balance parenting, marriage, career, activities, and friendships. The narrowly focused career man glorified in the 1950s is no longer the model. The downside is that the job market is more competitive, volatile, and unpredictable. Concerns over instability, not being promoted, downsizing, and being replaced by a less experienced person sweep the workplace. Males (especially white males) are concerned about being passed over for promotions because of cultural diversity. Although not "politically correct" the reality is that males feel threatened, if not intimidated, by a spouse who earns more. He wants the spouse to succeed and be satisfied with her career but not be more successful. Spousal economic competition is destructive for your intimate relationship.

A generation ago couples moved for the man's education or job. It might have been difficult and disruptive but was an accepted part of being a couple. Now married couples struggle with coordinating the needs of two careers. If her career is going well, what happens if he is offered a fantastic job in another city? If she wants to enter an MBA program, is he willing to give up his job and move with her? If both are interested in further schooling or a job change, do they apply to the same schools and cities? The choices and logistics can be mind-boggling. Practically and emotionally these are complex issues. We urge couples not to take the easy way out by saying we will live apart for 1 or 2 years or "compromise" by one spouse's going to a mediocre school or settling for a job she does not want. We encourage couples to talk out the hard emotional and practical issues, creatively explore alternatives, and reach an agreement that optimally would meet each person's needs but at a minimum each can live with and is protective of their marital bond.

Exercise—Integrating Individual Career Plans with Your Marital Bond

We are in favor of long-term (2- to 5-year) career planning. The plan needs to be flexible enough to allow for changes in opportunities, economic realities, and individual goals. Having a clear, concrete career plan wherein each spouse understands the other's goals, hopes, and concerns facilitates communication and planning.

This exercise involves two separate phases, each with a different focus. The first is an informal couple discussion in which you share dreams and hopes—your perfect life and career. Some couples do this over a glass of wine (a glass, not a bottle), sitting on the porch, during dinner, or on a walk. This can be fun, but do not make it frivolous. Career issues are important. Sharing helps you understand your spouse's ambitions and dreams. Verbalizing increases motivation. It allows the spouse to share your hopes and excitement and identify ways he can be supportive. We do something similar each year and have done so throughout our marriage. Several books have come out of this process; writing is our major shared career activity.

The second phase is realistic and rigorous, requiring a great deal of thought and preparation. This involves setting a long-term career goal (or goals) and detailing specific steps to reach the goal. In addition, a benefit-risk analysis is done. For people who enjoy computers, construct a decision-making tree detailing career plans with opportunities/advantages and risks/problems. This process has value for both the individual and the couple. Examining options in a concrete, step-by-step analysis allows both people to assess feasibility and likely success. For example, a husband had a goal of restoring houses and making large profits. However, when this was spelled out in terms of number of houses per year, amount of investment, amount of hours to do it yourself rather than pay a contractor, and profit needed per house, the massive amount of work and risk convinced him to focus on another profession (without any urging from his spouse). A woman who was committed to working at home so she could be the primary child caretaker found the husband a valuable consultant as they assessed space and equipment needs for a home office. When he realized what a complex undertaking this was, his respect for her career commitment grew.

In completing the second phase, discuss each spouse's career plans and integrate these with your marital bond. This is a complex, yet crucial, task.

Self-Esteem and Work

Ideally, one's career would account for a quarter of self-esteem, never more than one third. A career should not define a person (the traditional male trap), although competence and achievements are a major component of psychological well-being. What you do from 9-to-5 matters to you individually and also affects your marriage. When one or both spouses are unhappy or unsuccessful, it has a major detrimental impact. Each person is responsible for his or her work life, yet the spouse and marriage are affected.

When both spouses have careers it is even more important to be aware and supportive. Comparisons and competition around money, prestige, and success are a poison for marital intimacy. It is an especially virulent poison when there is a reversal of traditional male-female roles.

Newly married couples need to be aware of and take advantage of increased freedom and flexibility in each spouse's career path. In the most common example one person maintains a salaried job to provide security while the other takes the risk of starting a new business, making a career change, returning to school, or taking a high-risk, high-payoff job. Careers need not be controlled by gender stereotypes or rigid paths. Maintain awareness of individual, couple, and family values.

Closing Thoughts

The 21st century will be an exciting time for men and women in terms of career challenges. This can enhance people's lives with new opportunities, flexibility, support, and the freedom to take risks. It also has the potential to subvert the couple as they deal with conflict, competition, the unpredictable economic market, and need to reach agreements. Use your communication and problem-solving skills to enhance career functioning, life satisfaction, and your marital bond.

CHAPTER 13

Dealing with In-Laws
and Extended Family

The essential bond in a family is between the husband and wife. Through marriage you become involved with his or her nuclear and extended family. It is not a choice, it is a reality. We hope you will enjoy and feel accepted by your spouse's family. All families have strengths as well as problems. Ideally you enjoy the people without being caught up in stresses and conflicts. You form positive, meaningful bonds with in-laws and siblings while maintaining cordial relations with others. Extended family can be a positive resource for your life and marriage. Optimally, this would be true with both sets of families.

This ideal scenario occurs with only 15 to 20 percent of married couples. For the majority, it is a mixed picture, with more positives than negatives. The focus of this chapter is the 25 to 33 percent of couples who have significant problems with one or both sets of in-laws and extended family. Personality clashes and loyalty conflicts can be addressed so they do not stress or subvert your marital bond.

Sources of Conflict

There can be numerous sources of conflict involving in-laws and extended family. The most common is often overlooked: the spouse's conflict with his family. The new spouse feels caught in the middle of a conflict she did not start and usually was unaware of. The wish is that she and the new marriage will help resolve the conflict, an unlikely scenario. For a newly married couple the prime task is to build a marital bond of respect, trust, and intimacy while developing a couple style that is comfortable and functional. Resolving family-of-origin issues is not a priority, especially for the new spouse. Prime loyalty is not to the family-of-origin, but to your marriage, that is, family of creation. Spouses learn to respect and trust each other, not be distracted by taking sides (especially in opposition) in family-of-origin conflicts.

When the husband or wife has significant conflict with his or her family, the new spouse is advised not to get in middle. Do not try to be the impartial mediator or problem solver. It is not your issue or role. His loyalty is with her, not her family. Encourage her to deal directly with her family. He can serve a constructive role as a consultant and helper (but not do it for her). He is not an impartial observer; he is on her side. That means listening in a respectful, caring manner and validating her feelings. It does not necessarily mean agreeing with everything she says or does, nor seeing her as the innocent victim and the parents as evil perpetrators. Family conflicts are seldom black-white, right-wrong issues. A positive role for your spouse is to provide perspective, suggest alternatives, and support conflict resolution. He should not play the role of advocate, especially not the parents' advocate.

Focus on the present and future, specifically the present and future of your marriage. Do not be drawn into refighting old family battles. Being on your spouse's side does not mean being antiparent. Little in life is black-white, that is, the abusive parents and rescuing spouse. Help your partner learn from this conflict. Do not reinforce simplistic, dichotomous thinking. Awareness of strengths and vulnerabilities while refining problem-solving skills is optimal.

In a common pattern one or both spouses have blended families, so you have to integrate two sets of in-laws and extended families. The strategy of giving priority to your marriage remains the same. Reinforce family relationships that promote your bond and avoid unhealthy relationships that stress the bond. Do not pretend that everyone gets along equally well or that time and energy will be split fifty-fifty. Deal in a realistic manner. Some family members and situations are comfortable and inviting. The hope is that your spouse enjoys the same people, but this is not always so. Establish positive relationships with core family members while maintaining cordial relationships with others. Maintain a nonhostile distance with people you do not like; do not let hurt feelings or resentment control you. It is advisable to maintain socially appropriate relationships even with people you do not like.

A common problem is generational power struggles. The couple are in a different generation from the parental generation (there are exceptions, for example, a woman who marries a man the age of her parents). Newly married couples have different life issues than parents. This need not be a source of stress, yet often is. Differences involve career, money, leisure, or house issues. The parental generation has established (for better or worse) a life organization. Parents who are unhappy with their lives are insistent in their advice, particularly what not to do. Parents and in-laws offer unsolicited advice, especially on money issues. A generational theme across all kinds of families is that the young adult generation does not adequately plan, especially about finances.

During adolescence, fear is a major parental motivation. It is easy to remain stuck in that pattern with adult children, even when they are married. Being aware of this is helpful in reducing defensiveness and anger. Be cognizant of your agenda; do not just react to the in-laws agenda.

A helpful guideline is to differentiate between solicited and unsolicited advice. In-laws are pleased to be consulted and listened to. This does not mean you have to follow their suggestions, although sometimes it is helpful and wise. Unsolicited advice is better ignored than fought over. The in-laws' intention is usually positive, rather than controlling or a put-down. Feel free to solicit advice. Ignore unsolicited input, but not the person. If parents solicit your advice, count yourself lucky to have respectful, open-minded parents. Unfortunately, most older adults are not open to advice from young couples.

Another pattern, one of the most destructive, is a power struggle. The most common struggles are between a daughter-in-law and mother-in-law or son-in-law and father-in-law. Like most power struggles, there is seldom a winner. The essence of a power struggle is that people forget what they are fighting for but are intent on not losing. Much negative energy is expended in power struggles.

Your marriage is more important than the family-of-origin.

There is no need for a struggle. Fighting with in-laws to establish autonomy is unnecessary. You are married adults; in-laws and parents do not have a veto power. The way to stop a power struggle is not to play the game. Devote time and energy toward building your couple style. Do not be drawn into a family power struggle.

Exercise—Learning from the Family of Origin

As an adult, you have the maturity to view your parents as people, not just Mom and Dad. Consider each as a person with his or her strengths and weaknesses. Instead of seeing them through the lens of a child, view them through adult eyes. List positive personal (not parental) characteristics of your mother that you admire and want to integrate into your life. Do the same for your father. Then for each parent, weaknesses and personal vulnerabilities. View these as traps to monitor and avoid in your life. Do not just criticize. Use awareness as motivation not to repeat these patterns. Share these observations with your spouse and listen to his feedback, especially if it is specific, objective, and constructive.

What are positive attributes of their marriage you want to incorporate into your marriage? Review problematic characteristics, treating these as traps to monitor so they are not repeated. Do not blame the spouse's family of origin for your marital problems. This is an excuse and rationalization. Use awareness to empower change, not as an excuse to rationalize behavior and subvert change.

Loyalty Clashes

Balance loyalty to your marriage and to your family of origin. This is a matter of balance, not a win-lose struggle. Prime loyalty and energy belong to the marriage. Your priority is to create a viable, satisfying marriage. You want in-laws and extended family to be active supporters and resources for the marriage. This is not necessary but is beneficial.

A sensitive issue is in-laws who were initially opposed to or lukewarm toward your marriage. The joke is that no one is good enough for their child. Parents idealize the adult child and wish for the perfect mate. The decision of who to marry is the most important interpersonal decision in life.

Planning a wedding, especially logistics and expenses, can stress family relationships. Resentments last long after the ceremony.

Turning to parents or in-laws for support in a marital argument constitutes dirty fighting, exacerbating loyalty conflicts. Deal directly with your spouse, not through in-laws. Even if in-laws help you win a battle, you are in danger of losing the core of your marital bond (respect and trust). Do not misuse loyalty. Parents and in-laws do not want to be in the middle of your struggles; they would rather support your marriage.

Personality Conflicts

Each person has preferences and sensitivities. It is not surprising a son-in-law conflicts with the father-in-law. This can involve substantive issues like where to live or how to organize a career or mundane issues such as sports or lawn care. A daughter-in-law and mother-in-law clash over how important career is, when to have children, styles of entertaining, or couple versus family time.

Some people prefer an accommodating interpersonal style, others feel a need to assert autonomy. Ideally, in-laws are adult friends and you enjoy being together. Too often, especially among those who emphasize autonomy, this degenerates into uncomfortable interactions and avoidance of in-laws.

Typically, wives do the social negotiating, both with parents and in-laws. It is easy for males to avoid, using the excuse of work or sports. Although reducing the number and length of social interactions can be a reasonable coping technique, avoidance postpones dealing with issues and builds resentment and suspicion. Approach personality conflicts in a positive, realistic manner. Conflicts can be dealt with and a cordial, if not comfortable, relationship established. Other times you accept differences and work around them so high-risk situations are avoided; for example, not attending church together or not discussing financial issues. Recognize in-laws' positive characteristics and accept problematic ones.

Dealing with Birthdays and Holidays

Each family has rituals and traditions for birthdays and holidays. People assume their traditions are natural and the only right ones. When two people marry, there is often a clash of traditions and rituals. Stay away from right-wrong arguments—you can develop your style of celebrating birthdays and holidays. What happens when your newly developed traditions conflict with in-laws' traditions? A guideline is to take turns. When it is your house, observe your traditions; when it is the in-laws' house, observe theirs. Respect differences; they do not have to become a source of struggle. For example, if you are at the in-laws' house and they play classical music while decorating the Christmas tree, enjoy it. At your house you can play Christmas music.

Accept traditions you do not like, such as a formal Christmas dinner with candles, because it means so much to them. You do not have to come to Christmas dinner every year. You can have a light, informal Christmas Eve dinner before attending midnight mass if that is your preference.

For some, family birthday cards and presents are very important. For others, birthdays are celebrated with friends. This is a matter of personal and couple preference, not right or wrong. You can have a family birthday celebration, and the couple can have a separate celebration with friends. Sometimes traditions can be successfully blended, more often couples do events sequentially. Remember, the goal is to be comfortable and have a functional system, not for everything to be perfect. Establish couple traditions while enjoying family traditions.

What about personality conflicts? You have conflicts with friends, including your best friend. How do you handle it? Can you translate these coping strategies to in-laws? The most popular coping strategies are: (a) recognizing and accepting differences; (b) playing to the strengths of the person and accepting or downplaying difficulties; (c) accepting the person with his or her problematic characteristics; (d) structuring interactions so stress is minimal.

Extended Family Contacts

You establish relationships not only with in-laws but siblings, their spouses, aunts and uncles, grandparents, and a host of family, cultural, and religious traditions. Families are complex, with valuable characteristics as well as vulnerabilities. Some families come together in large groups, others in small subgroups. The first time Barry met his future in-laws was at a 60-person extended family picnic. Expecting to like everyone is unrealistic. The goal is to form at least two healthy bonds, whether with a cousin and her family, a sibling and his children, or grandparents. Enjoy them and share experiences. All families have problematic people and characteristics: the alcoholic uncle, the acting-out cousin, the depressed brother-in-law, the family fight over who is included and excluded. Some families provide practical support so when you move there are plenty of hands to help. Other families share social and leisure activities. Some families are particularly good with children; contact among cousins is highly valued. Other families provide a rich context for preserving cultural and religious traditions.

Sometimes your parents or siblings create positive relationships. If that occurs, count yourselves lucky. Most couples find in-laws easier to deal with separately.

Families convey negative legacies you want to be sure are not incorporated into your marriage. These include abusive relationships, racial intolerance, alcohol or drug abuse, gossip, putting people down. It is important to be aware of subtle but powerful family messages, including those which are not verbalized. For example, some families emphasize form over substance. Everyone pretends to be having a good time and feel close; the reality is people dread family gatherings. Some families downplay the importance of marriage. You marry and remarry because it is socially appropriate, but marital bonds are weak or meaningless. Other families have a powerful hidden agenda: vying for inheritance, secrets of spouse abuse, or illegal financial dealings. Confront subtle or unspoken family norms so they do not subvert your marital bond.

Competition between the Husband's and Wife's Families

Jealousy and competition between families is a difficult issue. You cannot split time or caring fifty-fifty. It sounds good but is neither possible nor healthy. Usually, couples are closer to the wife's family than the husband's, partly because she usually does the social arrangements and negotiations. Female socialization emphasizes the importance of maintaining social and family ties. The husband's family reacts by putting pressure on her to "be fair."

Ideally, each spouse would take responsibility to keep contact with their respective families. It should not all rest on the woman's shoulders. Develop healthy relationships with each family; make them noncontingent and noncompetitive. The relationship with one set of in-laws will be different than the other; they are different people. The trap to be aware of is playing one off the other. Do not fall into "my parents are good, your parents are evil" thinking.

A fear parents have is that adult children will "emotionally divorce" them. Parents want to keep contact with adult children, and especially grandchildren. They have devoted 18 plus years to the parenting endeavor; losing contact or being rejected is a hostile negation. Often, the conflict involves unresolved childhood or adolescent experiences, but sometimes it is about adult conflict. You cannot relive your childhood. Live your life in the present, not controlled by anger or resentment from the past.

A difficult situation is created by parents or in-laws who wish to maintain the myth that it was a perfect childhood, they were perfect parents, they are a perfect family. In reality, parents are people with strengths and weaknesses. There was good parenting, mediocre parenting, and bad parenting. Discussing parenting issues is difficult and emotionally painful, but it can be valuable if your goal is to improve understanding and psychological well-being. If the goal is to punish the parent, evoke guilt, or express hostility, the outcome will be destructive.

We suggest consulting a therapist before taking the step of emotionally divorcing parents or in-laws. This type of rupture causes unnecessary pain and turmoil and is seldom healthy for a marriage. Often the birth of a grandchild is an impetus to reconnect with parents and in-laws.

STACIE AND LEN

Stacie and Len were a couple 2 years before marrying. During the first year and a half they met parents and siblings on an informal basis. Len came from a blended family with eight siblings and step-siblings, most of whom lived in the area. Stacie's mother remarried 4 years after Stacie's father died. Stacie was not close to the step-father or his family who lived 2 hours away. Stacie's older brother and family lived 2,000 miles away. When they announced their intention to marry (they did not have a formal engagement), it was received in a lukewarm manner by Stacie's family. Len's family was opposed because Stacie was seen as not attractive enough and too career oriented. Stacie's career in computer marketing was more successful than Len's in hotel management. Len ignored family opposition, but Stacie found it hurtful. Paradoxically, Stacie's mother urged her to marry even though the mother did not like Len. She worried that Stacie's career success would make Len prone to affairs.

Since Len worked for a hotel chain, the wedding reception was held at the hotel. Stacie's family, especially the paternal grand-mother, were upset that it was not a church wedding. Stacie's brother attended, but without his family (he cited financial concerns). This caused a rupture with the sister-in-law. Stacie felt hurt that she was not important enough. Although she had not wanted to, Len convinced Stacie to invite the stepfather's family—Stacie felt they came for the free food and drinks, not for her. Len's step-siblings drank too much at the reception. With this large chaotic group, Stacie and Len felt out of place at their own wedding.

This inauspicious beginning continued on a stressful course. Len's coping strategy was to minimize family interaction and avoid, while Stacie wanted to talk and work it out. This caused stress each time there was a holiday or family event.

The first 2 years of marriage are the time the couple develop patterns of relating to others, but this was not working for Stacie and Len. Stacie talked to female friends who said she was right: Len was a typical male who stonewalled communication. Len talked to male friends who said he was right: Stacie was a typical female who wanted to talk everything to death and needed everyone's approval. With friends like that you do not need enemies.

Len suggested they go hiking and talk this out. Stacie was enthusiastic but wary of Len's assumption that all would be resolved through one talk. Len was insightful in pointing out that Stacie did not need the in-laws' or stepfather's approval to feel positive about herself and their marriage. Stacie's cogent point was she did not want them to be an isolated couple. They needed a healthy connection with family.

Len was fond of one sister and her husband. They engaged in joint activities and discussed family relationships. The sister noted that the larger the family event, the more chaotic and stressful. Stacie and Len decided not to attend large family events but enjoy smaller gatherings. What Len enjoyed best was a 12-person family picnic at the lake. Len and Stacie were cordial with everyone and played and ate with the relatives they most liked.

The family member Stacie most cared about was her mother. They did things one-on-one when the stepfather was out of town. Stacie enjoyed activities on her turf. To heal the rift with the brother's family she invited them for a three-day visit. Len enjoyed meeting his niece and nephew.

Stacie and Len developed two close couple friends. Couple friends who like both of you and are supportive of your marriage are a very valuable resource. Discussions with other couples about in-laws and extended family broadened their perspective. Len and Stacie decided to talk about career and money issues with friends instead of family. Friends understood the challenges and dilemmas more than family who were invested in a traditional view of career and money.

Some people and situations were difficult, but Stacie coped better since she and Len functioned as a team. Len learned a valuable lesson about dealing with Stacie and relationships. His tendency to ignore and avoid was not healthy. Working together to resolve issues increased his respect for Stacie and their marital bond. Stacie trusted that emotionally Len would be there for her; they could resolve conflicts and reach understandings. Relationships with in-laws and extended family were not perfect, but they established a comfortable way to relate. Len and Stacie built solid, healthy relationships with important family members.

The Meaning of Family

Americans are in favor of "family values," but dramatically differ in what that means. Is it the traditional family in which everyone stays married and men and women have well-defined roles? Or is it the new family in which people are accepting and loving no matter who you are or how you organize your life? People, marriages, and families are multidimensional and unique: There is not a "Walton" or "Cosby" family model in which everything and everyone is happy. All families have strengths and weaknesses. Extremists who claim 90 percent of families are dysfunctional are as wrong as those who claim the traditional patriarchal family is the only acceptable form.

Families provide a sense of context and continuity, both giving and needing support. Family contact allows you to experience a range of life events and feelings in a context of grandparents, older adults, young adults, and children. This sense of continuity and caring adds an important dimension to your marriage and lives. In our marriage, relationships with family, especially Emily's mother, provided an important base of meaning.

Exercise—Establishing Realistic Expectations about In-Laws and Extended Family

This exercise involves sharing feelings and perceptions as well as developing strategies for change. If you do this simply to complain, it will be counterproductive. Focus on constructive understandings and changes.

Since males tend to avoid family and in-law issues, he can go first. Identify people and family relationships he enjoys and values. Be honest and specific. She adds people and relationships she enjoys. How can you ensure these remain vital and satisfying?

He lists at least two and up to five problems involving in-laws and extended family. Be specific about people, relationships, and activities. She adds her perceptions of these concerns and problems. After each problem, discuss strategies to reduce or eliminate it. If that is not possible, what coping techniques will make the problem less frequent, intrusive, or severe? Reach understandings and agreements to deal with each problem. When that is not feasible, discuss how to monitor the problem so it does not become worse.

This sounds rational but requires full discussion of feelings, perceptions, and realities. Most important, it requires follow-through. For example, a brother-in-law's drinking and affairs have the potential to explode, stressing the extended family. Awareness is the first step, but the matter cannot end there. Discuss your attitudes and feelings about drinking and affairs. Decide whether you will take a proactive, reactive, or hands-off approach. You are an in-law and he is an adult—it is not your job to play God, judge him, or intervene when he is not open to advice or help. If he or his spouse asks for help, what are you willing to do (and not do)? How will this impact, directly or indirectly, your marriage?

She initiates her phase of the exercise by discussing strengths and problems with in-laws and extended family. Follow the same format, but be flexible. Every family is unique. Remember, the focus is to identify and problem-solve so these issues do not negatively impact your lives and marriage. This exercise is to strengthen interactions with in-laws and extended family while reducing stresses and problems. Do not let your marriage mimic negative stereotypes or jokes about in-laws. Families can play a positive role (emotionally and practically) in your lives and marriage.

Severe Problems with In-Laws

What if none of this is relevant or works? How do you deal with a serious in-law conflict? If the problem has stayed the same or gotten worse over a 6-month period, it is unlikely to spontaneously become better. Our suggestion is to seek consultation or mediation; a book is unlikely to provide the necessary level of help. The two most common sources of help are a trusted family member or a minister. A less common source, but the most appropriate, is a family therapist. Intergenerational conflicts are the special expertise of family therapy. Whether from a relative, minister, or family therapist, seeking help reflects good judgment. Conflict with in-laws can stress and even subvert a new couple. Establishing clear, healthy boundaries between the new marriage and family-of-origin is a crucial developmental task. If you find yourself stymied and caught in conflict, we urge you to seek consultation.

Ongoing Relationships with In-Laws and Extended Family

The quality of relationships you establish during the first 2 years of marriage are likely to continue. In-laws and extended family are part of your life. Relationships change as people become ill or die, while siblings and cousins have children. This is part of the family continuity process. The extended family has greatly changed since our marriage. All four parents have died, one stepmother is alive. Two older siblings have retired (one recently died), and nieces and nephews have adult children; we are a great-uncle and aunt.

Relationships with extended family do not remain static; they change with age and situations. Divorces occur, people move, and relationships improve or degenerate. Do not take family for granted. Welcome changes: They are opportunities for growth.

A guideline is not to bear grudges over past hurts or incidents. Focus on present relationships, not controlled by disappointment or anger from the past. The aunt who did not give you a wedding present should not be punished for 20 years. The sibling who pressured you to enter a marketing scheme 5 years ago and was angry when you said no is probably out of sales now; you can reestablish a relationship. The irresponsible sister-in-law might be a different person now and you could enjoy getting to know their child. If you do not like or relate to these people in the present, that is different. But do not let past hurts or anger control present relationships. Be especially aware of not taking a supportive in-law or sibling for granted. These relationships are valuable; be sure they remain vital. Quality relationships are meaningful for a sense of family.

Closing Thoughts

It is a great resource to develop healthy relationships with your in-laws and extended family. Forming positive bonds, especially with your mother-in-law and father-in-law, is important. Personality or loyalty conflicts put an unneeded strain on your marriage. Ideally you would form friendships with members of the extended family and maintain cordial relationships with others. Family can provide emotional and practical support throughout your marriage. Family provides continuity and a sense of meaning to your lives, marriage, and family of creation.

CHAPTER 14

Preventing Divorce

Divorce does not just happen; it is not a matter of bad luck. Many, if not most, divorces are preventable. If you build a strong bond of respect, trust, and intimacy and a comfortable, functional couple style during the first 2 years, you have the foundation to maintain a satisfying and stable marriage.

Prevention is the best and most cost and psychologically efficacious way to approach marital problems. Prevention is an active process, so be sure your marriage remains vital and satisfying.

Divorce prevention includes an early warning system that allows you to deal with issues and conflicts before they become a chronic problem. People and marriages change, but it is not change that causes divorce. Divorce results when the marital bond is strained by conflict and negative emotions that cascade into a cycle of negativity, defensiveness, and alienation, resulting in a loss of respect, trust, and intimacy.

Each couple style has specific vulnerabilities, requiring specific prevention strategies. For the complementary couple style, a major vulnerability is not attending to your marital bond and taking your spouse's contributions for granted. The prevention strategy is to set aside quality time involving couple dates, a weekend away, acknowledging and reinforcing each other's contributions, and the 5-to-1 ratio of positive to negative interactions and feelings. The conflict-minimizing style is vulnerable to ignoring problems until resentment builds or there is a crisis. The spouse feels betrayed, and the partner is blamed for breaking the marital bond. The intervention for conflict-minimizing couples is the courage to address conflicts or disappointments in a timely, productive manner. The best friend couple style is vulnerable to so much togetherness that there is no room for personal growth. The intervention is to promote both individual and couple growth, respecting autonomy and differences. The emotionally expressive couple style is vulnerable to pushing the limits, breaking the respect or trust bond. The intervention is to ensure conflict does not degenerate into personal criticism, put-downs, and contempt.

Divorce prevention involves strategies and techniques to nurture your marital bond and protect against poisons. Couples approach marriage with a take-for-granted, complacent attitude, only attending when there is a crisis. This reactive stance puts your marriage at risk. We advise a proactive approach to valuing your marital bond and nurturing your intimate relationship. Be aware of individual and couple changes; integrate these rather than resist them. A crucial strategy in divorce prevention is dealing with conflict in a manner that promotes respect and problem solving. Do not allow resentment, defensiveness, or criticalness to build. A marriage in which each spouse is responsible for his or her behavior, maintaining the 5-to-1 positive ratio, and a problem solving style which emphasizes the positive influence process are powerful divorce prevention strategies.

Expectations about Marriage and Divorce

The traditional assumption was that the couple stayed married no matter what. It required a major trauma to break apart a traditional marriage. The modern extreme is that couples stay together as long as there is love and everything is working. When that stops, the spouse says, "I'm out of here." Divorce is not expected, but ending the marriage is always a possibility. Neither extreme promotes marital satisfaction, although the traditional approach reinforces marital stability. Neither naive optimism nor cynicism about marriage serves you well.

The healthy expectation is that you commit to maintaining a

viable bond of respect, trust, and intimacy. This includes willingness to deal with conflicts and difficult situations: marriage for
worse as well as better, difficult as well as easy. The commitment
is not only to love and respect each other for stellar characteristics and good times, but love and respect each other with
weaknesses and vulnerabilities and through sad and difficult times.
You not only survive but can learn from bad times and take pride
in being resilient people. The commitment to prevent divorce is
contingent on your marriage not being destructive, physically
abusive, or undermining individual well-being. Respect and trust
are contingent on maintaining a healthy relationship.

Strategies to Prevent Divorce

Promoting individual and couple growth is the major strategy for
preventing divorce. Keep your marital bond strong so it is invul-
nerable to rupture. The most important technique is setting aside
quality couple time. Couples claim to have time together: They
see each other every day, sleep in the same bed 7 nights a week,
eat together, drive to work, do chores, deal with money issues,
engage together in child care. Is this quality couple time? It could
be but usually is not. The time is spent, as it should be, on the
nitty-gritty tasks of life. Quality couple time is different: You feel
close and nurture your marital bond. If you value your marriage,
both quality and stability, actively promote and reinforce your
bond. Quality couple time involves sitting in the living room, after
the children are asleep, sharing concerns and hopes, going for a
walk and discussing your dream house, lying in bed talking for 30
minutes before you go to sleep or when you awaken, taking a day
off work to go hiking and discuss hopes and dreams as you sit on
the summit.

An important strategy is to generate special feelings about your
spouse and marriage. This includes, but is certainly not limited to, a
regular rhythm of sexual experiences. Being loving is much more
than making love. Intimacy includes emotional closeness, affectionate touch, sensuality, playfulness, eroticism, as well as intercourse.
We encourage touching both inside and outside the bedroom. Nondemand pleasuring reinforces the value of touch; not all touching
results in intercourse. Emotional intimacy has value in itself. Affec-

tionate touch has value in itself. Sensuality has value in itself. Playful touch has value in itself. Each can serve as a bridge to sexual desire if your spouse is receptive. We encourage both planned sexual dates and spontaneous encounters. A full, satisfying marital life is enhanced by spontaneous as well as planned experiences. Intimacy nurtures your marital bond, while sexuality energizes your bond. Both generate special couple feelings.

An important strategy is to develop couple traditions (rituals) that have special meaning. These include religious traditions such as going to services together, lighting candles before Sabbath dinner, serving as volunteers on a monthly basis, involvement in a social action cause, developing special traditions for Christmas and Easter. Other couple traditions include going with your best couple friends on a 20-mile bike ride on Sunday afternoon, returning to your favorite romantic restaurant each year, going to the beach for a weekend each fall—walking in the sand during the day and making luxurious love in front of the fireplace at night. Traditions and rituals solidify your marital bond.

Another strategy is to build external support for your marriage. Religious, extended-family, and community support for marriage is weaker than in past generations. Marginal marriages were propped up by the stigma of divorce and the promarriage values of family, religion, and community. Unfortunately, marriages that were destructive or abusive stayed together; divorce would have been the healthy alternative. We are opposed to returning to the divorce stigma, but there is little doubt that marriage benefits from the concern and support of family, friends, and the culture.

We strongly recommend establishing couple friendships. A couple(s) who like both of you and support your marriage is an invaluable resource. Our closest couple friends live out of state, but we try to schedule at least 1 weekend a year with them. It is fun and allows us to keep up with each other's lives. More important, we discuss hopes, plans, and problems and receive their feedback. Knowing they have our best interest in mind makes their suggestions and perspectives particularly valuable. Observing how their lives and marriage are evolving motivate us to make changes. Extended-family members—in-laws, siblings, cousins who have healthy marriages—can serve as positive models and support. Some couples join church-sponsored marriage classes or prayer groups focused on marriage and family (see suggestions in Appendix B).

Another strategy is to find an interest or activity to add to your couple repertoire. This promotes stimulation and growth. It challenges treating your spouse and marriage as "the same old thing." Couples married over 20 years comment on how different their interests and activities are now as compared with the first 2 years. For example, couples who watched TV every night now spend 2 nights a week at community or hobby meetings. Another example is the couple who become involved in golf or bridge. Young couples who used to enjoy the bar scene find it becomes old. Replace this with fun and involving social activities. Couples add to their sexual repertoire so sexuality remains a vital part of the marriage. One couple developed a tradition of his writing flirtatious or erotic notes that he placed in her suitcase when she left on business travel. Taking your marriage for granted and falling into stagnant routines subverts satisfaction. Enhancing your couple repertoire is an important divorce prevention strategy.

Dealing with Problems

Maintaining a healthy marriage is not just increasing positives but, just as important, dealing with conflicts and problems. It is not conflict itself that threatens your marital bond but the ensuing emotions of frustration, resentment, and alienation. Many difficulties and problems cannot be successfully resolved. Yet you need to address these issues and reduce negative emotions. Criticism of your spouse reduces respect, the bedrock of your marital bond. Negative thoughts and feelings increase as one or both spouses withdraw from the dialogue or problem-solving process and become trapped in a helpless, hopeless cycle. The ideal strategy is to resolve the conflict. The backup is to continue dialogue about difficulties without attacking your spouse or negating your marital bond. Conflict need not become personalized nor dominate your relationship. Respect each person's individuality and choices. As long as you trust your spouse's intention is not to undermine you or the marriage, differences and difficulties can be accepted and many (but not all) can be solved or significantly remedied. Individual differences need not threaten marital viability.

There are no perfect spouses and no perfect marriages. All people and all marriages have weaknesses and vulnerabilities. Be aware of and acknowledge these rather than pretending everything is fine. This is not disrespectful nor a put-down of your spouse. It is an affirmation that you accept, respect, and love your spouse with his weaknesses and problems. It signifies you value and are committed to your marriage with its difficulties and problems rather than being demoralized when it does not meet your idealized dream. Positive, realistic expectations are a solid underpinning of marriage, integral to divorce prevention.

What is the distinction between realistically accepting problems and denying there is a problem? It is the difference between occasionally bouncing checks but recognizing and working on an accounting system in contrast to the spouse who regularly bounces checks and abuses credit cards while saying there is no problem. It is the difference between mediocre or unsatisfying sexual experiences once a month (which is normal) and avoiding sex because you are afraid of failure and embarrassment (which is self-defeating). Problems that interfere with individual functioning and undermine your marital bond must be addressed. You hope the resolution moves you forward but at a minimum halts the downward cycle. It might remain problematic, but it is no longer draining or controlling. Couples who approach change agreements with realistic goals have a major divorce prevention resource.

Another important technique is to ensure a lapse does not turn into a marital relapse. For example, if you have an agreement about home chores, that works well for 4 months and then the spouse reverts to a pattern of procrastination and making excuses, this is a lapse. A relapse would be to give up on the agreement and revert to charges and countercharges of being irresponsible or controlling. Few change agreements work perfectly; most require discussion, revision, and monitoring implementation. A lapse indicates a greater need for discussion and focus, not less. A lapse is acknowledged, not denied or minimized. Rather than being stuck in the guilt-blame mode, focus on getting the agreement back on track. The issue is learning from the lapse, not being on the defensive and arguing whether you are a good person or whether you love the spouse. Treat a problem as a lapse, and ensure it does not become a relapse.

A consistent theme among divorced couples is the frustrations and resentments caused by dashed hopes and broken promises. In a classic movie, *Love Story* the hero says "Love means never having to say you're sorry." Saying you are sorry is an integral component of a satisfying, stable marriage. Taking responsibility for a lapse, apologizing, problem solving, and working together to put things back on track are marks of a couple committed to preventing divorce.

BRYAN AND SYLVIA

At their 2nd anniversary, Bryan and Sylvia were feeling more solid about each other and the marriage than on their wedding day. Sylvia was 4 months pregnant with a planned, wanted baby. They realized parenting would be a major transition in their lives and marriage.

Bryan had thought of the marriage as a "done deal." Although Sylvia was satisfied, she did not want their marriage taken for granted. The year before they married, Sylvia's oldest sister divorced after 5 years of marriage. Sylvia knew her sister would struggle as a single parent. The marital bond was irretrievably broken with the ex-brother-in-law involved with another woman and working in a different city. Sylvia felt if they had recognized and dealt with problems earlier, their marriage could have been saved. Sylvia did not want this to happen with her and Bryan. She was a firm believer that prevention is the best way to deal with problems, especially confronting issues before they become chronic problems.

Bryan was less worried but equally committed to a satisfying, stable marriage. His parents were pregnant with him when they married, and separated 8 months after he was born. His mother married a difficult man with two children when Bryan was 4. Bryan did not keep contact with his biological father and had an angry relationship with the stepfather. His mother and stepfather divorced when Bryan was 17. Bryan was committed to being a different man, husband, and father than those male models.

Bryan and Sylvia were strong believers in the importance of commitment. In a mobile, changing world, marriage provided a solid foundation. Sylvia wished Bryan would focus on couple process issues. Commitment is not a substitute for talking, planning, problem solving, and nurturing intimacy: the nuts and bolts of marriage. Bryan assured Sylvia he did not take their marriage for granted and accepted the need to show involvement day to day.

Like many males, Bryan did not enjoy sitting around and talking about feelings and relationship issues. He feared being confronted and found wanting. Bryan felt it was more productive to discuss specific issues and problem-solve. Sylvia and Bryan learned to validate each other's communication style. Sylvia agreed to discuss issues while engaging in activities like driving, walking, cleaning, or a maintenance project. If he felt attacked, Bryan would check out whether her intention was to put him down (which was very seldom the case). Did Sylvia want to simply air feelings, or did she want this problem addressed and resolved? Bryan had the right to put a limit of a half hour on the discussion. This relieved his fear it would go on endlessly. Bryan realized how strongly Sylvia valued emotional connection. Her intention was not to make Bryan the bad guy. Sylvia being upset or angry was not a threat to Bryan or the marriage. Bryan realized it was normal to have differences and disagreements; not every problem was a crisis.

Core Prevention Strategies

Prevention has two parts. First, identify issues and intervene early and effectively so the problem does not fester and subvert your marital bond. The second component is positive: awareness of what you value about your spouse and marriage so you can nurture and reinforce healthy couple experiences. Do not take your spouse and marriage for granted: Marriage needs continual time, attention, and commitment. Your marriage will be vulnerable if you try to rest on your laurels.

With the birth of a child, your marriage changes. This was a planned, wanted child, and they were committed to parent together. They were aware from reading and talking to friends that couple time was a scarce commodity with a baby in the house. Bryan loved to walk, and they agreed to talk as they strolled the baby. Sylvia was excited about having a child but remembered the sermon that said, "The husband-wife relationship is the core of a healthy family." Sylvia wanted to be sure their marital bond remained strong and secure. They have two good couple friends, an affectionate and sexually satisfying relationship, and a shared passion for cross-country skiing in the winter and fishing in the summer. They vowed to keep these a vital part of their lives and marriage. Bryan and Sylvia are aware of the importance of primary prevention and early intervention to deal with marital issues and problems.

Daily Hassles and Major Problems That Tear at the Marital Fabric

When people are asked what causes divorce, they respond that it is major problems: an extramarital affair, spouse abuse, alcoholism, loss of job, conflict about children. These do stress a marriage and can break the bond. Yet major problems are not the core factor in divorce. It is the daily issues, resentments, and unresolved conflicts that tear at the bond of respect, trust, and intimacy.

The most serious attack on marital viability is the erosion of respect for your spouse and marriage. When you stop dealing with issues and conflicts and instead are critical of your spouse's personality, your marriage is in trouble. When criticalness turns to contempt and put-downs, you are heading toward separation. When you stop talking and give up on resolving issues, the marriage is on its way to divorce. An affair, differences about a child, or disagreement over whether to relocate serves as a lightning rod. The real issue is that the marital bond has eroded or is broken.

The earlier the destructive pattern is recognized, the easier to confront and to change. Treating marital problems with avoidance or benign neglect is risky. We advocate a proactive, preventative approach. This does not mean treating every disagreement or minor unhappiness as an impending crisis. The guideline is that if resentment or hurt feelings continue for more than 2 weeks and/or a problem has continued for over a month, you need to discuss feelings, perceptions, and ways to deal with this issue.

If the problem or negative feelings are not resolved or alleviated within 6 months, we advise seeking professional help. If the problem has not changed by this time, it is unlikely to spontaneously remit. When Barry sees a couple for marital therapy, he thinks how much easier this would have been if they had sought therapy 2 years before. They have to deal not only with the original problem but the frustration, resentment, and blaming that has built over the years. Dealing with a problem in the acute phase promotes positive motivation and expectation of success. A chronic problem lowers motivation. There is so much defensiveness and blaming that it is difficult to focus on the problem as an intimate team and communicate, problem-solve, and develop a change plan.

Couples with a vital marital bond are shaken by a crisis like a job loss, diagnosis of multiple sclerosis, inhibited sexual desire, conflict with in-laws, or bankruptcy. They are motivated to deal with the problem and put resources into play. When daily hassles or chronic problems have devitalized the marital bond, the couple find it hard to mobilize themselves.

It is preferable to plan and anticipate so you avoid life's major problems. Whether you are a strong or vulnerable couple, stresses and problems happen to everyone. Accept this reality. If you approach the problem as an intimate team, it is likely to be resolved. Even if it has to be accepted as unresolvable, you are able to incorporate the problem into your lives without its controlling well-being or draining your marital bond.

Dealing with everyday issues and stresses is crucial. This includes nurturing and reinforcing what you value about your spouse and marriage. Maintaining a respectful, trusting, intimate bond is the best divorce prevention strategy. This is not an abstract concept but one attended to on a day-by-day basis. Rather than letting hassles and stresses erode your bond while frustrations and resentments build, confront the issues. Disappointments are expressed and conflicts dealt with. Even if there is not a good resolution, at least the issue is on the table and its destructiveness contained.

Exercise: An Active Divorce Prevention Strategy

There is not one cookie-cutter divorce prevention program that applies to all couples. Individually and as a couple, identify vulnerabilities and potential traps that could subvert your marriage. Create a plan to monitor traps and implement an early intervention strategy.

Some people feel disloyal doing this exercise. Are you looking for trouble or betraying your spouse by even thinking about potential problems? There are no perfect people and no perfect marriages; everyone has weaknesses and vulnerabilities. Identifying sensitive issues and traps enhances rather than undermines marital health and viability. Feeling loved and respected with weaknesses and vulnerabilities promotes self-acceptance and a solid marital bond.

This is a two-part exercise. The first is awareness of personal characteristics which reinforce marital viability and those that could subvert your marriage. Most vulnerabilities are shared with your spouse. You might choose to not share those which would increase your spouse's defensiveness or result in unproductive anxiety. Examples of individual traps to share are a tendency to feel hurt and withdraw, angry thoughts that become stronger and more controlling over time, taking the marriage and sex for granted, becoming overly dependent on your spouse and giving up individual activities and friends, becoming apathetic and depressed unless you exercise on a regular basis, going along with things too easily, resentment builds, and you blow up. Examples of individual vulnerabilities that are probably not productive to share include parents divorced after 5 years and fear it could happen to you, the spouse's brother was opposed to the marriage and he is close to this brother, you wish the spouse had inherited a million dollars, you wish the spouse was 3 inches taller. A commonality underlying nonshared vulnerabilities is neither of you can change the reality.

Acknowledge individual characteristics that reinforce your marital bond. Examples include the commitment to deal with misunderstandings and hurt feelings within a day, religious beliefs that strengthen your marriage, keeping contact with a friend who respects your spouse and supports your marriage, being open to sharing affection and sexuality.

The second part of the exercise involves discussing couple strengths and traps. Honestly share what you can do as a couple to nurture a vital marital bond. In our marriage Emily feels the most important way we keep connected is taking walks. Walks can be used to make plans, talk out an issue, express hurt or angry feelings, or reconnect after a difficult time. For Barry, the most important strategy is setting aside couple time, especially a weekend away. Other important techniques are to set short- and long-term goals for your lives and marriage, have special time on a weekly basis to stay in touch emotionally, enjoy affectionate, sensual, playful, erotic, and intercourse experiences, maintain good couple friends, be involved with extended family.

Be aware of sensitive issues and problems. We have quite different traps to monitor. Barry becomes antsy and bored if he feels things are stagnating, becomes grumpy and critical of Emily and our lives. Emily gets into a comfortable rhythm of daily life, especially around house projects and friendships, and loses track of larger issues. When there is a problem or crisis she feels caught by surprise, feeling overwhelmed and devastated. We are more aware of individual differences and more accepting of these now than in the first 2 years of marriage. What are your individual and couple vulnerabilities and sensitivities, and how can you monitor them?

Discuss and share what you can do to nurture marital vitality and satisfaction, traps to monitor, and how to intervene effectively so your marital bond is not subverted. We strongly suggest discussing the state of your marriage at least every 6 months (whether on a walk or over dinner) to ensure it remains satisfying and stable.

What to Do When Your Marriage Is Off Track

All marriages get off track at times—it can be for days, weeks, months, or even years. It can occur during the 1st year of marriage, the 5th year, the 10th year, or even the 40th. If you use the strategies and techniques described, being off track would occur less frequently, last a shorter time, be less intense, but will not be totally eliminated. The core issue for divorce prevention is to deal effectively when conflicts and problems occur. Your lives, marriage, and situation change. You cannot prevent everything.

Face the reality that your marriage is off track. Do not waste time on the guilt-blame trap; focus on conflict resolution and problem solving. Resolving the problem is important; this can make you a stronger couple. What do you need to do as individuals and as a couple? Accept hurt feelings or disappointments, but do not let these turn into poisonous feelings that control your marriage. Life is meant to be lived in the present with planning for the future, not controlled by hurts or disappointments from the past.

If the marriage is not on track within 6 months, we suggest marriage therapy (Appendix A provides information and guidelines for choosing a marital therapist). Seeking therapy is a sign of good judgment, not weakness or craziness. A professional can provide a new perspective, empathize with your feelings, focus on critical issues, help you mobilize psychological resources, create alternatives, problem-solve, and maintain motivation until a satisfactory resolution is reached. Seek professional help when the problem is acute and you are highly motivated to revitalize your marital bond. Do not allow it to slip into a chronic problem with ambivalence about the value of your marriage. Many couples prefer taking a marriage enhancement course or going to a church-sponsored marriage savers program rather than marriage therapy. There is less stigma to this approach, and it provides a more optimistic, nonpathological approach to addressing marital issues. Appendix B lists resources for marital enhancement programs.

Closing Thoughts

Preventing divorce is an active process. Marriage cannot rest on its laurels, whether after 2 years or 40 years. A healthy relationship requires consistent attention and nurturing. Divorce prevention is a one-two combination. The first is to nurture and reinforce your marital bond of respect, trust, and intimacy. Ensure the 5-to-1 ratio of positive experiences and feelings is maintained. Recognize and reinforce individual and couple strengths. Maintain respect for your spouse, and value your marital bond.

Equally important is identifying individual and couple vulnerabilities and traps. Be aware there will be lapses and problems, but be sure these do not turn into a relapse or a chronic problem. Ambivalence and loss of motivation erode your marital bond. Monitoring traps and early intervention, including marital therapy or a marital enhancement program, are the recommended strategy.

You made a healthy marital choice and developed a solid marital foundation. Devote the time and energy to promote individual and couple growth and prevent erosion of your marital bond.

CHAPTER 15

Valuing Your Spouse and Marriage

Maintaining a satisfying, stable marriage that promotes individual and couple growth requires time, psychological energy, and commitment. Two concepts facilitate maintaining a vital marriage. The first is that each spouse values and nurtures the marital bond. The marriage is not treated with benign neglect. Second, do not settle for a mediocre or marginal marriage. More than fifty percent of marriages are vital and satisfying. You want yours to be in that group.

Awareness and good intentions are necessary, but not sufficient, to ensure a satisfying, stable marriage. This book has focused on strategies and techniques to build a strong marital bond and a healthy couple style during your first 2 years. The theme of this chapter is a natural follow-through, actively valuing and nurturing your marital bond. We have been married 37 years and are still careful to put time and energy into our marriage, although it requires less thought and time than 35 years ago. It is easier to reinforce a marital bond than build it.

There is a tendency to take marriage for granted and treat it as a "done deal." That is not all bad because security is one of the advantages of marriage. In traditional cultures, marital stability was a given. Family, religious, and community pressures were anti-divorce, so only a catastrophe or death would end a marriage. Unfortunately, although stable, these marriages were often a hollow shell and unsatisfying, especially for women. We value stability and security, but not at the cost of individual well-being and couple satisfaction. We advocate healthy marriages, not those which are abusive, alienated, or propped up by fear of divorce, stigma, or loneliness. We encourage you to value both satisfaction and security.

Core Elements in Marriage

Two core elements anchor a healthy marriage. One is respect for your spouse and marital bond. The second is maintaining a 5-to-1 ratio of positive to negative experiences and feelings.

Respecting and valuing your marriage is both a symbol and an active process. Valuing means speaking positively of your spouse and marriage, not indulging in the cultural stereotype of complaining about being married (the male trap) or the spouse (the female trap). The best friend marital style involves thinking of and treating your spouse as a valued friend. The complementary style means recognizing the spouse's contributions to your life and marriage. The emotionally expressive style involves verbally and emotionally expressing special feelings. The conflict-minimizing style means being protective and supportive of your spouse and marital bond. Valuing is an active affirmation, not just refraining from negative behavior.

Respect for your spouse and marriage is crucial. Maintaining a respectful relationship includes acknowledging what your spouse does that you admire and appreciate. When she is doing things you do not respect, instead of complaining to others or putting her down, try to positively influence her. A powerful technique is to say "you're a better person than that." You can deal with problems in a respectful, effective manner. A hallmark of a healthy marriage is that both people utilize the positive influence process rather than issuing ultimatums or making threats.

The 5-to-1 ratio of positive to negative interactions and feelings sounds mechanical but has received strong empirical and clinical support in enhancing the quality of marriage. This validates the folk saying "love is what love does." Both words and actions matter. This ensures that your spouse and marriage will not be taken for granted.

Maintaining a positive marital tone is particularly important when going through stressful or depressing times. Our marriage has had four periods lasting from 2 months to 2 years that were difficult and unhappy. During those times, Barry's favorite saying was "we'll survive this." Even in the worst times, we set aside time to do our favorite activities of taking walks, going to ethnic restaurants, and having weekends away. These helped reenergize us and maintained motivation to deal with difficult issues. During these times we tried to keep our ratio at least 3 to 1. Positive reinforcement and good feelings are just as important during mundane times.

Rituals that symbolize valuing your marriage are important. These serve as a reliable means to acknowledge your relationship. Couples create planned and spontaneous ways to nurture their bond. These are not mechanistic things you do for the spouse, but genuine shared means to demonstrate caring for each other and your marriage. For example, couples put on music and dance late at night, on Sunday go to church and have friends or relatives over for brunch, wake early and spontaneously decide to take a day trip, make hot chocolate and watch their favorite sitcom, once a month go for a hike or camping trip with couple friends, on weekday mornings one makes coffee while the other gets fruit and cereal, take their niece and nephew to the zoo once a month, every other Saturday is an all-day house project that finishes with beer and pizza, planned or spontaneous sexual dates twice a week, engaging in affectionate touch and nondemand pleasuring three times a week, establishing couple rituals to celebrate birthdays and holidays, working toward one major goal each year.

A variety of feelings, activities, and experiences can nurture and reinforce your couple bond. The important thing is not what you choose but that there be ways to share and stay connected.

Special Events/Mundane Activities

What keeps a marriage healthy? Is it the special events of having a baby, buying a house, starting a business, taking a trip to Europe? Or is it mundane life activities such as giving backrubs, talking on the phone daily, making dinner together, feeling support when stressed, doing chores in tandem? Both count and reinforce your marital bond, but it is everyday living and mundane activities that are the underpinning of a healthy marriage. Barry saw a couple who seemed to have done everything right in their first 2 years of marriage: Both received job promotions, they had money set aside for a house down payment and a great vacation in Hawaii, and were ready to start a family. The problem was the wife did not enjoy dinner because they had nothing to say to each other. They made better business and traveling partners than spouses. She did not enjoy being with him and sharing life: Money, Hawaii, house, and baby could not overcome that.

Couples find comfortable and enjoyable ways to be with each other, including cuddling, house chores, eating together, and just hanging out. Special events are anticipated and savored, but it is the nitty-gritty of marriage that counts. If you do not enjoy eating hamburgers together, a gourmet meal at a luxury restaurant will not revitalize your relationship.

Develop comfortable and functional patterns of sharing your lives. The house is vacuumed, food bought, dishes cleared, toilets cleaned, garbage taken out, bills paid, and the checkbook balanced. Who does what is less important than an equitable distribution of the mundane, yet important, tasks of a shared life. Housework can involve doing tasks in tandem or autonomously, but there needs to be some organization and predictability. Feeling good about your spouse and marriage on a day-to-day, nitty-gritty basis is core. Remember the guideline of 5-to-1 positive to negative experiences and feelings. In our society the symbol of marriage is valued, but there is not sufficient attention to the process of developing a strong marital bond and a satisfying way to share your lives.

The unrealistic expectation is that marriage automatically makes life better. Vital, intimate, secure marriage is a major component in self-esteem, but not more than 25 percent. Do not hide behind your marriage. Each spouse is an autonomous, fully functioning person. Your partner can complement and support you, but not function for you. For example, the spouse who has a public speaking phobia needs to confront this and build comfort and skill with public speaking. She should not be dependent on her husband to make speeches for her. The husband cannot say now that I am married, I no longer have to cook or iron; that is her role. He needs to be able to take care of himself. Each spouse has special areas of interest and competence, but each is a fully functioning person. Marriage is a positive, integral component of self-esteem, but it is not marriage that gives the person a sense of worth.

Traditional Roles, Equality, and Equity

Traditional marital roles provide the most stability but not the most satisfaction. Two generations ago (in the 1950s) there were external supports for traditional marriage (extended family, religion, and community) and different expectations of marriage (security, economic well-being, social acceptability, raising a family). With the cultural upheaval of the 1960s, the role of marriage was questioned, divorce laws were reformed, less stigma was attached to divorce, and divorce rates dramatically rose (as did remarriage rates). The traditional assumption was that people stayed married unless there was child abuse, spouse abuse, abandonment, or public infidelity. This is no longer true (and was not healthy). Traditional roles did not support marriage as a respectful, trusting, intimate relationship.

Extreme feminists advocated replacing the traditional marital model with one that demanded equality in every aspect of the relationship. Equality was defined as sharing everything fifty-fifty, a rigid and unrealistic criterion. The equality model increased frustration, resentment, and relationship instability. It sounded logical and good, but for the great majority of couples it does not work. People have different competencies and interests; life does not split fifty-fifty. In our marriage some tasks are divided along traditional gender roles: Emily does the cooking because she is more skilled and interested and Barry manages the finances and investments. In other areas tasks are divided in a nontraditional manner, on the basis of skills and interests. Emily does house and mechanical repair while Barry does dishes and food shopping.

We advocate the equity model of dividing roles and tasks. This can be functional and satisfying but requires thought, time, and negotiation. The model emphasizes contributions to the marriage that are respected and valued, leading to a sense of equity in roles and responsibilities. When one spouse feels responsible for 80 percent of the tasks or is carrying the partner, the marriage is in trouble.

In the complementary marital style, each spouse's contribution is acknowledged and valued. Each spouse makes contributions in his or her domain. The conflict minimizing style utilizes traditional roles that are appreciated, not resented. Emotionally expressive couples lobby the other to do more, but each spouse's contribution is a symbol of caring. Sometimes best friend couples try so hard to have an equitable marriage that they shy away from the hard discussions necessary in maintaining equity.

An advantage of the equity model is that you do not treat your marriage as a "done deal." By the nature of the equity model, tasks are discussed and adjustments made as situations and life circumstances change. The best example is the birth of a baby, which dramatically changes responsibilities and challenges facing the couple. The main reason for the guideline of waiting at least 2 years before having a child is to develop a couple style and solidify your marital bond. So much changes after you start a family, you need to ensure your bond is solid and strong. The danger with a child is that the couple fall into traditional, less equitable ways of dividing tasks. The division of labor will change, but a sense of equity can be maintained. For most couples, marital satisfaction decreases during the year after the baby is born. Partly, this is because there is less individual and couple time. Times of transition bring stress. Change is necessary and healthy but not problem-free or easy.

We suggest couples discuss perceptions about martial equity at least every 6 months. The trap is ignoring the issue for years until there is a major blow-up. Some couples discuss tasks weekly, but this becomes tedious. We suggest a 6-month time frame with the format of sharing perceptions and requests. Reach understandings and agreements; do not threaten nor placate. An equitable distribution of tasks combined with acknowledgment of each person's contributions strengthens your marital bond.

Change and Acceptance

A satisfying, stable marriage involves balancing change with acceptance. In discussions before marriage the couple are optimistic they can do anything and be everything. That is an exciting and special feeling. Unfortunately, this romantic promise has a built-in unreality. We encourage you to have positive, realistic expectations toward each other and your marriage. The danger is abandoning positive expectations when confronted by the inevitable disappointments, hard choices, and reality constraints.

We encourage growth for each spouse and your marriage. Change is welcomed, not avoided, both because it is inevitable and can enhance individual and marital satisfaction. On the other hand, change can negatively impact your marital bond—even planned, desired transitions cause stress. Many changes are a result of necessity, not choice, which is more stressful. For example, the spouse loses a job, a parent becomes ill, the building is sold and rent increased. A common issue is that one spouse's decision—to return to school, join a church, run for a community board—impacts the partner. One of the hardest issues is when a job change or transfer necessitates the couple's moving to a different city or state.

Some couples thrive on change, others value stability. Be aware of your comfort level and organize your lives to play to your strengths. Some couples love the challenge of living overseas for 3 years, for others it would destroy their marriage. Conflict-minimizing couples value stability while emotionally expressive couples thrive on change and challenge.

Trusting Your Spouse and Marital Bond

Trust is more than not having affairs. Trust means believing the spouse has your best interest in mind. Trust involves the expectation you will deal with differences and conflicts. There are some problems that are not resolvable. These are dealt with in a manner that minimizes harm to your spouse and marriage. Trust in the spouse's intentions is a bedrock of the marital bond. This is true across all marital styles. One of the reasons divorce is so painful is that the person you once trusted is now an angry stranger who treats you badly and wants to do harm. Reinforcing trust is crucial in maintaining a vital marital bond.

Respect as the Core Component

Empirical research has traced the process by which a relationship cascades toward divorce. Criticism of the behavior changes to criticism of the person; defensiveness, hostility, and put-downs increase; characterizations of the spouse are disrespectful and contemptuous; avoiding and stonewalling increase; you no longer believe you can influence each other. In the final stage, the bond of respect, trust, and intimacy is irrevocably broken. The marriage might limp along for a few months or even years, but the bond and satisfaction are gone.

The more you do to strengthen and reinforce respect, the better. Be aware of and acknowledge, in words and feelings, what you admire about your spouse. What do you value about your marriage? This can include material items like furniture, a house, a collection of antique dishes, workout equipment, or paintings. It can be friendships with neighbors and couples, parenting together, a community group, an organization. It can include life experiences like learning a sport together, being cochair of a political or religious group, being experts on wallpapering or the best places to listen to music, creating a lovely garden, integrating emotional intimacy and sexuality. Respect what you have created and who you are as a couple. Reinforcement and admiration from others add to respect.

Respect is reinforced by positive events, feelings, and experiences. In addition, dealing with disappointments, problems, and weaknesses is vital to personal and couple respect. Respecting your spouse includes accepting problematic characteristics, inadequacies, and areas of vulnerability. Being accepted for who you are, warts and all, is validating and creates a marital bond that can withstand almost anything.

Accepting weaknesses and problems is not to encourage them. For example, the woman who is phobic of driving on freeways is not advised to stop driving or avoid highways. Ideally, she would overcome this problem with professional help and the support of the spouse. If that goal is not achieved, accept this as a weakness. He does not berate nor put her down. He encourages her to build comfort and confidence in driving, but if she requests he drive on freeways, he does so without complaining or holding a grudge. Another example is the husband who feels uncomfortable at social events involving people he does not know. Ideally, he would develop a comfortable manner of relating and she would encourage this. When that is not possible, they are not controlled by the problem but remain sensitive to it. For social events where his attendance is not required, he does something else. She goes with friends to the event and later they meet for dinner or a movie. For events he needs to attend, she stays close, introduces him to people, and they converse about mutually interesting topics. Barry has a perceptual-motor learning disability that severely hampers his ability to repair items, type, or use computers. This is a major problem for Barry to deal with, and Emily encourages his coping techniques. She accepts this as an unfortunate reality, does not put him down for it, nor does this reduce her respect for him.

You cannot be good at everything. Accept the reality of deficits, weaknesses, and disappointments. You may not be good at entertaining, have as nice a house as friends or siblings, have the close relationship with extended family you had hoped for, have financial success, or be knowledgeable about political or cultural matters. All couples have strengths and weaknesses. If weaknesses dramatically reduce satisfaction, they are addressed, and it is hoped, remedied, but they are unlikely to become strengths.

Respect involves dealing with reality and establishing realistic expectations. For example, the couple uninterested and unskilled at financial management cannot afford to deny or avoid dealing with money or it will subvert their marriage. Ideally, one or both people take a course or seminar and improve money management skills. The trap is to feel deficient and ignore the problem until it becomes a crisis. When neither is capable, accept this is a couple weakness and explore coping mechanisms. Examples include setting up an arrangement with their bank, hiring a money manager, asking a relative or good friend to help with financial affairs, paying in cash or using only one credit card. Ensure that the weakness does not control or subvert your marriage.

Respect for your spouse and your marital bond is the cornerstone of a healthy, stable marriage. Maintain respect while accepting weaknesses; be sure these do not undermine respect.

Reenergizing and Reaffirming Your Marital Bond

Positive motivations and intentions are crucial in maintaining a satisfying, stable marriage. Devote time and energy to keep your marital bond vital. Each couple find techniques that work for them. In our marriage, Emily emphasizes the core role of walks: Seldom a day goes by without going for at least a short walk. Sometimes the walk is for exercise and pleasure, more often it is to talk, catch up, discuss feelings, hash out a disagreement, explore a concern or worry, plan an event, share good news. Barry emphasizes the reenergizing effect of special events: a couple trip, a weekend away, a special lovemaking experience, dinner and a play. This protects us from taking our relationship and each other for granted. Emily enjoys special events but not in lieu of attending to day-to-day feelings and issues.

Some couples utilize structured, planned activities to reenergize their marriage. Others emphasize spontaneous, emotion-based experiences. The latter feels better. The danger is that unless you are consciously aware of the importance of affirming your marital bond, opportunities slip away and your relationship suffers from benign neglect. Marriage, even the best marriage, cannot rest on its laurels.

The following are a smorgasbord of techniques couples utilize to reenergize their marriage: going to church together and/or joining a couple support group, at least twice a month going out as a couple, being sexual one to three times a week, playing golf and going to lunch with couple friends, going to the in-laws for dinner once a month, bringing flowers or a small gift on occasion, talking by phone each day, when out of town bringing home something special, doing one zany and/or romantic activity a month, being playful and spontaneous when the mood strikes, special holiday traditions, once a quarter both take a day off work to play, going skiing with a group of friends, doing at least one house project in tandem each summer, a week winter vacation at a romantic destination, family traditions that reinforce the value of your marriage, every 6 weeks have a pleasuring date with a prohibition on intercourse, when attending a wedding reaffirm your marital commitment, after a stressful period doing something fun to acknowledge you survived. Each spouse and each couple develop special activities, experiences, and symbols. What is valuable for your marriage? Whether planned or spontaneous, be sure special experiences and rituals are a valued part of your relationship. Empirical research emphasizes the importance of a 5-to-1 ratio of positive to negative couple interactions and feelings. Reaffirm and reenergize your marital bond.

The Crucial Role of Dealing
with Loss and Disappointment

A test of a healthy, viable marriage is the ability to deal with loss and disappointment without losing respect or trust. All individuals and couples experience defeats and disappointments. This is normal, part of the human condition.

Some crises and problems could have been avoided if you had talked and planned, but some are inevitable. Either way the problem has to be dealt with. The process involves addressing the crisis or loss, discussing feelings and perceptions, looking at a range of alternatives, doing a practical and psychological cost-benefit analysis, making a problem-solving agreement, and having a plan to successfully implement and monitor the agreement. Accepting losses and disappointments rather than pretending is crucial. Address the problem and resolve it as successfully as possible.

Acceptance is healthier than feeling controlled by the loss. Some problems can be overcome, others significantly changed, and some must be accepted. Do not allow chronic anger or blame the spouse. Chronic problems can devitalize your marital bond, especially when blame and disrespect become dominant. The test of marital viability is dealing with crisis and loss without turning on your spouse or causing a rupture in your marital bond. This is especially important with chronic problems. Cope with the problem as a marital team.

Feeling loved and respected even though your weaknesses and failures are exposed is a sign of a healthy marriage. This allows you to accept a loss and move on rather than its being a self-definition. For example, the spouse who starts her own business that fails or runs for elective office and is defeated needs to accept the reality of the loss, but not treat it as a negation of her worth. Let go of things you cannot change. Focus on present issues and reinvest in new ventures and activities. Your spouse provides reality feedback and emotional support in helping deal with defeats. She helps you avoid the extremes of denial or obsessing. Accept the defeat, learn from it, and reinvest in new projects, people, and experiences.

Your spouse is a supporter: She should not take on the problem as if it were her own. In healthy marriages, each spouse maintains individuality and personal boundaries. Being an intimate team does not mean being enmeshed and losing autonomy. The person who was defeated was the spouse, not you. If you take the defeat as your own, it robs you and the marriage of perspective. If one spouse is depressed, it does no good for you to become depressed. You will be better spouses and friends if you maintain personal boundaries. You are not looking down on your spouse. Rather, you are a respectful, trusting friend providing perspective and support. Surviving hard times with an intact marital bond reenforces resilience and viability.

Keeping Your Marriage Special

Your marital bond of respect, trust, and intimacy needs continual attention and reinforcement. A satisfying, stable marriage cannot be taken for granted. You have put energy into creating a healthy marital style during the first 2 years and built a solid marital foundation. You need to keep building, modifying, and reinforcing. Welcome individual and couple changes and be open to dealing with differences and conflicts. The positives of your marriage are acknowledged and enjoyed: the good times, talks, making love, building a life, fun days, caring days, children, friends, trips, a sense of pride and satisfaction. Maintain a 5-to-1 ratio of positive feelings and experiences. Respect, trust, and intimacy are the cornerstones of a satisfying, stable marriage. Commit the time and psychological energy to your lives and marriage, enjoying and valuing your spouse and marital bond.

Choosing a Couple
or Individual Therapist

As stated in the first chapter, this is not a "do-it-yourself therapy" book. People are reluctant to consult a therapist, feeling that to do so is a sign of "craziness," a confession of inadequacy, or an admission that your life and marriage are in dire straits. In reality, seeking professional help is a sign of psychological wisdom and strength. Entering marital or individual therapy means you realize there is a problem and you have made a commitment to resolve the issues and promote individual and couple growth. The first 2 years of marriage are a particularly good time to seek therapy and deal with issues before negative thoughts, behaviors, and emotions grow and subvert your marital bond.

The mental health field can be confusing. Couple and individual therapy are clinical subspecialties. They are offered by several groups of professionals including psychologists, social workers, marriage therapists, psychiatrists, and pastoral counselors. The professional background of the practitioner is of less importance than his or her competence in dealing with your specific problems.

Some people have health insurance that provides coverage for mental health and thus can afford the services of a private practitioner. Those who do not have the financial resources or insurance could consider a city or county mental health clinic, a university or medical school outpatient mental health clinic, or a family services center. Clinics usually have a sliding fee scale (i.e., the fee is based on your ability to pay).

When choosing a therapist, be assertive in asking about credentials and areas of expertise. Ask the clinician what will be the focus of the therapy, how long therapy can be expected to last, and whether the emphasis is on individual, communication, relationship, conflict resolution, or sexuality issues. Be especially diligent in questioning credentials, such as university degrees and licensing. Be wary of people who call themselves personal counselors or marriage counselors. There are poorly qualified persons—and some outright quacks—in any field.

One of the best resources for obtaining a referral is to call a local organization such as a psychological association, marriage and family therapy association, or mental health clinic. You can ask for a referral from a family physician, minister, or trusted friend. For a marriage therapist, check the Internet site for the American Association of Marriage and Family Therapy at Therapistlocator.net.

Feel free to talk with two or three therapists before deciding on one with whom to work. Be aware of comfort with the therapist, degree of rapport, and whether the therapist's assessment of the problem and approach to treatment make sense to you. Once you begin, give therapy a chance to be helpful. There are few miracle cures. Change requires commitment and is a gradual and often difficult process. Although some people benefit from short-term therapy (fewer than 10 sessions), most find the therapeutic process will require 4 months to a year or longer. The role of the therapist is that of a consultant rather than a decision maker. Therapy requires effort, both in the session and at home. Therapy helps to change attitudes, behavior, and feelings. Do not be afraid to seek professional help to assist you in assessing and changing individual and marital problems.

Marriage Enhancement Programs and Marriage Support Groups

Many couples find a marital enhancement or educational program more acceptable and inviting than marital therapy. Preventing problems is easier than trying to change an over-learned negative personal or marital problem. Primary prevention involves learning attitudes and skills to promote healthy marriages by learning communication, conflict resolution, and intimacy and sexuality skills that build a solid marital foundation. The best time to do this is in the first 2 years of marriage.

Secondary intervention refers to addressing a problem when it is in the acute stage (has existed for less than a year) and the couple is highly motivated to resolve the problem. In secondary intervention the layers of disappointment, frustration, and resentment that marital therapists so often have to confront have not been built. Another way to conceptualize secondary intervention is as a way to deal with normal developmental phases of marriage such as the transition from romantic love/passionate sex to developing an intimate, interactive couple sexual style: the transition from idealizing your spouse and believing you can be a perfect couple to accepting your spouse and marriage with vulnerabilities and weaknesses as well as strengths and positive characteristics; the transition from being a couple to becoming parents; the transition from being carefree people to managing time and finances as you buy your first house and balance careers and parenting.

There are a growing number of resources for married couples, ranging from a church-sponsored free weekend seminar for newly married couples to a 4-month marital training class sponsored by a fee-based marital enhancement program. An excellent resource for finding a program that could meet your needs is on the Internet at www.smartmarriages.com. The Smart Marriages coalition sponsors a yearly convention with a variety of speeches, workshops, and training sessions. In addition, it has a directory of training programs, classes, and groups for couples listed by geographic area. It also lists a number of other resources including recommended books and tapes. An excellent premarital resource is PREPinc.com that includes training classes, articles, information on risk factors, and prevention resources. Another Internet resource is lovegevitity.com that is dedicated to promoting healthy marriages and has both premarital and marital resources.

The largest sponsors of both premarital and marital enhancement programs are religious organizations. Many of these programs are free or quite inexpensive. There are also community organizations, including community college programs, adult education programs, and a variety of other sources, that sponsor large- and small-group programs to promote healthy marriages. We hope these offerings will increase in the future as awareness grows about the need to promote satisfying, stable marriages.

Recommended Books

Christensen, Andrew & Jacobson, Neil (2002). *Reconcilable differences*. New York: Guilford.

Doherty, Williams (2001). *Take back your marriage*. New York: Guilford.

Fowers, Blaine (2002). *Beyond the myth of marital happiness*. New York: Wiley/Jossey-Bass.

Glass, Shirley (2002). *Not just friends*. New York: Free Press.

Gottman, John & Silver, Nan (1999). *The seven principles for making marriage work*. New York: Crown.

Jordan, Pam, Stanley, Scott & Markman, Howard (1999). *Becoming parents*. New York: Wiley/Jossey-Bass.

Markman, Howard, Stanley, Scott & Blumberg, Susan (2000). *Fighting for your marriage*. New York: Wiley/Jossey-Bass.

McCarthy, Barry & McCarthy, Emily (1998). *Couple sexual awareness*. New York: Carroll and Graf.

McCarthy, Barry & McCarthy, Emily (2002). *Sexual awareness*. New York: Carroll and Graf.

McCarthy, Barry & McCarthy, Emily (2003). *Rekindling desire*. New York: Brunner/Routledge.

Spring, Janis (1996). *After the affair*. New York: HarperCollins.

Waite, Linda & Gallagher, Maggie (2002). *The case for marriage*. New York: Doubleday.

Weiner-Davis, Michele (2001). *Divorce remedy*. New York: Simon & Schuster.

Weiner-Davis, Michele (2004). *The sex-starved marriage: boosting your marriage libido: a couple's guide*. New York: Simon & Schuster.